New Zealand Wild

Nic Bishop

New Zea

Wild

land

The greenest place on earth

REED

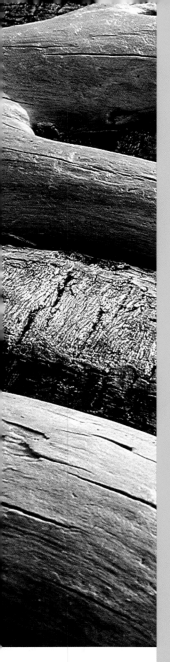

Acknowledgements

For help with the photography I wish to thank Dawn Wilson of the Queenstown Kiwi and Birdlife Park, and Brian Lloyd of the Department of Conservation. My thanks to Holger Leue for the use of his photographs on pages 28 and 73. Thanks also to my wife Vivien Pybus for the photograph on page 80.

Front cover: Red-crowned parakeet (kakariki)
Back cover: Leaf litter

Published 1995 by Reed Consumer Books, a division of Reed Publishing (NZ) Ltd, 39 Rawene Rd, Birkenhead, Auckland. Associated companies, branches and representatives throughout the world.

Edited by Deirdre Parr
Text and cover design by Chris Lipscombe
Type set in Futura Heavy and Janson Text
Film separations by The Image Centre

Produced by Mandarin Offset Ltd., Hong Kong

ISBN 0 7900 0431 3 paperback
ISBN 0 7900 0441 0 hardback

© Nic Bishop 1995

Previous page:
Karamea Basin
from
Mt Patriarch,
Kahurangi
National Park

Above:
Driftwood

Above right:
Waxeyes

Contents

one of

the most

fascinating

stories of

life on

earth

New Zealand has an unusual natural history. One scientist has suggested that it is the closest many of us will get to observing life on another planet. Others have said it is the nearest approximation to life as it was at the time of the dinosaurs.

There is truth in both these points of view. Isolated by thousands of kilometres of sea, New Zealand has produced some anomalies of the living world — birds that cannot fly, insects that occupy the niche of rodents, and bats that crawl through the leaf litter. There are also many plants and animals, such as the coniferous podocarp trees and the tuatara, that seem little changed from ancestors fossilised millions of years earlier.

There is a third curious feature. Some plants and animals have close relatives in countries many thousands of kilometres away. For instance, the beech forests covering large areas of New Zealand have an uncanny similarity to those growing in Tasmania and South America, even to the point of sharing similar associated fungi. Yet beech seeds cannot spread far by floating and are not carried by birds. They have

Top left:
Fern frond

Bottom left:
White heron

Above:
Rocky tideline

Left:
Tuatara

7

Top:
Hygrophorus
fungus

Bottom:
Sea tulips

Right:
Powelliphanta snail

failed even to cross the 30 kilometres of Foveaux Strait to populate Stewart Island from the South Island. So how has beech managed to colonise such widely separated lands?

The answers to many of these mysteries have been threaded together by the combined sciences of geology, palaeontology and biology, producing what is surely one of the most fascinating stories of life on earth.

To follow this story we must return to the earth as it was some 200 million years ago. At that time the southern continents — Australia, South America, Africa and Antarctica — lay locked together in a single supercontinent called Gondwana. Thick forests of primitive conifers, cycads, tree ferns, horsetails, and mosses covered much of its surface, including what is now Antarctica. There was also a rich fauna of insects, spiders, snails, and amphibians. The dominant forms of animal life, however, were the dinosaurs.

The site of New Zealand at this time lay submerged beneath a shallow sea off the south-eastern coastline of Gondwana. For millions of years, erosion from the adjacent land, now corresponding to Australia and Antarctica, poured deepening layers of sediment into this sea. As they grew in thickness, so these sediments were compresssed and heated into rock. Then, about 130 million years ago, earth movements lifted them from the waves, creating a proto-New Zealand, many times larger than the present-day landmass.

At first this new landmass was part of coastal Gondwana, so it inherited the supercontinent's flora and fauna. These included not only the dinosaurs, but also the ancestors of New Zealand's modern-day tuatara, frogs, weta, land snails, earthworms, and many other small invertebrates. Among the plants would have been ancestors of the podocarps, kauri, and some tree ferns, ferns, and mosses.

New Zealand's birth coincided with a time of great biological and geological change on Gondwana. During the Cretaceous period, 135–65 million years ago, three major living groups were starting to diversify and spread across the land — the birds, flowering plants, and modern mammals. Yet, at the same time, earth movements began to cleave the continent apart, severing the land links across which these groups could spread.

South America and Africa were the first to start breaking ties,

creating the beginnings of the South Atlantic and Indian Oceans. Similar rifts opened between Australia and New Zealand, so that by 100–80 million years ago an infant Tasman Sea had crept between them. This had a profound effect on the passage of immigrant plants and animals. Some early flowering plants, such as beech trees, managed to spread across the southern continents (including New Zealand) while they were still attached to one another. A number of primitive bird groups had also probably become widely distributed; but for the modern mammals, which were last to spread across the fragmenting supercontinent, it was too late. By the time they reached the New Zealand region, seas are thought to have barred the route to further migration. The young island continent had drifted into isolation.

This early isolation sealed New Zealand's biological identity for ever more. Some life forms were able to survive here which, on other continents, would have been dominated by the overwhelming success of mammals and flowering plants. This is not to say that New Zealand remained some sort of isolated biological paradise, protected from the forces of evolutionary change. Its passage through time was testing, with extreme changes of both climate and landscape. For the inhabitants of the island continent, there was also no easy option of migrating to more pleasant lands when things got tough. It was adapt or perish.

Neither was New Zealand completely isolated. New colonists — particularly flying animals and plants with wind- or bird-dispersed seeds — could arrive by sea or air, especially if they rode the westerly weather systems that blow from Australia. Among bird colonists were ancestors of the rock wren, kakapo, and takahe, which, not having ground-dwelling mammalian predators to contend with, lost some or all of their powers of flight.

The ancestor of the short-tailed bat was another early arrival, probably originating in South America and crossing the then-green Antarctica to reach New Zealand. It too became partially flightless. During a semitropical phase in the country's history, about 25 million years ago, colonists migrated from warmer latitudes. For a while coconut palms fringed the shore and corals grew off northern coastlines, until a return to temperate conditions forced their extinction.

The New Zealand landscape we are familiar with today has taken shape within the last 2–3 million years. Until 20 million years ago the island continent that split from Gondwana had been whittled away by erosion until it was reduced to a few low-lying islands. Then, just as it seemed destined to vanish beneath the waves, earth forces started to lift the land once more. Movement along the boundary between two crustal plates, the Indian–Australian Plate and the Pacific Plate, began to heave up the land, giving birth to the Southern Alps.

No sooner had these mountains started to rise than they were besieged by ice. By 2 million years ago, cooling world temperatures initiated the Ice Age. Large snowfields and glaciers smothered the young high country and reached into the lowlands, particularly in the south. It was an unforgiving period, which not only carved New Zealand's magnificent glacial terrain, but also sorely tested the survival of the flora and fauna. Many species, which until then had only experienced millions of years of warm–temperate conditions, became extinct. Some managed to hang on by finding refuge in the warmest parts of the country. Yet

Top left:
Ice fall,
Tasman Glacier

Middle left:
Kauri bark

Bottom left:
Sand dunes,
Farewell Spit

Below:
Alpine weta

11

others, including the kea, rock wren, alpine weta, celmisias, hebes, and other alpine plants, evolved apace with the change, producing species that could cope with the cold and mountainous terrain.

When the glaciers retreated some 12,000 years ago, New Zealand was left with a truly unique natural history. It combined an eclectic mix of archaic organisms, such as the tuatara that had managed to survive the 80 million years of isolation from Gondwana, with more recent immigrants that had managed against considerable odds to cross the surrounding oceans. All had evolved in response to extreme environmental changes and to the unusual community of organisms that had assembled on the emergent New Zealand.

Notably, in the absence of mammals, many insects and birds evolved mammal-like roles, filling feeding niches similar to those usually filled elsewhere by mice, shrews, rabbits, and deer. Not only did some birds become flightless ground feeders, they also lost defensive strategies to cope with mammals. The only predators they had to contend with were others of their own kind, such as a giant eagle — far larger than any eagle alive in the world today — that once preyed on moa.

Thus it was that the flora and fauna, which had been sheltered from mammals for so long, was simply unable to cope when the isolation was finally broken. Maori arrived about 1000 years ago and within 500 years had largely hunted the moa and other large birds into extinction. The dog, or kuri, and Polynesian rat, or kiore, which Maori brought with them had a similar impact on smaller flightless birds, insects, and reptiles. The arrival of Europeans, with a multitude of imported plants and animals, continued this process. Predatory stoats, ship rats, and Norway rats rapidly

Left:
Short-tailed bat
and weta

13

lowered the numbers of many native birds, including kakapo, kokako, and the native thrush. Grazing by deer, possums, and thar meanwhile destroyed vulnerable plant species.

Although comparatively recent, human colonisation has proved overwhelming for many plants and animals. Birdlife has been particularly hard hit, with half of all endemic species being lost. Gone are the giant moa, as well as the flightless wrens that scurried like mice through the leaf litter. Yet wonders do remain. Because of its very isolation, New Zealand was one of the last habitable landmasses on earth to be settled by humans. It retains vast tracts of virgin forest and wildernesses that embrace ecosystems stretching from snow summits to surf beaches. In many parts of the country, it is still possible to wander from the roadside and lose oneself in another age.

Northland
beach

profoundly at ease with their environment

Situated on the Pacific 'ring of fire' — a geological belt of earthquake and volcanic activity — New Zealand is one of the world's most active mountain-building regions. Beneath its surface the Pacific and the Indian–Australian crustal plates slide against each other, shattering and lifting great blocks of land into mountains. Along the Alpine Fault, which extends from Milford to Marlborough in the South Island, these forces are literally tearing the country in two. Rock that was once part of Fiordland has been pushed northwards to form the Paparoa Range 400 kilometres away. The uplift of the land has also been vigorous. During the past few million years some 20 vertical kilometres of rock have been raised. The process continues today, pushing up the Alps by as much as two centimetres per year.

Scouring by rivers and glaciers has seen to it that little more than three out of the 20 kilometres of lifted rock remains standing on the horizon. Erosion and plate tectonics have nevertheless been creative adversaries. From Mount Hikurangi in the north to Fiordland in the south, their handiwork is as spectacular as it is varied.

The alpine landscapes found in the eastern North Island — the Raukumara, Kaimanawa, and Ruahine ranges — are a thickly forested complex of ridges, relieved by open mountaintops of alpine tussock. It is a rugged back-country and largely off the beaten path for all but the experienced tramper. Further west, Tongariro and Egmont National Parks give well-tracked and popular access to outstanding volcanic terrain. The former, in particular, is an outdoor lesson in physical geography. Craters, vents, thermal pools, and lava flows are exposed to view. The landscape is palpably young and of uncertain destiny. The main peaks of Ruapehu and Ngauruhoe are both given to periodic out-bursts of steam and ash.

The South Island is home to the most extensive alpine areas. The Southern Alps, the island's backbone, rise from the drowned river systems of the Marlborough Sounds and reach their zenith in the glacial summits of Mount Cook National Park before ending in the labyr-inthine ranges of Fiordland. It is a distance of 800 kilometres, which offers an outdoor adventure almost without end.

On one hand there is the vast and largely untracked wilderness of the western ranges of Fiordland, Mount Aspiring, and Kahurangi

Left:
Kea

Top right:
Cloud forest,
Westland

Bottom right:
Odd-leaved orchid

High country

National Parks, where one may walk for weeks without seeing any sign of humanity. On the other hand there are well-formed walks, such as the Heaphy, Routeburn, and Milford, where the less experienced can find a route into exceptional scenery. Between these extremes are large and moderately tracked mountain regions such as Nelson Lakes National Park, Arthur's Pass National Park, and Lewis Pass, which suit those who have already served some apprenticeship in the hills.

Access to alpine landscapes does not necessarily entail long hours of climbing steep trails. Several areas are within relatively easy reach of the road. In the North Island, both Egmont and Tongariro National Parks have well-formed roads that take you within striking distance of mountain habitats. In the South Island, impressive areas include Arthur's Pass and Mount Cook National Parks, as well as the Milford Road.

To venture into the alpine zone is always an experience. The world opens up, expanding into a sea of mountains that seem to go on forever. But beyond the physical dimensions you are struck by the wealth of biological detail. Almost half of all native plants are found here, and some of their diversity can be viewed by wandering steadily uphill.

Immediately above the bushline are waist-high tussocks and small-leaved shrubs. As you climb higher, the vegetation diminishes in size in response to the increasingly harsh demands of mountain life. Feathered expanses of low tussock shelters species of delicate flowering gentian, celmisia, and olearia. In the Southern Alps you may also find showy clusters of the Mount Cook lily, which is actually the world's largest buttercup.

Left:
Milford Sound
from Sandfly Point

Go higher still and the plant life shrinks back to tiny green islands in an ocean of grey rock. Miniature gardens of buttercups, daisies, and edelweiss crouch in the lee of boulders and along sheltered streambeds. In the higher South Island ranges live the curious hummocky plants called vegetable sheep. These are actually shrubs that have adopted an extreme growth form to survive conditions that would defeat most other plants. Their growing tips are sheltered within whorls of felt-covered leaves. These are, in turn, packed together to form a rigid domed canopy almost impervious to the outside world. Thus the plant creates a modified microclimate, warmer and moister than the outside environment, and one that is better able to recycle the products of its own decay. It is about as close as the plant world comes to creating a 'space ship' to colonise an inhospitable world.

The success and diversity of alpine plants presents biologists with a puzzle. New Zealand's alpine habitats have come into existence only during the past 2–3 million years, which is rather a short period for so many specialist plants to have evolved from lowland ancestors. Yet this

Left:
Needle frost

Below:
Paradise
shelduck

Mt Cook lilies

must be what happened in many cases, given that the nearest overseas mountain range that could offer an ancestral source of plant colonists is thousands of kilometres away. It seems that evolution was swift and home-grown, with lowland species adapting to the mountains as they were created. As a result, 95 per cent of the New Zealand alpine flora is found nowhere else in the world.

It is also the case that many alpine animals evolved from lowland ancestors. Among them is the alpine weta, which scientists have discovered has the dubious distinction of being the largest insect that can survive being completely frozen. The most noticeable alpine insects, particularly on calm sunny days, are those that take to the air, pollinating the sea of alpine flowers. The majority of small colourful 'butterflies' seen in alpine areas are actually moths, which fly in daylight to take advantage of the warmer conditions. There are several hundred species, vastly outnumbering the handful of true butterflies that live above the bushline. Of the latter, you may see orange-brown tussock butterflies and black mountain ringlet butterflies. Crawling and chewing through the alpine foliage are cicadas, beetles, weevils and grasshoppers.

Among birds, the pipit is regularly encountered in the mountains. It is easily mistaken for the introduced skylark, but has the distinctive habit of making short runs, bobbing frequently and flicking its tail. One bird there can be no mistaking is the kea. This inhabitant of the Southern Alps is a large parrot, closely related to the kaka of the lowlands. It has an insatiable curiosity, particularly about humans and their possessions. For this reason kea often loiter near car-parks in the mountains, particularly at Mount Cook and Arthur's Pass. They are amiable intelligent rogues and their antics can be both entertaining and infuriating, depending on whose car they have chosen to relieve of its windscreen wipers.

Kea are seen in their best light when further from human settlement. In the mountains they seem profoundly at ease with the fickle nature of the environment. They sometimes perform aerobatics in the midst of storms, presumably for the sheer exhilaration of it. Yet despite their mountain savvy, kea do retreat below the bushline to nest.

Only one bird remains in the alpine zone all year round — the rock wren — but it is not easy to find, living as it does in fairly high and remote places. It is also very small, weighing little more than a 50-cent coin. The rock wren's favourite habitat is a place jumbled with boulders and small shrubs. Here it can be seen making short flights and constantly bobbing up and down on its seemingly oversized feet. How so tiny a bird survives the winter remains a mystery. Some ornithologists speculate that it seeks a dry resting place beneath the snow and goes into a torpid state, allowing the body temperature to drop.

In prehistoric times the mountains were home to takahe and kakapo, which ranged above the bushline in summer to browse on tussocks and alpine herbs. Both have now been pushed to the brink of extinction by the competition and predation of introduced mammals.

The takahe, a large relative of the pukeko, numbers fewer than 200 in the wild. These are restricted to the Murchison Mountains and Stuart Mountains of Fiordland, where they are protected by the Department of Conservation. Captive birds, however, can be seen at Te Anau and at Mount Bruce, and individuals are being released on offshore islands open to the public, such as Tiritiri Matangi in the Hauraki Gulf. The kakapo, the world's largest flightless parrot, has fared worse than the takahe. There are fewer than

Left:
Granite boulders,
Stewart Island

50 birds left and these are the subject of an intense conservation effort on the protected islands of Codfish and Little Barrier.

The only large herbivores to be found above the bushline today are introduced mammals — deer, chamois, and thar. Alien to the native ecology, they damage the alpine vegetation if allowed to go unchecked, and any plant loss is irreplaceable given that so much of the flora is unique. Nevertheless, it is hard to reconcile the label of ecological villain with the magnificent chamois nimbly picking its way along a remote mountain ridge. The true criminal is human folly for bringing these animals to a land where they do not belong.

Left:
Shaler Range,
Arthur's Pass
National Park

Above:
Takahe chicks

Top:
Sunset behind
Mt Taranaki
(Holger Leue)

Top right:
Mt Ngauruhoe

Right:
Sunrise from
Mt Luna, Kahurangi
National Park

Above:
Winter sunset on
Mt Rintoul,
Richmond Range

Far right:
Franz Josef Glacier
terminal, Westland
National Park

Above:
Mt Christina
from the
Livingstone
Mountains,
Fiordland
National Park

Right:
Main Divide and
moraine pool,
Tasman Glacier

Top right:
Otago skink

Far top right:
Black mountain ringlet
butterfly

Middle right:
Giant mountain dragonfly

Bottom right:
Tussock butterfly

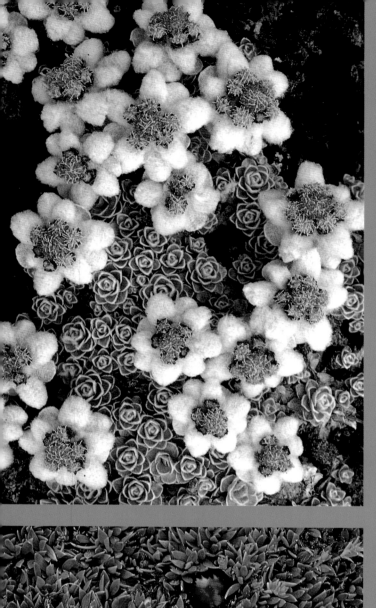

Top left:
Edelweiss

Top middle:
Vegetable sheep

Top right:
Sundew

Bottom left:
Coprosma

Bottom middle:
Ranunculus
sericophyllus

Bottom right:
Hebe

a green and watered land

Above:
Arahaki Lagoon,
Whirinaki Forest Park

Right:
Common river galaxiid

With mountains braced against the roaring forties, New Zealand is a green and watered land. On western coastlines that face the prevailing weather systems, the annual precipitation is measured in metres. Even a single storm can deposit half a metre in its wake. During the Ice Age, when this fell in frozen form, snow-fed glaciers carved the magnificent

Above:
Pukeko

Right:
Arahaki Lagoon
(detail)

landforms of the South Island, and also left their mark on upland areas of the North Island. Today, rivers continue the erosion, cutting gorges and spreading the rubble across riverflats and broad floodplains.

Trout, and to a lesser extent salmon, are the most conspicuous fish in these waterways. Both were introduced as sport fish, although one could be forgiven for concluding that they were native, so successful have they been. Brown trout is widespread, with rainbow trout having a more limited distribution. Of the three species of salmon introduced, quinnat is the best established. Like its Northern Hemisphere relatives, the fish spend several years at sea before returning to spawn in their river of birth.

Native fish, of which there are about 30 species, tend to be small, cryptic, and nocturnal, so are rarely noticed. In fact, they would not exist at all in the minds of many people were it not for whitebait. Considered a culinary delicacy, whitebait are the young of several species of galaxiid fish, netted in late winter and early spring as they enter estuaries and swim upstream. The 'season' is a major event on the nation's calendar, when whitebaiters pack their nets and head for a favourite spot by some remote river to endure cold, rain and clouds of bloodthirsty sandflies — all in the hope of a bucket full of the tiny transparent fish.

Above:
Little Arch,
Oparara Valley

For the whitebait shoals, entering the estuary represents the end of the first major hurdle in what is an unusual life cycle. Adult fish live inland, in rivers and swamps. In autumn they migrate downstream to spawn at the rivermouth, somehow timing their arrival to coincide precisely with the high flood tide of the new or full moon. The fish lay their eggs on vegitation well up on the riverbank, where they are left high and dry until the next flood tide a fortnight later. Then the eegs hatch and the the fish larvae are swept out to sea where they live and grow during the winter months.

The few fish that survive this episode assemble offshore to enter the rivermouth as whitebait and head upstream to grow to adulthood. Sad to say, even if they elude the whitebaiters' nets, worse may lie ahead in the headwaters. Many inland waterways have been modified by human activity, so suitable habitats for the adult fish have become scarce.

In their natural state, New Zealand's rivers typically flow clear, across bouldery beds and between corridors of forest. This is the ideal situation in which to find native aquatic species, whether they be fish or the many insect larvae, such as mayflies, stoneflies, and caddisflies, that live on the underside of submerged rocks. The most remote of these

environments are also the only places you are likely to encounter the threatened blue duck, a species unique to New Zealand, and one of the few ducks worldwide to have adapted to life on fast-flowing water.

Likely areas to see blue ducks in the North Island are in the head-waters of the Whirinaki and Wanganui Rivers, as well as in the mountain catchments of Urewera National Park. In the South Island, this threatened species can be found in all of the larger national parks, with the greatest population being in Fiordland National Park. Those walking the Milford Track will often see the birds at Clinton Forks.

It is the call of a blue duck that will first attract your attention — the male's high-pitched fluty whistle is commonly heard near dusk when the birds are most actively feeding. If you can find a spot to sit and watch, the sight is pure enchantment. The blue duck has extraordinary grace, dodging and darting among the rapids with consummate ease. In the gathering darkness it floats over the turbulent surface like a grey shadow, diving occasionally to pluck insect larvae from the bottom with its unusual soft-tipped bill.

Forming a complete contrast to these forested waterways are the river systems that drain from the eastern flanks of the South Island mountains. Over the past 2 million years, glacial erosion and frost shattering of the Alps' greywacke rock have produced an enormous outflow of shingle, which rivers have spread across broad flats, colonised by lichens, tussocks, and small scattered shrubs.

Surrounded by snowy peaks, these braided river systems are awesome landscapes, exposed to all the physical extremes of the environment. Yet, perhaps surprisingly, they are also vital habitats for many waterbirds, which migrate here to nest in spring. On the inland riverbeds of Canterbury and Otago you are likely to encounter dotterels, pied stilts, Canada geese, pied oystercatchers, paradise shelducks, terns, and gulls.

The rarest of the riverbed nesters, the wrybill and black stilt, can be found in the upper Waitaki Valley. Both are endemic and endangered. The tiny wrybill, with its unique laterally curved bill, spends most of the year feeding at estuaries in the North Island, but comes to nest

Below:
Jumping spider

Bottom:
Lichens

Left:
Blue ducks

39

Purakaunui Falls,
Catlins

here in early spring. The black stilt may remain on inland riverbeds all year, still feeding in mid-winter when the days are so cold that water freezes a bib of ice onto its chest.

Wetland — that other vital water habitat — is found in pockets throughout the country, from the coast to the mountains. Wetlands are enigmatic and seemingly ill-defined landforms, covering a number of often quite separate habitats.

Freshwater wetlands are of two main types, swamps and bogs. Swamps usually form where a river is blocked and the water seeps across soggy ground. They are fertile habitats because the river continues to contribute mineral-rich sediments and maintains a throughput of fresh water. Bogs form in areas of poor drainage where the water supply comes directly from falling rain rather than via rivers. They therefore lack an input of minerals and tend to be infertile while at the same time have stagnant oxygen-depleted water. Not only does this inhibit growth, it also stifles decay, with the result that dead vegetation (mostly sphagnum moss) accumulates as layers of waterlogged peat. In the long run this can cause the bog to spread, as the ever-growing mass of peat spills sideways and smothers surrounding areas.

In the North Island, fine wetlands can be found in the Waikato, notably at Kopuataii, with its striking example of a peat dome. This is a bog where the central portion, which is the wettest part and so accumulates the most peat, has become raised over the centuries, lifting the water-table with it. As a result the bog is a few metres higher in the middle than at the edges. It is a curious phenomenon, rather like an island of water in a sea of land. Living on its surface are numerous specialist plants and animals, nine of which are vulnerable or threatened, making this one of the nation's prime wetland sanctuaries.

In the South Island, one of the most distinctive regions for diversity of wetland habitat is Southland, with relatively well-known examples near Te Anau and at Waituna. The latter, which lines the gale-swept southern coastline, contains bog plants normally found in the alpine zone. Less well known, even to those who drive past it, is a large and virtually pristine wetland ecosystem near Haast on the West Coast. Just metres from the road are vast areas of swamp forest, broken by looking-glass lakes of peaty water.

While wetlands are not easy to explore on foot, they are nevertheless superior locations for birdlife, much of which can be observed from the safety of the margins with a pair of binoculars. Most visitors will soon recognize the ubiquitous mallard, introduced from the Northern Hemisphere and now New Zealand's most common duck. With time you will also see less familiar species — shoveler, grey teal, and

perhaps grey duck. Scaup can be observed on the deeper water of lakes, diving underwater in search of aquatic invertebrates. Visitors to some lakes, particularly Alexandrina in inland Canterbury, may also be fortunate to watch the exquisite nuptial dances of the crested grebe, one of the rarest and most beautiful of waterbirds.

Among swamp-dwelling rails, by far the most obvious and common is the pukeko, a close relative of the takahe. Not confining itself to reeds and rushes, it is often seen strutting across adjacent farmland, resplendent with royal-blue plumage and a bright orange beak. Of all the native wetland creatures the pukeko has fared best since human settlement, happily devouring pasture plants and their various insect pests such as grass grub. Other rails, the crakes, and coot are very shy and uncommon, as is the bittern. Sightings of any of these would be rare indeed.

One of the wetland's most unusual birds, the fernbird, is its least pretentious in appearance — small, brown, and with a rather bedraggled tail. An endemic member of the warbler family, it lives in the scrubby margins of bogs and swamps, and once you learn to recognize its brief metallic call it is a sound you will hear in many of the less disturbed wetland habitats. The caller is almost always invisible, but if you stay still and 'call' back by snapping your fingers, the fernbird will investigate, hopping through the dense vegetation to materialise suddenly before you. Such moments, so intimate and filled with life, are the magic of wetlands. Though lacking the scale and immediate appeal of alpine landcapes, thay can hold you just as surely if given the chance.

Top left:
Thermal sinter stone,
Rotorua

Top right:
Ice forms

Left:
Champagne Pool,
Rotorua

43

Pyke River and
Darran Mountains
Fiordland
National Park

Sutherland Falls
and Staircase Creek,
Fiordland
National Park

Lake Mavora,
Southland

Top left:
Blue damselfly

Top middle:
Wrybill

Top right:
Grey teal and chicks

Bottom left:
Black stilt

Bottom middle:
Pied stilt

Bottom right:
Black swan and chicks

a multitude of plants and animals

The first encounter with the podocarp forests that cover moist lowland regions of New Zealand can be a surprise. Immediately, you are engulfed by a damp world of wall-to-wall vegetation. With a luxuriance more typical of the tropics, the greenery leaves no space untouched. Even the trunks of fallen trees are smothered with seedlings competing in a mad scramble for light.

While it may take time, it is possible to find order in the apparent confusion. Dominant are the coniferous podocarp trees — rimu, kahikatea, totara, and matai — whose tall crowns pierce through a main canopy of broadleaved flowering trees such as towai, tawa, and kamahi. Below this are sub-canopies of smaller trees and large spreading tree ferns entwined in vines and epiphytes. Finally, at ground level, is a twilight world of ferns, mosses, and forest-floor orchids.

The term 'dinosaur forest' has been coined for these forests, with some justification. With their multi-storey layering they are considered to have similarities in structure to the forest that covered New Zealand at the time it split from Gondwana. Some of the trees are also of ancient

Forest

Far left:
Praying mantis

Above:
Ferns

Left:
Mountain
ribbonwood

51

Top left:
Kauri grove,
Puketi Forest

Middle left:
Kahikatea trees,
Whirinaki Forest

Left:
Goblin forest,
Urewera
National Park

Top right:
Moss forest on
Milford Track

Above:
Rain forest,
Stewart Island

lineage. Fossil records indicate that rimu and kahikatea have changed little in 70 million years, and were surely browsed by dinosaurs.

One of the best examples of podocarp forest is at Whirinaki in the central North Island. An enormous eruption of Lake Taupo about 1800 years ago decimated the plant life that grew here, setting in motion a process of succession that has culminated in breath-taking forest stands. Many trees are more than 800 years old and have grown into veritable giants on the fertile volcanic soils. The whole region is also an important showcase for forest wildlife, including rare species such as the blue duck and kaka.

While podocarp forests appear tropical, beech forests are definitely temperate. The dominant tree, one of four species of beech, presides over a relatively simple understorey of small shrubs and beech saplings. Beneath the canopy it is open and airy, with dappled light filtering down to the carpet of ferns and soft mosses on the forest floor. There is an orderliness akin to the deciduous woodlands of the Northern Hemisphere, which is perhaps not surprising considering that New Zealand beeches come from the same family (Fagaceae) as the northern beeches, oaks, and chestnuts.

Beech forest thrives in drier and cooler parts of the country, so as a rule it is found by travelling east away from high-rainfall areas or by heading into the hills. Thus, it holds sway over vast tracts of the eastern mountains of the South Island, including most of Fiordland. Throughout much of this range it extends an unbroken mantle from the valley floor to the bushline.

The most common beech species in any area depends on the prevailing conditions. Black and hard beech prefer warmer lowland areas, while red beech usually occupies the foothills, particularly on more fertile ground. Montane forests are the domain of

silver and mountain beech (a subspecies of black beech). The former, which predominates in moister regions, is responsible for the wonderful cloud forests of gnarled moss-cloaked trees that cover the western slopes of many ranges.

A third major forest type, though less extensive than podocarp and beech forests, is perhaps the most commanding. The kauri forests of Northland and Coromandel feature one of the world's largest species of tree. It is not the height of the kauri tree that is impressive, so much as the girth. A kauri will have completed most of its vertical growth by the tender age of 200 years. For the remaining 2000 to 3000 years (no one is sure how long they live) the tree adds weight to its enormous cylindrical trunk, which can measure more than 20 metres in circumference, with barely a taper for the first 25 metres from the ground.

But to look at a forest and see just trees would be to miss the truth that this is a community, comprising a vast multitude of plants and animals. The greatest living diversity is found among the 'lower' animals or invertebrates, and New Zealand forests are no exception to this. They contain an extraordinary 200 or so species of earthworm, 600 species of millipede, and perhaps more than 1000 species of snail.

Notable among invertebrates are weta. These large, flightless, cricket-like insects are another 'dinosaur' relic from the time when New Zealand was part of Gondwana. In the absence of terrestrial mammals (bats excepted) they have thrived and diversified to occupy the niche of scavengers and herbivores, which on most landmasses is occupied by rodents. Sadly, with the introduction of rats and mice, weta have suffered both predation and competition. Worst affected have been species of giant weta, which are now virtually restricted to rodent-free offshore islands. The smaller bush weta remains relatively easy to find, usually spending the daylight hours sheltering in the hollow of a rotten tree trunk or behind loose bark.

First meetings with a weta may be a little alarming (for both parties) as the weta is of fearsome looks and dimensions. However, it is a harmless and fascinating creature. Despite its brutish reputation, zoologists have found the weta to have quite sophisticated social and courtship interactions.

The thriving invertebrate community is the mainstay for several

Left:
Red beech, Lewis Pass

Right:
New Zealand pigeon

insect-eating birds. Robins, tomtits, and fantails are the most conspicuous of these, often approaching you out of territorial curiosity or in the hope of a feed of insects disturbed in your wake. The only specialised fruit-eater is the large New Zealand pigeon, or kereru. Between spells of snoozing on a full belly of forest fruit, it flies through the canopy with a slow, distinctive wingbeat.

Other forest birds are omnivorous, taking a mixed diet of insects, fruit, and nectar, which they vary according to season. The bellbird and tui are the most vocal of these opportunist feeders. Both are gifted songsters, performing an extraodinary range of chuckles, rasps, and fluty, melodious tunes. One of the most hauntingly beautiful sounds in the forest, and now unfortunately one of the rarest, is the call of the kokako. Once plentiful throughout the country, kokako now inhabit only a few North Island forests. Puketi Forest and the Kaimai–Mamaku Ranges are two areas where you may find these birds, which do occasionally come down close to ground level where they can be readily seen. They scramble and hop along branches with unusually strong, agile legs, but are indifferent fliers, usually making just short glides between trees.

Another increasingly rare song is that of the kaka, the lowland relative of the kea. This large parrot exists in small populations in North Island forest areas, but is most common in the western South Island. It feeds in the canopy, often noisily ripping apart rotten trunks and branches in search of grubs and dropping the debris to the ground. At other times the kaka laps up nectar from flowering rata with its brush-tipped tongue. Then at dusk it flies to its roost, calling late into the evening with musical garrulity.

After dark the forest offers a whole new world to be investigated. This is when most of the invertebrates — the spiders, snails, moths, and millipedes — come out of hiding. On a night walk you may hear the whispered 'zit-zit-zit' of a weta calling to its neighbours. Damp sheltered banks shine with magical pinpricks of light emitted by glow-worms, waiting to snare small flies with beaded curtains of sticky threads.

New Zealand's only surviving endemic owl, the morepork, or ruru, can be heard in almost any bush patch, calling a softly repetitive

Below:
Huhu beetle

'more-pork' and sometimes breaking into a more guttural and spine-chilling screech.

One of the few places you are guaranteed to hear the whistling call of a kiwi is on Stewart Island. Here, kiwi not only exist in significant numbers, they also frequently come out in daylight, making sightings quite common. Elsewhere in New Zealand the kiwi population is scattered and, in many areas, even declining, although it is always worth keeping an ear to the darkness when you are out in the forest. Kiwi have been established on some offshore islands, most notably Kapiti, which is now the stronghold for the little spotted kiwi. Kapiti is also a haven for other rare birds, such as the stitchbird and saddleback. To ensure its security as a sanctuary, the island is accessible only to permit holders.

Night is also the domain of New Zealand's only native land mammals, the long-tailed bat and short-tailed bat. In evolutionary terms the long-tailed bat is a newcomer to New Zealand, with close relatives in Australia whence its ancestors came. The short-tailed bat has a more ancient and obscure ancestry, perhaps originating in South America many millions of years ago. In the absence of ground-dwelling mammals it has become the most terrestrial of bats, able to fold up its wings and forage on the forest floor like a small rodent. This has been its downfall in the face of introduced predators, and the healthiest populations now exist on offshore islands, such as Little Barrier and Codfish. The long-tailed bat, although more common, is itself not seen very often. It flies at dusk, hunting in open areas and near water. In the half light it can easily be mistaken for a swallow.

Top left:
Brown kiwi

Top middle:
Weka

Above:
Litter of Hector's
tree daisy

Left:
Hygrophorus
fungus

59

Top left:
Forest creek,
Mount Aspiring
National Park

Far left:
Peripatus

Left:
Hamilton's frog

Top:
South Island
robin

Above:
Bush weta

61

Top:
Red admiral and
epiphytic orchids

Above:
Elephant weevil

Top right:
Northland
green gecko

Far right:
Violet pouch fungus

Right:
Basket fungus

Top left:
Clematis

Top middle:
Tree fuchsia

Top right:
Easter orchids

Bottom left:
Spider orchids

Bottom middle:
Kowhai

Bottom right:
Wineberry

65

a surprising
variety of life

The coastline is a diverse habitat. From the dunes of Ninety Mile Beach to the plunging cliffs of Fiordland, the landscape constantly changes. Muddy inlet yields to ocean beach, then rocky headland and sheltered bay, each sustaining a myriad of living communities uniquely adapted to the prevailing conditions.

Exposed rocky shores, which seem so inhospitable to us, support a surprising variety of life, which either glues itself onto wave-thrashed surfaces or seeks refuge in tiny fissures and beneath boulders. At low tide, visitors can explore miniature seaweed jungles inhabited by starfish, sea urchins, crabs, mussels, barnacles, and sponges. By contrast, the beaches — so favoured by humans — are inhospitable to most sea creatures, which cannot tolerate the constantly shifting and abrasive nature of sand. Those that do live here, such as toheroa and tuatua, usually manage by burying themselves out of sight.

Perhaps the most rewarding coastlines to visit, especially for bird-watchers, are estuaries. Here rivers deposit deep beds of fertile mud, creating one of nature's most productive ecosystems. The prolific growth of algae lays the foundation for a food chain that supports crustaceans, molluscs, and worms living buried in the sediment. These in turn attract flocks of wading birds — oystercatchers, godwits, stilts, herons, and others — that pick and probe in search of food.

Estuaries, with their attendant birdlife, can be found near most

Far left:
Ice plant

Above:
Beach detail

Left:
Mangrove and aerial roots

67

coastal centres. Fine examples exist at Ohiwa, Kawhia, Foxton, and the Firth of Thames in the North Island, and at Bluff and Farewell Spit in the South Island. Large flocks of birds wheel through the air, and, by looking through a pair of binoculars, you can tick off a checklist — dotterel, knot, stilt, plover, turnstone, sandpiper . . . Most of these birds are migratory, departing for the breeding season. Some species, such as pied oystercatchers, stilts, and wrybills, head inland at the end of winter to nest. Others, including godwits, knots, and sandpipers, depart in autumn to travel the enormous distance to their nesting grounds in Siberia and Alaska.

A close encounter with the finer points of estuarine ecology is difficult unless you are willing to don boots and wade into the mud. Boardwalks, however, have been erected at a few locations. At Waitangi in Northland it is possible to wander through stands of mangroves, which so dominate the ecology of estuaries in warm parts of the country. Near Haast in South Westland another walkway explores the Hapuka Estuary, winding among tall rimu, groves of kowhai, and sea-washed fringes of rushes.

Some sites offer sea-borne viewing, made possible by hiring a canoe to float across the submerged mudflats at high tide. Okarito Lagoon on the West Coast of the South Island ranks as the most spectacular location for this. From the water an almost seamless transition of ecosystems rises before you, from saltmarsh, through podocarp forest, to the fellfields and snowy glaciers of the Southern Alps beyond.

Among the wildlife at the lagoon is the white heron, or kotuku, whose ice-bright form shines against the sweep of dark forest beyond. The birds become common in September when they congregate to nest in kahikatea trees lining the banks of the nearby Waitangiroto River. This is the only nesting site for white herons in New Zealand. For the rest of the year the birds disperse throughout the country, feeding in estuaries, swamps, and even damp paddocks.

Seabirds can be watched from almost all exposed coastal cliffs or headlands, many of which serve as nesting sites for colonies of shags, seagulls, and terns. Occasionally you can spot petrels and shearwaters, skimming the wave crests with outstretched wings. In fact more than half of the world's 100 or so species of albatross, shearwater, petrel, and prion (collectively called the tubenoses) are seen in New Zealand waters.

A few of these tubenose species maintain small colonies on the

Top left:
Godwits at Miranda

Bottom left:
Heaphy coast

Above:
White-faced heron

Ohinemaka beach
and Mt Strachan,
South Westland

mainland, but mostly they crowd onto the many islands offshore, where they are spared the problems caused by introduced predators. Breeding densities can be phenomenal and burrow nesters can honeycomb islands. The 328 hectares of the Snares Islands host almost 6 million sooty shearwaters, which is said to be as many seabirds as inhabit the entire coastline of Britain.

Gannets are often seen off the coast, diving for fish by folding their wings and plunging from the air like spears. To study them at closer range it is possible to visit one of the few mainland nesting colonies, Cape Kidnappers and Muriwai in the North Island being the most accessible. The birds pack together tail to beak, although the sense of community is not all that it might at first seem. Each bird vigorously defends its territory, fiercely snapping at any neighbour that strays within reach. Individuals recognize their mates from the sea of identical-looking birds with the aid of specific postures, often followed by mutual preening sessions. The behavioural complexities are a treat to observe, particularly as gannets usually nest on inaccessible islands.

Another rare opportunity presents itself on the Otago Peninsula, near Dunedin in the South Island. The royal albatross, which ranges throughout the subantarctic seas, nesting mostly on remote islands, maintains a small colony at Taiaroa Head at the tip of the peninsula. Between long spells spent circling the southern latitudes of the earth, each albatross returns faithfully to the same nest site and partner, where they greet each other with elaborate courtship postures.

The Otago Peninsula is home to another rarity, the yellow-eyed penguin, which is possibly the world's rarest penguin. It comes ashore at a number of nesting areas along the south-eastern coast of the South Island, from Banks Peninsula to Southland and Stewart Island. In contrast to the gregarious habits of other penguins, breeding pairs prefer to nest out of sight of one another, preferably in the shelter of thick coastal scrub. The clearance of habitat for farmland, introduction of predators, and disturbance from people have made the yellow-eyed penguin's future uncertain. Nevertheless, it struggles on, with such determination that it has won the hearts of a growing band of supporters who have made wonderful efforts to restore and secure the bird's habitat, as well as provide viewing hides for visitors.

Less of a celebrity but equally endearing (and probably just as rare) is the Fiordland crested penguin, which frequents the isolated

Top:
Kaipo coastline,
Fiordland

Above:
Hooker's sea lion

Top right:
Doughboy Bay,
Stewart Island

Bottom right:
Blowhole,
Punakaiki

south-western coastline of the South Island. It nests in small and sometimes noisy colonies among scrub-covered boulders. Much of the penguin's coastal habitat is remote, although there are opportunties to see this bird at beaches near the Haast Highway. The most successful and responsible tactic is to take binoculars and sit quietly at a hidden vantage point, for if the penguins see you they will not come ashore to feed their young. With luck you will be able to watch them hop from the surf after a day's fishing and waddle across the beach before vanishing into the scrub.

The south-western corner of New Zealand is also a stronghold for the fur seal, which last century was pitched into a precipitous decline by commercial hunting. Recent protection has witnessed a steady recovery, with seals becoming an increasingly common sight on rocky coasts. Individuals are even encountered hauled out for a snooze and sunbathe north of Auckland. The breeding colonies, however, remain further south, with one of the most accessible being near Cape Foulwind at Westport.

There have been recent hopes for the recovery of another seal, the Hooker's sea lion, which is considered the world's rarest sea lion. It is thought that this species bred on mainland New Zealand in prehistoric times, but disappeared, possibly through over-hunting by Maori. Today, while breeding colonies are restricted to the subantarctic islands, batchelors, not yet able to defend a harem, often visit the Otago and Southland coasts, where they haul out to wallow on ocean beaches. Recently, female sea lions have also been sighted and a first newborn pup was discovered in 1993, raising a tantalising possibility for the future.

The largest of all seals, the elephant seal, maintains a small yet steady presence in the south of the South Island. There is no mistaking this animal. Males weigh three tonnes and have a prominent snout that allows them to make an impressive bellow. From the cliffs of Nugget Point in the Catlins, they can sometimes be watched swimming with ponderous grace among swirling fronds of bull kelp. Out at sea, these creatures travel enormous distances and can dive to a depth of 1200 metres, an extraordinary feat equalled only by the sperm whale.

Hunting for whales in New Zealand waters continued until the middle of this century, and caused severe depletion of species such as the right whale. Sperm whales and orca, however, can still be seen, and swim

close to shore where the continental shelf is narrow. Whale-watching ventures operate in both the North and South Islands, with Kaikoura being the best known region for such observation. Here the shelf gives way to deep water just a few kilometres offshore and upwelling nutrient-rich seawater provides good feeding grounds for whales and many other marine mammals, including the rare Hector's dolphin. On a fine day you can even watch whales from a small hill by the township, their spouts issuing from the ocean below.

Sooner or later, anyone who spends time walking by the coast will encounter dolphins — in any bay and, in calm weather, even close to exposed coasts. First there is a splash and a small dark shadow, then the sea is alive with fins arching and dipping through the waves. The sudden spectacle of wild lives is invigorating and reassuring, a reminder of undisturbed relationships of the sea.

Top left:
Coast musk

Top middle:
Fiordland
crested penguin

Above:
Yellow-eyed
penguin

Left:
Elephant seal

77

Fiordland crested
penguin and
fur seal

Nic Bishop,

photographer

TRAINING
YOUR
DOG

TRAINING YOUR
DOG

JOAN PALMER

a Salamander book

Published by Salamander Books Limited
LONDON • NEW YORK

A Salamander Book

Published by Salamander Books Ltd.,
52 Bedford Row,
London WC1R 4LR,
England.

ISBN 0 86101 229 1

Distributed by Hodder and Stoughton Services,
PO Box 6, Mill Road, Dunton Green,
Sevenoaks, Kent TN13 2XX.

Credits

Editor: Jilly Glassborow
Designer: Roger Hyde

Colour reproductions: TrendAdd Ltd., Essex, England
and Melbourne Graphics Ltd., London, England.
Filmset: Modern Text Typesetting Ltd., Essex, England.

Printed in Belgium by Proost International Book
Production, Turnhout, Belgium.

Author

Joan Palmer is a former honorary official of the National Dog Owners' Association of the United Kingdom, a voluntary organization which pioneered pet owner education and the setting up of instructors courses in dog training. She is currently a member of the Society for Companion Animal Studies, the Scottish Kennel Club and several breed clubs, and has exhibited Airedales, Chihuahuas and Chinese Crested dogs in the show ring. Other hobbies include riding, gardening, travel and historical research.

Joan has written a considerable number of full length works, including two previous dog books for Salamander. One of these, *A Dog of Your Own*, won a Best Multi-Breed Book award from the Dog Writers' Association of America. A former staff journalist, Joan now works as a freelance author, writing regularly on consumer affairs and show business as well as on animal subjects. She also occasionally lectures on public relations at the School of Media Studies at the Polytechnic of Central London. Her time is divided between her London flat in Hampstead and her home in Moffat, Dumfriesshire, in Scotland.

Consultants

Harold Bellamy is a member of the National Dog Owners' Association of the United Kingdom, and the Society for Companion Animal Studies. He is interested in establishing a better standard of informed dog ownership and, as one of the founders, has been helping to run a dog training club for the household pet in the Birmingham area for over 20 years. He is also a Championship Show judge of both obedience trials and Samoyeds, his own principal showing breed, and is an Open Show judge of several other breeds.

Michael A. Findlay B.V.M.S., M.R.C.V.S. is a veterinarian who has been particularly involved with dog obedience training and has written or contributed to several books on pet animal care. He is an honorary veterinarian to several dog clubs and shows in England, notably Crufts, and is a member of the UK Kennel Club.

Peter Lewis is a Championship Show judge and a prolific winner in working and obedience trials. When agility tests were introduced by the Kennel Club in 1980, he immediately rose to the top of the sport as a handler. He has since written a book entitled *The Agility Dog*, and become chairman of the Agility Club. His expertise is sought across the world in this exciting new sport.

Hal Sundstrom, as president of Halamar Inc., publishers of North Virginia, has been editing and publishing magazines on travel and pure-bred dogs since 1972. He is the recipient of six national writing and public excellence awards from the Dog Writer's Association of America, of which he is now president, and he is the past president of the Collie Club of America.

Hal has an extensive background and enormous experience in the dog world, as a breeder/handler/exhibitor, match and sweeps judge, officer and director of specialty and all-breed clubs, show and symposium chairman, and officer of the Arizona and Hawaii Councils of Dog Clubs.

CONTENTS

Introduction

Dogs, like children, have to be trained to conform to an acceptable standard of behaviour, and to do so they have to learn to obey commands and not to make a nuisance of themselves. Once the rules have been learnt, the dogs are ready to take their place in society, and to live full and happy lives in their rightful role as man's companion.

People that enter the world of dogs — dogdom as it is so often called — will be amazed at the diversity of interests for which the hobby caters. The countryman, for instance, may wish to train his dog to the gun, to trek or hunt with a Bloodhound pack, or even to learn the skilful art of sheepdog trialling. A town dweller, on the other hand, may be more drawn by the attraction and excitement of showing. Dog ownership is also a sociable activity, and many a new friendship may be formed while exercising a pet in the park, attending a training class or competing in the show ring.

Choosing the right dog

It would be foolish to expect a gentle gundog to take on the job of a fierce guard, or to choose a hound as a prospective obedience champion; these breeds have not been bred for such a task. In order to avoid the disappointment of buying a dog that is not well suited for the role you wish it to fulfil, it is important first to study the various groups into which dogs are divided, according to the roles for which they were bred. And even if you are not looking for a working dog, but simply want a loving companion and a playmate for the children, studying these groups will still help you to make a sound decision.

Caring for your dog

Of course, different breeds are not only suited to different roles in life, they also have different requirements with regards to accommodation, feeding, exercise and grooming. Owners must be aware of their dog's particular needs. Small breeds, for example, require less food than larger ones, and puppies must have their daily food ration divided into several portions. Dogs also require varying amounts of exercise, though the main criterion here is not necessarily size; a medium-sized working breed will often require more exercise than a larger non-working breed. And long-haired dogs need far more time spent on grooming than short-haired ones, particularly if they are to be exhibited in the show ring.

Even with regards to health there are differences among the breeds. Some dogs are renowned for having breathing difficulties: the Boxer for example. Others, such as the German Shepherd Dog and the Golden and Labrador Retrievers, are prone to hip malformation which can cripple them in middle age. Understanding these problems, as well as more widespread complaints such as worms and fleas, and appreciating the necessity for regular inoculations and health checks, are all important aspects of dog ownership.

Training your dog

For many, the first step in training their dog is to take the animal to a dog training class. Usually the aim is to train the dog in basic obedience so that it responds to the commands 'sit', 'down', 'come', and 'heel'. But by the time this standard has been reached, many owners are firmly hooked on the more advanced stages of obedience, and before long they are competing in obedience and working trials.

For the more athletic owner, excitement and fulfilment is attained by teaching their dogs to compete in agility tests, in which the handler must run with the dog, against the clock, as the animal negotiates an obstacle course of jumps, ramps, hoops and tunnels.

But whatever your ultimate aim as a dog owner, it is your duty first and foremost to train your dog to obey simple commands. Remember that only a well trained dog is able to fulfil its natural instinct, which is to please and obey, while the owners of such a dog can pride themselves in having a dog that is the envy of all their friends and which, more importantly, never gives anyone cause for complaint.

1

Man and his Dog

The relationship between man and dog has existed since man first recognized the animal's potential as a hunter and protector, and welcomed it to his fireplace. Since then, by the mixing of various native types, and the selective breeding of individuals to perpetuate their working qualities, man has created a wide range of breeds to fulfil an ever-broadening range of functions.

The dog's role has diversified even over the last century. Not only are dogs herding sheep and hunting game as they have done for hundreds of years, but today they are also leading the blind, acting as ears for the deaf, and sniffing out drugs and explosives. They have even played their part in times of war, earning medals for their bravery and heroism in rescuing people trapped under bombed buildings or carrying messages along the front line.

Right: An Assyrian hunting scene depicts a ferocious ancient breed of dog.
Below: The Ibizan Hound has changed little over the last 5,000 years.

F ew pleasures can equal that of buying a puppy, unless it is the delight that follows when we witness the affection the animal bestows on us, or the eagerness with which it contrives to understand and carry out our commands.

Most dog owners believe that the relationship they have with their pet is unique. Yet man and dog are simply re-enacting a partnership that has existed for thousands of years, since people first enticed dogs to their camp fires with pieces of meat.

Evolution

Dogs, wolves, foxes and jackals all belong to the family Canidae, one of seven families in the mammalian order Carnivora—the flesh-eating mammals. The carnivores have a common ancestor in a small, long-tailed, tree-climbing mammal called *Miacis* that lived in prehistoric forests over 40 million years ago. A small fox-like descendant of *Miacis*, called *Tomarctus*, is widely regarded as the forerunner of the dog, wolf, fox and jackal.

The dog's most likely close ancestor is the grey wolf, which was once commonly found throughout Asia, Europe and North America; the jackal is another likely candidate. It is highly improbable that the dog evolved from the fox.

It is significant that matings between a wolf and a dog prove fertile (as do some matings between a dog and a jackal), and that any dog that escapes into the wild will, before long, revert to the wolf-like behaviour of its ancestors.

Of all breeds, the German Shepherd Dog (or Alsatian) most closely resembles the wolf. In fact, when it was first recognized by the British Kennel Club it was known as

Below: The dog is most likely a descendant of the wolf, a theory backed by the resemblance between the German Shepherd and the wolf.

the Alsatian Wolf Dog. It is interesting to note that fewer than 250 years have elapsed since the last wolf was killed in Britain. The species survived longest in Scotland, the last recorded killing being in Sutherland, north-west Scotland, in 1743. In other parts of the world wolves still continue to survive, though their numbers are dwindling. They are found largely in Asia and in North America, from Alaska down to the states of the northern plains.

Canine Characteristics

Zoologists often divide the dog family into two distinct groups: dogs and wolves; and foxes and jackals. Even so, all members have in common a number of characteristics. They are all largely carnivorous, with 42 teeth, and four or five toes on their fore-feet and four on their hind-feet. The animals run on their toes and, unlike cats, their claws are non-retractable. The females have a 63-day gestation period and give birth to large litters. The pups' eyes are closed at birth.

Most members of the family tend to live in packs and are gregarious by nature, characteristics which cause the domestic dog to regard its human owner as 'pack leader' and to look to him for both companionship and leadership.

Domestication

How the dog came to be the friend and servant of man can only be conjecture. It would seem that such a state of affairs has existed since the Stone Age, judging from fossil

Below: The Pharaoh Hound is an ancient breed which has changed little over the past 5,000 years. It is as fast as a Greyhound and has acute hearing.

remains found in early encampments dating back 10,000 years. Indeed, excavations in some villages have revealed the remains of dogs not unlike many of today's breeds

Early man recognized in the dog a likely friend and protector. Later he must have realized that the dog could assist him in hunting. The most successful guards or hunters would have been bred from to perpetuate their special qualities, although it would be some time before selective breeding along the lines we know today came about.

What we do know is that as man travelled from country to country his dogs accompanied him, interbreeding with native types, so that eventually there were many varieties, ranging from small lap dogs to the Roman Molossus dogs which had to fight gladiators, and in which the Mastiff, Bulldog and Boxer share a common ancestor.

The Pharaoh Hound is the oldest domesticated dog in recorded history; an inscription recording the burial of a dog named Abuytiyuw was found in the great cemetery west of the Pyramid of Cheops at

Above: The Ibizan Hound is an ancient breed that hunts predominantly by sense of smell.

Right: Bulldogs are descendants of ancient Mastiffs. Established in Britain, they were used by the Romans to fight in the arena.

Giza. We know that dogs like the Ibizan Hound were also owned by the ancient pharaohs because hunting dogs of this type were drawn on rock and papyrus as early as 3,000 BC, and bones of similar dogs have been found even earlier.

Interest in the dog and in the development of its mental and physical capacities is nothing new. The oldest book of Persian (Iranian) religion, the *Zend-Avesta*, tells us that 'The world exists through the dog's intelligence'. Xenophon (430-355 BC), who is credited with writing the first dog book, laid down that the bodily structure of a good dog must be created; and Aristotle (384-322 BC) tells us that lap dogs were kept and bred in his day, becoming favourites of the ladies.

DOGS AT WORK

On 21 January, 1788, Napoleon Bonaparte of France wrote to one of his commanders in Egypt: 'There must be at Alexandria many dogs which would be of much service to you in the outposts'. Even as far back as 1788, Napoleon was able to appreciate the importance of a dog's role in times of war, presumably as that of a guard. Yet few could have envisaged the enormity of the role dogs were later to play, both at war — carrying messages and locating the wounded — and during peace — helping the blind and sniffing out explosives.

Colonel Konrad Most began training service dogs in 1906, while serving as police commissioner at the Royal Prussian Police Headquarters at Saarbrücken. He spent the next eight years giving instructions to the constabulary on the management of police dogs, using methods he himself had devised, and in 1912 he was appointed principal of the newly formed State Breeding and Training Establishment for Police Dogs at Berlin, where he carried out much research in training dogs for service personnel and for the tracking down of criminals.

At the outbreak of the war, Colonel Most was attached to the staff of Field Marshal Von Hindenburg, Commander-in-Chief in the East, to direct the use of army dogs on the Eastern Front. And in the following year he was put in charge of the organization of all canine services on both the Eastern and Western fronts.

It was after witnessing German Shepherd Dogs working in Germany during the First World War that a band of British dog fanciers, including Colonel J. Y. Baldwin and Air Commodore Cecil-Wright (a past president of the British Kennel Club), introduced the breed into the United Kingdom and strove to make full use of the abilities they had seen so ably demonstrated in Germany. Later, Colonel Baldwin founded the RAF Police Dog School in England, and to this day the Royal Air Force maintains a police dog museum, known as the Baldwin Room, in his honour.

At the beginning of the Second World War, the British Royal Air Force recognized the potential for properly trained dogs for safeguarding airfields and equipment; and in November 1941 the Ministry of Aircraft Production Guard Dog School was founded. However, in April 1944 the school became known as the RAF Police Dog Training Centre, since when the training of all dogs employed on RAF stations throughout the world has taken place there. But it is not only German Shepherd Dogs that are recruited into the Royal Air

Right: A German Shepherd Dog in the United States Air Force carries out a baggage check to ensure that drugs are not being smuggled aboard the plane.

Force. Labradors, spaniels, pointers and any other retriever or gundog breed can be signed on, and even an Irish Water Spaniel is on the pay-roll.

Police dogs are now commonly used in various parts of the world. They may become patrol dogs taught to detect, pursue and capture intruders or they may become search dogs used in the detection of drugs or firearms. Recently in Britain a Springer Spaniel named Pip made the headlines and was described as a 'canine sleuth' when he sniffed out a massive haul of cannabis which had a street value of £6 million. The dog had been with the Customs and Excise for two years, and is one of a squad of 30 British sniffer dogs trained by the Royal Air Force.

At RAF Newton dogs are trained not only for the Royal Navy, the British Customs and Excise and other British services, but also for the United States Navy and the United States Air Force. In America there are also many dog training centres which train service dogs for the detection of narcotics and bombs. While many dogs are used in the armed services, many are also active in search and rescue work for the local police.

Dogs accompanying civilian policemen on the beat is nothing new. As early as the fifteenth century, police constables in Britain patrolled with their dogs, although it is generally supposed that the sole function of the animals was to provide companionship. It was not until 1946 that the police force took the idea of working dogs seriously, and added six Labradors to their strength.

Today there are nearly 300 police dogs working in London alone, the most popular of which is the German Shepherd Dog. However, Labradors are used for patrol and detection work, and other breeds, including a Belgian cattle dog, the Bouvier des Flandres, have been used with considerable success as guards.

Above: A police dog is taught to detain a criminal by getting a grip on his arm. In training, the arm is heavily padded for protection.

Above: Labrador Retrievers are expert at sniffing out narcotics, even when they have been concealed in a telephone!

Below: This young Labrador is being taught to seek out explosives. It looks upon the task as a game and is taught on a reward basis.

Above: The close interaction between man and dog is clearly apparent during an agility performance by the RAF police dogs' display team.

Below: A dog in the RAF display team weaves its way through the poles. Exercises like this prove very popular with spectator audiences.

Right: An RAF dog leaps through a hoop of searing flames. To perform such a feat, the dog requires both courage and confidence.

Sight and hearing dogs

In 1916, a German doctor in charge of war wounded had reason to leave a blind patient for a time in the company of his German Shepherd Dog. Upon his return he was so impressed with the way in which the dog had discharged its responsibility that he made a vow to commence training dogs for that purpose. However, it was not until 1928 that America produced its first guide dog owner, Morris Frank, the United Kingdom following suit three years later.

The Hearing Dogs for the Deaf scheme was first launched in the United Kingdom, in 1982, under the auspices of the Royal National Institute for the Deaf. The idea of the scheme is to train dogs to act as 'hearing ears' for deaf people by responding to everyday sounds, such as a knock at the door, the whistle of a kettle, the ring of an alarm clock in the morning, or the sound of a baby crying, thus offering the owner a greater degree of independence and greatly increasing the quality and enjoyment of his or her life.

Therapy dogs

Only in the last few years have psychologists, animal behaviourists, veterinarians and the dog owning public become aware of the true value of the relationship between dog and man. Now, not only can dogs help the blind to 'see', and the deaf to 'hear', they also have an important task to perform for the old and the sick, and for disabled and emotionally disturbed adults and children. It has been discovered that the mere presence of a dog can be of great theraputic value to such people, helping to brighten their often dreary days. There are in existence various pet visiting schemes whereby dogs are taken to establishments such as children's homes or homes for the aged, places where the residents would not otherwise be able to benefit from the warmth and affection that dogs can bestow on them.

Sled dogs

In many countries of the world, dogs are used for carting and sled pulling. In Switzerland, it is not unusual to see a sturdy Bernese Mountain Dog pulling a milk cart. In Germany, before its abilities as a police dog and guard were fully recognized, the powerful Rottweiler — originally a hunter of wild boar, and later a reliable cattle dog — was the tradi-

Right: The Eskimo Dog is making a welcome comeback after becoming almost extinct. Here, these excellent sled dogs are seen competing in a race in Alaska.

Below: A guide dog will undergo training for seven to eight months at a training centre before joining its new master, after which dog and master train together for a time.

tional butcher's dog that pulled the meat cart; it was known as the Rottweiler Metzgerhund (the Rottweil butcher's dog).

In America the Newfoundland and several other large breeds, are sometimes harnessed up to take children for a ride. In the United Kingdom the use of dogs for draught purposes is forbidden, but a growing band of enthusiasts regularly harness up their dogs for charity events.

Sled dog teams have time and time again proved their worth. In 1873, the Royal Canadian Mounted Police brought law and order to the northern frontiers with their dog patrol teams; and throughout Alaska and Canada mail teams delivered news and post to the outlying settlements.

Visitors to Central Park in New York may see a monument that records one of the proudest chapters in sled dog history. In January 1925 a case of diptheria was diagnosed in Nome, Alaska. The antitoxin supply in that city was insufficient to combat an epidemic. A relay of 22 native and mail teams fought their way through the rough interior of Alaska and across the Bering Sea to bring serum to the grateful citizens. The inscription on the monument reads: 'Dedicated to the indomitable spirit of the sled dogs that relayed antitoxin 600 miles over rough ice, treacherous waters, through arctic blizzards, from Nemana to the relief of the stricken Nome in the winter of 1925. Endurance. Fidelity. Intelligence!'

Sheepdogs

In recent times, few dogs and trainers have won more admiration than those who take part in sheepdog trials. Such trials provide ample evidence that, without a good trained dog, the work of a hill shepherd would be impossible.

The first recorded sheepdog trials were held in Bala, North Wales, in 1873, but it was not until 33 years later that the International Sheep Dog Society was formed. A meeting of English and Scottish sheepmen met in July 1906; and soon afterwards the first international trials were held in Gullane, Scotland. Now, 78 years later, the International Sheep Dog Society has over 6,000 members world-wide.

The considerable growth of interest in sheepdog trials has obviously been enhanced by the television coverage it has received. However, the stars, the dogs themselves, have been totally unspoiled by this recognition of their abilities, and it has often been said that it is the unaffected joy that they show in their work that gives trialling its undoubted charm.

Below: A shepherd and his dog pen sheep. This type of work is instinctive in a Border Collie which, even as a pup, will crouch on seeing sheep in a field.

CANINE HEROES

Dogs in art, films, television series, books and story telling have always performed unusual, daring and heroic deeds. Stories of dogs saving lives, physically or by signal, or acting as guards, messengers and 'soldiers' on the front line of battle are familiar to many people. The stories have been told through the years and these real life dog heroes are a dramatic testament to the interaction of man and dog.

Famous historical canine heroes include little Peritas, the pet dog of Alexander the Great who did battle with an elephant and sacrificed his life for that of his master; Soter who, during the Peloponnesian War, was presented with a silver collar engraved 'Defender and Saviour of Corinth'; and Moustache, a Poodle who was at the battles of Marengo and Austerlitz, during the Napoleonic Wars, and once saved the flag of his regiment.

Many dogs have been awarded medals for their bravery and heroism. A German Boxer, Mathias, saved 15 wounded men, for which he was awarded the Iron Cross in 1943. In the United Kingdom, Maria Dickin, founder of the charitable organization The People's Dispensary for Sick Animals (PDSA), instituted the Dickin Medal, popularly referred to as the animals' Victoria Cross. The medal was awarded to any animal displaying conspicuous gallantry and devotion to duty while associated with, or under the control of, any branch of the armed forces or civil defence units during the Second World War and its aftermath. Of the 53 Dickin Medals awarded, 18 were presented to

Below: Judy, the brave English Pointer bitch who was awarded the Dickin Medal in 1945 for her superb behaviour in Japanese prison camps.

dogs, three to horses, one to a cat and 31 to pigeons.

Dogs awarded the Dickin Medal include Irma, an Airedale bitch who, while serving with the Civil Defence Service of London, was responsible for the rescue of 233 people trapped under blitzed buildings. Judy, a pure-bred English Pointer born in Shanghai in 1936, was adopted as a mascot by the Royal Navy, and served in several gunboats. She was torpedoed and captured by the Japanese, and spent two years as a prisoner of war under horrifying conditions in Sumatra, where prisoners were used as slave labour to lay 3,000 miles (4,800km) of railway track. During that period she distinguished herself by her devotion to Leading Aircraftsman Frank Williams, to whom she had attached herself; by her hatred of the Japanese guards who on several occasions tried to shoot her; and by threatening and distracting the guards when they beat the prisoners. She was liberated with her fellow prisoners in 1945, and was awarded the Dickin Medal. Her citation reads: 'For magnificent courage and endurance in Japanese prison camps, thus helping to maintain morale among her fellow prisoners and for saving many lives by her intelligence and watchfulness'.

Since the war, two other British organizations have awarded dogs medals for bravery and services to humanity—Pro Dogs and the National Canine Defence League. The former of these two animal welfare bodies, Pro Dogs, makes annual Gold Medal Awards to dogs for devotion to duty, life saving or for earning the title 'Pet of the Year'. Golden medals were recently awarded to a police dog named Khan who, despite being run down and badly injured when in pursuit of criminals, managed to drag himself up and continue the chase; to Judy, a Jack Russell Terrier who alerted

her deaf and paralysed owner to a fire; and to Sandy, who accompanies her window-cleaning master on his rounds and arouses considerable amusement and admiration by climbing adeptly up ladders and balancing on narrow ledges.

The National Canine Defence League awarded the coveted Medal for Bravery to Hanna, a Dobermann bitch who was shot twice in the leg when she leapt to the defence of her master during a raid by an armed robber on a London pub. Hanna had to have her injured leg amputated, but has since recovered and is now able to run around happily on three legs.

Other countries have their dog heroes also. For the past 32 years in the United States an annual search has been conducted to find the dog most worthy of receiving the title Ken-L Ration Dog Hero, given for an exceptional moment of heroics. All winners are selected from hundreds of entries and represent an interesting cross-section of heroic acts and canine breeds. Ten pure-breeds and eight all-American mixed breeds have numbered among the United States' most courageous canines. Past winners include five Collies, five German Shepherds and five St Bernards. There has even been a German Shepherd/wolf mix.

Forty-five persons have been saved by US dog heroes, and the 32 winners have helped rescue or protect people from almost every type of catastrophe—including 14 near-drownings, six animal attacks, one illness, five fires, several traffic accidents, and one burglary.

The US programme began in 1954 when the first Ken-L Ration Dog Hero title was awarded to a Collie named Tang. Twice Tang saved children from potential traffic accidents, once in Texas and once in Alaska. Numerous other youngsters owe their lives to dog heroes. In 1969, a Great Dane named Top

Above: Avalanche dogs have excellent scenting ability and brave all kinds of weather to find those who have become buried in the snow.

Right: The massive Newfoundland is as much at home in water as on land. Its ability to rescue a swimmer in distress is instinctive.

pushed a young girl out of the path of an oncoming truck. The girl was not hurt, but Top suffered a broken leg. One week after his cast was removed, Top proved to be a hero again when he alerted his owner to a drowning child. Six other US dog heroes risked their own safety to save humans. The 1966 winner, Hero, lived up to his name when he distracted a wild horse which was about to trample a little boy. The horse attacked Hero, pitching the dog into a tractor. Hero was badly injured, but eventually made a full recovery.

All such great feats were performed by dogs who had no thought but to save and protect their human masters, regardless of their own safety.

2

Choosing a Dog

*O*nce the decision has been made to buy a dog it is always tempting to rush out and buy one of the first ones you see advertised — all puppies tend to look adorable. But buying in haste without first giving the matter due consideration is a chancy way of finding the right canine companion.

Many breeds have been bred for a specific purpose, for instance, hunting, herding or guarding, and may therefore be accustomed to the kind of life-style which you are unable to provide. So that the breed types can easily be identified, dogs are generally divided into groups. Study of these groups will enable readers to select the dog which is most suited to their home environment and most able to perform the role for which it was bought, be it that of family pet, guard or obedience champion.

Right: Some dogs, such as the Labrador, are renowned for their reliability with children.
Below: Whether pure-bred or mongrel, time and care must be taken in choosing the right dog.

When one considers the immense time and care that most people take in selecting a house or an item of furniture, it is surprising that the family dog, which could be sharing its owners' lives for anything up to 14 years or more, is often bought on the spur of the moment. It is frequently chosen because of the breed's physical appearance rather than its character, temperament and requirements in terms of environment, exercise and feeding. Indeed, every year a lamentable number of dogs are discarded, or put down, in circumstances that could have been avoided if the owner had taken the trouble to choose a suitable animal in the first place.

You may be tempted to buy a large breed, such as an Afghan Hound or an Old English Sheepdog, but if home is an apartment, or a house with a small garden, then it would be more sensible to think in terms of a toy dog or a medium-sized dog which does not require a great deal of exercise.

If all members of a household are out at work during the day it is certainly not advisable to get a dog unless someone can return home at lunch-times to take the lonely animal for a walk; and such an arrangement is suitable only in cases of an adult dog, which is able to control the urge of nature for a reasonable time. Puppies need someone on hand during the day to feed and house-train them.

THE DIFFERENT GROUPS OF DOGS

For showing purposes the breeds are divided into a number of clearly defined groups, though these may vary from one country to another. The United Kingdom has six groups: toy dogs, hounds, terriers, working dogs, gundogs and utility dogs. The United States, on the other hand, has seven groups: toy dogs, hounds, terriers, working dogs, sporting dogs (similar to the UK gundogs), non-sporting dogs (similar to UK utility dogs) and herding dogs.

Studying these various groups (see page 172) may help you to select the dog that is most likely to meet your requirements in terms of behaviour, appearance and size.

Toy dogs

Toy dogs include breeds such as the diminutive Chihuahuas, the Affenpinscher, Miniature Pinscher, Pekingese, Pomeranian and other small pets often referred to as lap dogs, though it should be noted that the term 'toy' or 'miniature' does not necessarily imply that a dog belongs to this group; the Miniature Poodle for instance is classed as a utility breed in Britain.

The largest dogs to be found in the toy group are the Cavalier King Charles Spaniel and the King Charles Spaniel, the latter being known as the English Toy Spaniel in the United States. These attractive, friendly little dogs are an ideal choice for a family who simply wants a charming and obedient pet that will prove a reliable play-mate for the children.

Hounds

Hounds are of two distinct types; those which hunt by sight and are capable of great speed, such as the Afghan Hound, Borzoi, Greyhound, Saluki, Scottish Deerhound and Irish Wolfhound; and those which hunt by scent, such as the Basset, Beagle, Bloodhound and Foxhound.

The sight hounds will give their hearts to anyone prepared to offer them sufficient exercise and interest, though they should not be kept in cities. They have an inherent love of speed and open spaces, yet are usually obedient in the home and will lie peacefully for hours in their favourite sleeping place.

Foxhounds in the United Kingdom are the property of foxhunting packs, and they are not kept as domestic pets; as a rule it is not possible to purchase them for this purpose. The American Foxhound is exhibited in the show ring in the United States as well as being used for hunting, but is just as unsuitable for a pet as its close relative.

The scent hounds are friendly hunters with an irresistible urge to follow their noses. Members such as the Basset, the Beagle and the Bloodhound are sometimes kept as pets and are usually good with children. However, like the sight hounds, these dogs are not recommended for town life unless they have an energetic owner. And

Left: Cavalier King Charles Spaniels make excellent, obedient and good-natured companions. Neither too big or too small, they enjoy exercise without being demanding.

Above: Without adequate exercise and play, puppies will often expend their energies in being destructive — one reason why pups must not be left on their own for too long.

Below: Borzois are large dogs with an enormous exercise need. They are not suited to life in an apartment, nor to small, town gardens, and are definitely a breed for the country.

immense care must always be taken to prevent them escaping from the confines of a garden, which they will undoubtedly attempt to do.

Finally, it should be mentioned that hounds, although amiable enough, are not ideal for obedience work; many a wayward Beagle has driven its owner to near despair by its indifference to command.

Terriers

Terriers are busy, energetic dogs which were bred to go to ground and hunt small mammals. They are alert and loyal and would be unlikely to admit a burglar without giving noisy warning. Certainly well worth considering to perform the dual role of companion and guard would be the Airedale. It is a hardy dog and usually gets on well with children. Despite its relatively large size—the male grows up to 24in (60cm) in height—it usually adapts happily to life in town providing its owner gives it adequate exercise. This British breed was performing guard-dog duties before many other more popular breeds came into vogue, and it has never been spoilt by over-popularity.

With the possible exception of the Scottish Terrier, the Yorkshire Terrier (classified as a toy breed) and the Dandy Dinmont, a terrier's lively nature does not make it an ideal choice for an elderly person seeking a quiet, albeit affectionate, companion. The terriers, especially the males, are also noted for their aggression towards other dogs, which makes them more difficult to handle than other small breeds.

Working and herding breeds

Although categorized separately in the United States, working and herding breeds are combined in a single group—working dogs—in the United Kingdom. If you are looking specifically for an obedience dog or guard dog, it is not necessary to look beyond these categories. Here one finds the German Shepherd Dog and the Border Collie, breed names which have become synonymous with obedience. Along with many other sheepdogs, such as the Belgian Sheepdog, Bearded Collie and Shetland Sheepdog, the groups also include a number of Spitz varieties, such as the Alaskan Malamute and Samoyed (a strong intelligent sled dog which benefits from obedience work and training) and, of course, the Boxer, the Mastiff and the vigilant Dobermann and Rottweiler.

Below: Jack Russell Terriers cope with lots of exercise and can be aggressive towards other dogs. If allowed off the lead they may go to ground as a natural instinct for several days.

Above: The Gordon Setter is a big, gentle companion, but ideally needs several hours of exercise daily if it is to retain its figure.

Below: Working collies are ideal one-man dogs which tend to herd naturally. Though very intelligent, they become mischievous if bored.

Gundogs

Gundogs, or sporting dogs as the equivalent group is known in the United States, make a first class choice for buyers in search of a good-natured family pet which will also share their sporting interests. They are not natural guard dogs but are good as a warning or deterrent against burglars. The group includes the setters, pointers, retrievers and spaniels.

Utility breeds

The utility breeds (or non-sporting breeds in the United States) include dogs that have been bred for any number of purposes, such as the Dalmatian, which was originally used for hunting in the Mediterranean countries, but was latterly used in England and France as a carriage dog. It is not only a first-class companion for anyone who wants a dog to follow a horse, but is frequently overlooked as a candidate for the obedience class in which it often works well.

Right: Gundogs such as Labrador Retrievers and English Springers make hardy and loyal companions. Adequate exercise is essential.

With the unfortunate increase in crime, more and more people are looking to dogs as a form of protection. They are sensible to do so: it takes a stout-hearted burglar to continue with his break-in while a furious dog barks a warning of his presence. Breeders and canine societies are inundated with calls from people wanting dogs to combine the role of guard with that of family pet, or merely to guard their business premises against intruders. They also receive calls from elderly people, often those living alone and scared of attack, who feel that a guard dog would provide them with protection and companionship.

Left: Guard dogs at rest. Apart from the German Shepherd Dog, other breeds such as the Boxer should not be overlooked for guard work — this was originally the Boxer's prime use.

Above: Even a small non-aggressive dog such as a Cavalier King Charles Spaniel can be a good burglar alarm, especially for the elderly.

Left: Dogs of any breed will act as a burglar deterrent by barking a warning to its owner if suspicious.

Many such inquirers have had long experience of dog-keeping and so understand the responsibilities involved. Others are simply looking for an animated burglar alarm, and show scant regard for the requirements of the dog. And some people do not appreciate that the perfect guard dog does not necessarily make the most suitable play-mate for their children.

The most popular guard dogs are undoubtedly the Dobermann, German Shepherd Dog and Rottweiler, all admirable and highly-intelligent breeds. However, they are, without exception, animals that need training, firm but kind handling, and space. They have an inherent restlessness, are continually on the alert, and often overguard their owners' property, even against visitors to the home.

Accidents can happen when these dogs' keen intelligence and working ability is not put to good use and the animals become bored. Also, in common with many other animals, they are quick to recognize nervousness on the part of their owners or their visitors. This nervousness may be transmitted to the dog, and a nervous dog is often a dangerous one.

Most important is that the choice of dog has the whole-hearted approval of the entire family, and that anyone who is secretly rather scared of big dogs is not presented with, say, a Dobermann as a fait accompli.

Of course, it is not always necessary to buy a traditional guard dog for a domestic situation. Mastiffs make formidable guard dogs as well as loyal and devoted pets. Boxers, too, are a good choice, though they are rather boisterous and tend to knock or pull small children over. In fact, it is likely that the sight and sound of any largish dog will prove a deterrent to most burglars providing it is not an obviously friendly animal.

It is unnecessary for an elderly person, who would find a large dog difficult to handle, to think that only large dogs make suitable guards. An intending burglar is unlikely to be able to determine the size of a dog by its bark, especially from the other side of a door. Few burglars would in any case risk having their ankles bitten or their work disturbed by a snappy toy breed.

The table above shows the various breeds that make good guard dogs in the home. Those breeds that are also good with children are marked with an asterisk, but it is important to note that there are good- and bad-natured dogs in all breeds, and though the Bull Terrier, for instance, has been marked as a reliable dog with children this does not mean to say that any one individual will be trustworthy.

GUARD DOGS

Airedale Terrier	Collie	Mastiff
American	Corgi, Pembrokeshire	*Newfoundland
Staffordshire Terrier	Welsh and Cardigan	Puli, Hungarian
(also known as Pit	Welsh	Pumi
Bull Terrier)	Dachshund	Pyrenean Mountain
Anatolian	Dobermann	Dog
Sheepdog	German Shepherd	Rottweiler
Belgian Shepherd	Dog (Alsatian)	Schnauzer, Standard
Dog	Great Dane	and Giant
Boston Terrier	Hungarian Kuvasz	*Scottish Deerhound
Bouvier des Flandres	*Irish Wolfhound	*Shipperke
*Boxer	Japanese Akita	Staffordshire Bull
*Buhund, Norwegian	Komondor	Terrier
*Bull Terrier	Leonberger	Weimaraner
Bullmastiff	Maremma Sheepdog	

An asterisk denotes those breeds renowned for their reliability with children.

Above: A Cocker Spaniel is getting used to being positioned on a table, or dias, in preparation for learning ringcraft. Smaller breeds are exhibited standing on a dias and must learn to remain calm while they are examined by the judge.

Dogs for Obedience work

Two of the best breeds for obedience work are undoubtedly the German Shepherd Dog and the Border Collie. But should circumstances dictate that you need a smaller or less exacting pet (if, for instance, you are a town dweller) then there are plenty of other possibilities. The Shetland Sheepdog, for example, is an intelligent Rough Collie in miniature which does well in obedience work. It is happiest living in the home, rather than kennelled, and makes a good family pet.

Gundogs (sporting dogs) such as the Labrador and Golden Retrievers, the Weimaraner, the Cocker and Springer Spaniels, and even

Above: This Springer puppy is being rewarded for successfully retrieving its rubber ring. Basic obedience training can be combined with play so that the dog enjoys learning.

members of the toy group (such as the Papillon) or the utility group (Toy and Miniature Poodles, Keeshonden, Leonbergers and Schnauzers) can also give a good account of themselves in obedience work, even though they may never reach the top. A list of dogs suitable for obedience work is shown below. Again, emphasis has been placed on those breeds that are often good with children.

Selection for the show ring

In choosing a dog for showing in the conformation ring, you must not only look for an animal with show potential and sound temperament, but also bear in mind the time you have available for its show preparation. If time is strictly limited, any idea of choosing an Airedale, Afghan Hound, Old English Sheepdog, Poodle, or any other breed that requires elaborate grooming, should be forgotten. Select a smooth-coated breed such as a Chihuahua, Boxer, Bull Terrier, Dobermann, Greyhound or Pug, all of which require comparatively little pre-show attention.

If you are keenly competitive, this must also have some bearing on the choice of breed. Classes for the more popular breeds are likely to be much larger than those for rare and less fashionable varieties, and consequently the competition is more intense. On the other hand, if you do well with an Afghan Hound, a German Shepherd Dog or a Golden or Labrador Retriever you will certainly have cause to feel pleased with yourself.

Choosing a rare breed may enable you to get into the winners and make a name for yourself in that variety. However, classes for rare breeds are limited, so it is often

necessary to exhibit alongside other varieties in a special class, known, in the United Kingdom, as an Any Variety (AV) non-classified class. In the United States, such a class is known as the Miscellaneous class, which is only open for specific breeds designated by the American Kennel Club.

Generally speaking the most sensible course for a person who is new to exhibiting is to choose a breed that, although not in the 'top twenty', is assured of good representation, and which has a fair and reasonable chance of achieving a degree of success.

In selecting a dog for the show ring you must also consider whether you require a dog or a bitch and whether you wish to have a puppy or an adult dog.

Obviously the successful show bitch is most desirable, as her line may be perpetuated. On the other hand, if you have no thought of breeding, but merely wish to have the fun exhibiting and, hopefully, owning a winning animal, you may decide on a dog. Classes for dogs are often smaller, and if the animal does well the owner can command a good stud fee.

Generally speaking, it is not a good idea to use a dog for stud

OBEDIENCE DOGS

Airedale Terrier	German Shepherd	Rottweiler
*Bearded Collie	Dog	Rough Collie
Belgian Shepherd	*Golden Retriever	Schnauzer
Dog	Keeshond	*Shetland Sheepdog
Border Collie	*Labrador Retriever	Smooth Collie
Bouvier des Flandres	Leonberger	Springer Spaniel
*Buhund, Norwegian	Papillon	Weimaraner
Cocker Spaniel	*Pointer	
Dalmatian	*Poodle	

An asterisk denotes those breeds renowned for their reliability with children.

work, irrespective of its pedigree, if the animal has simply been kept as a pet. It is a fallacy that pet dogs, leading a celibate life, suffer from sexual frustration. Indeed, rather than providing a pet with a service by using it as a stud, an owner could be doing himself a far greater disservice, for the dog which has mated is far more likely to urinate on the furniture and take off in hot pursuit after every bitch on heat in the neighbourhood.

Anyone choosing a dog for almost any other purpose than the show ring, should first and foremost consider buying a puppy; the earlier a puppy enters the home, the closer the bond it is likely to develop with its owner. However, with few exceptions, it is extremely difficult to pick out a prospective show-winner at six, eight or even twelve weeks; and it is usually six months, or even a year, before anyone can determine, with any degree of accuracy, whether or not a dog has show potential.

If you do wish to show your dog, but still prefer to buy a puppy, the breeder will do his best to select a promising specimen for you and, from long experience and knowledge of the breed, the chances are good that the choice will be sound. But there can be no guarantees, and in buying a pup there must always be some element of risk.

Left: A Miniature Pinscher is examined in detail at an open-air show in America. Here, judging is not very different from that in the UK.

HEREDITARY COMPLAINTS

In choosing a dog it is important to be aware of a number of hereditary complaints to which certain breeds are prone, such as hip dysplasia (HD), which is a malformation of the hip joint, entropion and ectropion (diseases of the eyelid), and progressive retinal atrophy (PRA, an irreversible degeneration of the retina which results in blindness.

In order to reduce the incidence of such problems, no dog or bitch suffering from an hereditary defect should be bred from. But despite the considerable advances being made in the diagnosis of hereditary diseases, and the enormous care taken by breeders to breed only from registered disease-free stock, cases do continue to turn up.

Many owners who, having discovered that their pet has HD, PRA or some other hereditary disease, want to know if they have any redress against the breeder. Naturally they feel bitter about the money they have spent on buying a pure-breed and wonder why an apparently healthy dog has been so afflicted. Unfortunately, provided the necessary precautions have been taken by the breeder, as is usually the case, they cannot be held responsible for the condition of the dog.

Hip dysplasia This condition is found in all breeds, but the German Shepherd Dog, and the Golden and Labrador Retriever are those most commonly afflicted. An animal with severe HD may walk rather slowly and laboriously, with 'clicking' hips. But only x-rays at one or two years of

Below: The normal hip is a perfectly smooth fit between the top of the thigh bone and the pelvis, like a ball and socket. In dysplasia, close contact is lost and the edges of the ball and socket become rough and uneven, causing uneven gait, pain and weakness.

Above: The Cocker Spaniel is one of the breeds which suffer from the inherited condition entropion — inturning of the eyelid.

Right: Rough Collies can suffer eye problems which cannot be cured. First signs of PRA are bumping into objects and twilight blindness.

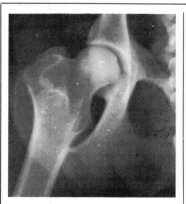

Normal Hip

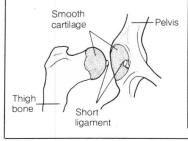

Smooth cartilage — Pelvis

Thigh bone — Short ligament

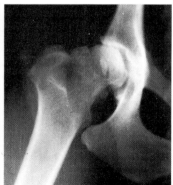

Advanced Dysplasia

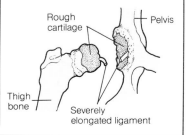

Rough cartilage — Pelvis

Thigh bone — Severely elongated ligament

age will give conclusive diagnosis. The carrying of excessive weight will aggravate the situation. HD can, in some cases, be helped by an operation.

In an attempt to eradicate the disease, stock that is disease-free is registered as such and this fact can be used when selecting breeding stock.

Entropion A condition in which the eyelids tend to turn inwards onto the eye. Usually it is detected because of a watery discharge, and because the puppy continually paws and rubs the eye. This condition can be corrected by an operation. Eye ointments will give temporary relief from irritation. However, dog owners should not resort to home remedies. Many breeds exhibit entropion, notably the Chow, Pekingese and Labrador.

Ectropion A less common hereditary disease, most frequently found in St Bernards and Bloodhounds, but it can occur in other breeds. In this complaint the lower lid falls away from the eye to show the red conjunctiva. As with entropion, the condition can be corrected with surgery.

Progressive retinal atrophy This disease is more serious than those mentioned above. PRA often first shows as 'night blindness', and is usually discovered when the dog shows impaired vision at dusk, when the light is poor. At a later stage, the size of the pupil of the eye may increase and cataracts often develop in the lens at a later stage.

Schemes similar to that in existence for hip dysplasia have been set up by national breed clubs in an attempt to eradicate PRA. Dogs are examined by a qualified veterinary ophthalmologist (eye specialist), and certificates are provided for those that are clear of the disease. Conscientious breeders breed only from registered-free stock. However, to eliminate PRA is by no means an easy task, because it is virtually impossible to detect early signs of the disease.

Those breeds most likely to suffer from PRA are listed in the table opposite.

Breeds that suffer from progressive retinal atrophy (PRA)

Border Collie
Briard
Cairn Terrier
Cardigan Welsh Corgi
Cocker Spaniel
Dachshund,
    Miniature Long-haired
Elkhound
English Springer Spaniel
Golden Retriever
Irish Setter
Labrador Retriever
Poodle, Miniature
Poodle, Toy
Rough Collie
Shetland Sheepdog
Smooth Collie
Tibetan Spaniel
Tibetan Terrier

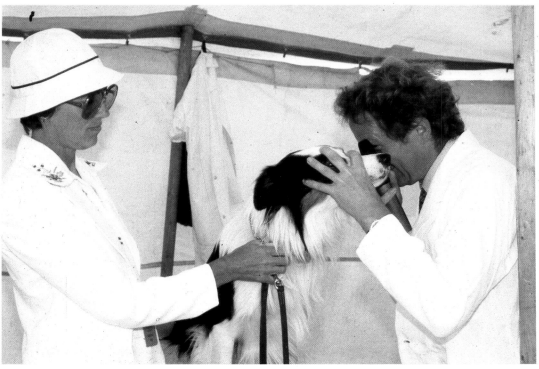

Right: A thorough examination by a veterinary eye-specialist is necessary to detect some serious eye problems. Special equipment such as an ophthalmoscope may be used.

MONGRELS AND CROSS-BREEDS

Of course, when considering what type of dog to buy, many people decide against buying a pure-breed. The reasons may be charitable — it is certainly a charitable act to give a good home to an abandoned pup that has landed in a dog home or pound — or they may be financial — a mongrel is not nearly as costly a buy as a pure-breed. Unfortunately, it is because they are so cheap that they make up such a large proportion of the dogs found in dog homes and pounds; they can be acquired all too easily and, in many instances, are abandoned just as readily.

There are certain drawbacks to buying a mongrel puppy. It is not easy to know how large the adult dog will be if the parents are unknown. Nor will a buyer have any idea about the dog's temperament, such as whether it is likely to be good with children or be a natural guard. A cross-breed, on the other hand, is the result of a breeding between a dog and a bitch of known but different pedigrees and is therefore less of an unknown quantity. Again, it may not be as costly as a pure-breed, but the buyer has more idea about its possible size and nature.

Many people believe that in obtaining a cross-breed they are getting the best of both breeds, and certainly many cross-breeds give a very good account of themselves in the obedience ring. However, although cross-breeds may be entered in obedience classes in the United Kingdom, only pure-bred dogs may compete in obedience in the United States.

It is worth noting that there is no truth in the commonly held belief that mongrels and cross-breeds are more intelligent than pure-breeds. But, as pets, they are just as loyal and affectionate as their pedigree contemporaries. It is true to say, however, that they may be less likely to suffer from the various hereditary complaints which afflict many pure breeds of dog.

BUYING YOUR DOG

Whether pure-bred or mongrel, puppies should ideally be selected while still with their littermates, using two main criteria — health and temperament.

Avoid puppies which have evidence of coat staining from diarrhoea or vomiting, those with dirty eyes or ears, and those with any patches of hair loss.

Above: Mongrel temperament can be very variable. It is essential that no risk to children is seen during a pup's 'probation' period.

Above right: Cross-breeds, such as this Bearded/Border Collie cross, often combine the best of both breeds

Right: Pure-bred puppies are more predictable than mongrels as regards size and temperament.

As an indication of further temperament, you should also avoid puppies that isolate themselves from the other littermates, and those that retreat in response to a sudden noise such as a hand-clap, or the dropping of a large bunch of keys. The better puppies will regard such provocation with interest and will want to investigate the cause.

Adult dogs acquired from dog homes, animal charities and breed rescue organizations should be subjected to the same general health checks as puppies. However, they may have been rejected by the owners because of some inherent vice, such as biting humans, aggression towards dogs or other livestock, over-sexedness or indoor incontinence, and these can rarely be spotted by a cursory glimpse.

Sale or return

Acquisition or purchase of a new dog or puppy should be subject to a health clearance by a veterinarian. If for any substantial reason the animal is found to be unfit, it should be (and is, by law, in the United Kingdom) returnable to the source for a full refund of any monies paid, providing a veterinary certificate is produced stating clearly the reason for rejection, and providing this is done within a reasonable time of acquisition — say, seven days.

Similarly, adult dogs acquired from sources as stated above should have a seven or fourteen day 'warranty' which should allow a return and refund if any vice is discovered which renders the animal unacceptable to the new owner. Most organizations involved with dog rescue not only volunteer this, but insist on this as a condition. The reason, of course, is to stop the highly undesirable practice of 're-cycling' unsatisfactory dogs from one home to another, possibly involving maltreatment and certainly unsettling and causing unhappiness to the dog.

Where to go

Having decided what type of dog you want and the role you wish it to fulfil, be it that of guard, companion or show champion, there may be several options open to you with regards to where to buy your pet.

In the case of almost every recognized breed of dog there exists a relevant breed society, or breed club as it is known in the United States. Each society liaises with the national kennel club in matters appertaining to its breed, holds regular events, and generally assists members in all matters relating to the breed. If you decide to buy a pure-breed, a request to the relevant club or society will bring forth addresses of reputable breeders. (The national kennel club will help you contact the breed club.)

You may, of course, have to travel some distance to find the breed of dog you require, particularly if it is a rare one. You must also be prepared to go some distance if you live in a town: with the exception of breeders of small dogs, most breeders tend to live in rural areas. You will need to give the breeder a full description of the type of dog you are looking for; for example, whether you want a dog that is bred from a long line of working stock, or if you want a promising show prospect which you can actively campaign. And bear in mind that with dogs, as with most other things, you only get what you pay for. A puppy with some slight defect as far as coat, colour, size or some other show fault is concerned, may not cost as much as a more perfect specimen, but then neither will it be of show standard.

Breeders pride themselves in their kennels' reputation and their

Below: Homes for unwanted dogs are an ideal source for a new pet, but beware of problems. Have a vet check the pup soon after acquisition and allow a settling-in period to confirm your choice.

wins in the show ring, so they tend to be very choosy about the people to whom they sell their most likely prize-winners, regardless of the amount of money they may be offered. If you do wish to show your pet, it is important to convince the breeder that you are keen to succeed and will make a caring owner. Providing you do this, the breeder should do his or her very best for you, as well as give endless help and advice.

Most breed societies or clubs operate a breed rescue scheme, whereby any misplaced breed member is housed by a representative of the society pending a suitable home being found for it. In the United States, the Humane Society also has many shelters which care for misplaced dogs. Dogs find their way into rescue schemes for any number of reasons —they may be the victim of a broken home, bereavement or simply an unwanted pet—and such schemes provide an ideal source for the buyer who is not looking for show

stock and does not mind giving a home to an older dog, providing it is of the desired breed.

It must be remembered that, although breed rescue schemes try to find out as much as they can about a dog's background, there may be some element of risk in buying a dog about which little or nothing is known. The same, of course, applies to buying a mongrel or any other dog from a dog home or pound.

A reputable pet store will probably be able to obtain the pure-breed of your choice providing it is not too rare. However, if you are considering showing, the chances of such a dog conforming to its breed standard are slender. It is more likely to be a sub-standard specimen, such as the runt of a litter, which the breeder has passed on to the dealer in the hope that it will find a good home. Such an animal can make a healthy and attractive pet but is unlikely to be a show-winner.

If you are prepared to take a chance with buying a mongrel, bearing in mind that you will have little or no idea of how it will grow up with regards to size, appearance and temperament, then you may find what you want either advertised in the local paper, in a pet store or in a dog home or pound.

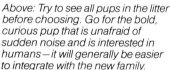

Above: Try to see all pups in the litter before choosing. Go for the bold, curious pup that is unafraid of sudden noise and is interested in humans — it will generally be easier to integrate with the new family.

Below: New puppies need special attention having just left the litter. In addition to warmth and food they need much companionship to establish them in their new home.

3

Popular Breeds

F ashions in breeds are undoubtedly influenced by the publicity given to the winners of big national shows, such as Crufts in the United Kingdom or America's Westminster Dog Show. And dogs appearing on television or photographed with celebrities always generate large numbers of enquiries about buying puppies.

Many breeds can be seen almost every day in city parks. But one of the best ways to examine the varieties is at a dog show, where you will be able to discuss the various breeds and their given characteristics with the exhibitors.

Study of this chapter will also help you to make that all important decision – which breed? Here you will find most of the more popular breeds, with advice on their temperament and suitability for various roles, and on the amount of time that needs to be devoted to their exercise and grooming.

Right: The Rottweiler makes an ideal guard dog.
Below: The Dachshund is an affectionate dog with a great sense of fun.

The following dogs represent a wide selection of popular breeds, and though some may seem unfamiliar in one country they may rate highly in another. The Alaskan Malamute, for instance, is still a relatively uncommon breed in Europe but is extremely popular in the United States. Other breeds of course, such as the German Shepherd Dog, are renowned world-wide.

Many dogs have alternative names, and where this occurs the names are shown in brackets beneath the dog's official title (according to the UK Kennel Club). Measurements such as height (taken from the shoulder) and weight are according to the breed standard in the United Kingdom unless otherwise stated.

AFFENPINSCHER

The Affenpinscher is an ancient German breed that was depicted by Jan van Eyck (1395-1441) and Albrecht Dürer (1471-1528). It has an almost monkey-like appearance, whence the prefix 'Affen', which is the German word for monkey. In its country of origin it is often called the 'Zwergaffenpinscher' ('Zwerg' means dwarf). The French have dubbed it the 'moustached devil'. In any event it is an appealing comical little dog, the smallest of the Schnauzers and Pinschers, alert, gentle and affectionate, but always ready to defend.

Size
Height: 9½-11in (24-28cm).
Weight: 6½-9lb (3-4.1kg).

Exercise
Like most toy dogs it will be content with a walk around the park, but it will gladly walk you off your feet if that is your pleasure.

Grooming
Regular brushing will keep the Affenpinscher in good condition.

AFGHAN HOUND

The Afghan is dignified, aloof and fond of comfort. Though it enjoys nothing more than surveying the scene from a cosy armchair, the Afghan is not the ideal choice for apartment dwellers or even those with a small house and garden. For despite its beautiful house manners, the Afghan is basically a hunting dog, warmly affectionate to its owners and usually trustworthy with children, but independent in character and often quite fiery in temper, particularly in adolescence.

It is impossible to show an Afghan too much affection, and it shouldn't be bullied. But it is important to maintain superiority from the first, especially during showing and training sessions, or later you may suffer the indignity, and physical near-impossibility, of publicly wrestling with a powerful creature armed with a mouthful of large teeth.

Size
Ideal height: dog 27-29in (68.5-73.5cm), bitch approximately 2-3in (5-7.5cm) smaller.

Exercise
Afghans need free running to keep fit and happy; their original task was to hunt wolves and gazelles in the deserts of Afghanistan, so a stroll in the park or a run up and down the suburban garden will not be enough to subdue their boundless energy. A puppy, from the first, should be allowed unrestricted exercise in its waking hours. This should be in a safe enclosed place. An adult should have a minimum of half an hour's free galloping a day, as well as disciplined walking on the lead.

Grooming
Daily grooming is vitally important to prevent the dog's thick coat from matting; the well-groomed Afghan is a delight to behold, the neglected specimen an abomination. Indeed, this breed is definitely not for those with little time on their hands for grooming and exercising.

The only type of brush capable of getting through an Afghan's coat is one with an air cushion behind the tufts. Best of all is a real bristle brush made for humans, though this is expensive. The nylon version is cheaper but remember to use a coat lubricant with it, otherwise static electricity will build up and cause the hair to become brittle. An air-cushioned brush with steel pins is excellent, and is not expensive.

AIREDALE

The Airedale is the king of the terriers and the largest of the terrier group. It is a splendid-looking animal with plenty of stamina and a sound temperament. It combines ideally the roles of family pet and guard, but can sometimes prove to be over-protective.

Prior to the First World War, the Airedale worked as a patrol dog with dock and railway police. It served during the war in the Russian Army and the British Army. It also worked for the Red Cross, locating the wounded and carrying messages. Indeed, at that time its abilities as a messenger and guard were considered superior to those of the German Shepherd Dog. The Airedale also took part in the Second World War, but was gradually superseded by the German Shepherd Dog, the Dobermann, the Boxer and others.

Size
Height: dogs 24in (61cm) at the shoulder, bitches slightly less.
Weight: approximately 55lb (25kg).

Exercise
One of the useful features about this dog is that although large it will adapt easily to living in a reasonably

Above: The Airedale is a good, all-purpose dog that makes a reliable guard, obedience dog and show-man. It can also be trained to the gun.

confined space, provided that it has at least two good 20-minute walks and an off-the-lead run every day. Alternatively, it will be in its element running with horses in the country and squelching, with wagging tail, through muddy fields. The Airedale can live indoors, if the owner wishes, or outside in a heated kennel with an adequate run.

Grooming
The Airedale needs daily grooming with a stiff brush, and if you plan to enter the dog in the show ring it is essential that its coat is regularly hand stripped. Ask the breeder to show you how this is done and don't be ashamed if you eventually resort to having the job done by a skilled canine beautician. If you do not plan to show, you need have your Airedale stripped only in spring and summer for coolness and neatness, but allow it to keep its thick coat for winter protection.

ALASKAN MALAMUTE

The Alaskan Malamute is an Arctic Spitz-type that is popular in the United States. It is an affectionate and sociable dog, capable of being

Below: The Alaskan Malamute is a sociable, intelligent dog which is good with children. A superb sled dog, it needs plenty of exercise.

driven in sled races by children. It is highly prized as a sled dog, and capable of immense speed. Do not be put off by the wolfish appearance: the kindly expression is genuine!

Size
Height: dog 25-28in (63.5-71cm); bitch 23-26in (58.5-66cm). Weight: 85-125lb (38.6-56.7kg).

Exercise
Needs plenty of vigorous exercise to stay healthy.

Grooming
Regular brushing will keep the coat in good condition.

AMERICAN COCKER SPANIEL

The American Cocker Spaniel is an excellent hunter, and excels in flushing out and retrieving birds. It is also extremely popular as a house-hold pet, and is an attractive, affectionate, adaptable animal and an excellent companion.

Size
Ideal height: dog 15in (38cm); bitch 14in (35.5cm). Height may vary ½in (13mm) above or below this ideal.

Exercise
It must be remembered that the Cocker Spaniel was originally bred for hunting and, although it adapts happily to the role of companion and family pet, it will obviously fit in best with families who are prepared to give it two good walks a day and have a garden for it to romp in.

Grooming
The American Cocker, with its luxuriant coat, needs daily brushing and combing, and a bath and trim every 8-10 weeks. It is best to ask the breeder for advice, or to visit a professional dog groomer, because the skull and muzzle hair must be trimmed to precise accepted lengths with electric clippers, the neck and shoulders carefully scissored, and feathering left on the legs, ears and belly. Feet must also be trimmed.

Above: The American Cocker is a keen hunter and makes an ideal family pet. It requires meticulous presentation for the show ring.

Obviously you may wish to attend to this ritual yourself, but it is advisable to be shown the procedure by an expert first.

AMERICAN STAFFORDSHIRE TERRIER
(Pit Bull Terrier)

The American Staffordshire Terrier is not to be confused with the English Staffordshire Bull Terrier, which is a lighter dog with smaller bones. At one time the American Kennel Club was allowing the American Staffordshire Terrier to be shown with the Staffordshire Bull and, indeed, crossbreeding of the two was allowed. However, although the American Stafford-shire's ancestry does originate in England, it has evolved as a quite independent breed.

It is a fearless breed, but some-what controversial in the United States where it has been bred for illegal dog fighting, as a result of which it has a tendency towards over-aggression. It therefore requires firm discipline from an early age.

Size
Height and weight should be in proportion. A height of about 18-19in (46-48cm) at shoulders for the male and 17-18in (43-46cm) for the female is preferable.

Exercise
This breed should be kept firmly under control while exercising as it has a tendency to fight with other dogs if given a chance. It is a first class ratter and a good companion in the field but will adapt to a more enclosed life in a house and garden provided regular walks are given.

Grooming
This breed requires little attention other than a good daily brushing.

AMERICAN WATER SPANIEL

The American Water Spaniel is little known outside its country of origin, where it has found great favour as a working gundog. In some parts of America it is still known as the Boykin Spaniel after Whit Boykin, one of the pioneers of the breed in Boykin, South Carolina. It is a strong swimmer, an excellent water-fowler and an efficient retriever of game.

Size
Height: 15-18in (38-46cm). Weight: dog 28-45lb (12.7-20.5kg); bitch 25-40lb (11.3-18.1kg).

Exercise
Needs plenty of exercise.

Grooming
Daily brushing and weekly combing required. Seek advice on stripping of unwanted hair. Take care that mud does not become caked in the toes.

AUSTRALIAN CATTLE DOG

The Australian Cattle Dog is an intelligent dog, amenable and first-rate at its job of driving cattle, sometimes covering vast distances. It has an equable temperament and makes a loyal companion.

Below: The Australian Cattle Dog has many working ancestors, having emerged from various collie crosses.

Size
Height: 20in (51cm). Weight: 35lb (15.9kg).

Exercise
The Australian Cattle Dog is accustomed to plenty of exercise in the great outdoors.

Grooming
This breed will benefit from regular vigorous brushing.

AUSTRALIAN SILKY TERRIER

(Silky Terrier, Sydney Silky Terrier)

The Australian Silky Terrier is a dainty little dog, similar to the Yorkshire Terrier in appearance. It is alert and hardy, and has a merry and affectionate nature.

Size
Height approximately: 9in (23cm). The most desirable weights are 8-10lb (3.6-4.5kg).

Exercise
Despite its small stature the Silky has well-developed terrier instincts and is a first-class ratter. It will adapt well to apartment living and town walks, but is in its element chasing across the field, getting that straight, silky coat into complete disarray.

Grooming
Ideally the Silky should have a well-groomed appearance, which calls for a coat length of 5-6in (12.5-15cm) from behind the ears to the set-on of the tail. Legs from knees and hocks to feet should be free from long hair.

AUSTRALIAN TERRIER

The Australian Terrier is a loyal and devoted dog, game, hardy, and utterly reliable with toddlers. It has no human enemies, but will give a good account of itself when called to do battle with other dogs. It is an exceptionally alert watchdog but, having given the alarm, is more likely to kill intruders with kindness. It makes an excellent companion, and its alertness and speed combine to make it an excellent ratter. The

Above: The Australian Terrier is a useful companion, combining the qualities of a loyal pet with those of an alert guard.

Aussie's coat is weather-resistant, so it can be kept either in the home or in an outdoor kennel.

Size
Height: approximately 10in (25cm). Average weight: approximately 14lb (6.4kg).

Exercise
This is an active and keen scenting dog with the skill and courage to hunt and attack food for itself. Nowadays it is rarely asked to use these abilities, but it should have the opportunity to unleash its energy with regular walks and off-the-lead scampers. Nonetheless, it will adapt to apartment living.

Grooming
Regular grooming with a bristle brush will stimulate the skin and encourage a good coat growth. If you are planning to show your Aussie, bath it at least a fortnight before the show; but during the spring and summer, when show dates may be close together, don't bath on each occasion, as frequent washing will soften the coat.

BASENJI

(Zande Dog, Belgian Congo Dog, Congo Bush Dog, Bongo Terrier, Congo Terrier, Nyam-Nyam Terrier)

The Basenji (the name is the translation of a native word meaning 'bush thing') is an interesting and attractive breed, its main claim to fame being that it has no bark. But only the bark is absent; the Basenji will growl and whine like other breeds, and can express itself

feelingly with a distinctive chortle or yodel. The breed's vocal cords are present and it is believed that training, over thousands of years, to hunt game silently may account for their characteristic quietness.

The breed is well known for its gentle disposition and love of children, though it can be aloof with strangers. It has a great curiosity and mischievousness.

Appealing features are its curling tail, high set and lying over to one side of the back, its habit of washing with its paw like a cat, and its forehead full of 'worried' wrinkles.

Size

Ideal height: dog 17in (43cm); bitch 16in (40.5cm); but an inch either way should not penalize an otherwise well-balanced specimen. Ideal weight: dog 24lb (10.9kg); bitch 21lb (9.5kg).

Exercise

The Basenji is a great hunter and if not exercised has a tendency to put on weight. It is fleet-footed, tireless, and enjoys a daily walk and off-the-lead run. It is, incidentally, a breed that is particularly good with horses.

This is a breed that should not be kept in an outside kennel. It is essentially a house dog, which loves to stretch out in front of the fire, or to indulge in its strange habit of re-clining in places off the ground. It is suitable for apartment living as long as it is given sufficient exercise.

Grooming

Regular use of a hound glove is recommended.

BASSET HOUND

The Basset Hound is an affable dog that gets on with most people and makes the ideal family pet. It does, however, retain strong hound instincts and will wander miles if a

Below: The Basset Hound is a friendly dog and is reliable with children. Not renowned for obedience, it none-theless makes a lovable pet.

gate is left conveniently open. It is up to the owners to see that their property is adequately fenced. Like the Beagle, the Basset has a mind of its own; it is eminently lovable, but not always obedient — unless it chooses!

Size

Height: 13-15in (33-38cm).

Exercise

Most important: if you can't give a Basset Hound plenty of exercise, don't have one.

Grooming

Daily brushing and combing required. You should also pay attention to ears and toe-nails.

BEAGLE

The Beagle is a merry, affectionate little fellow, loving humans and other pets alike. It adores children and is a wonderful companion, equally at home in a small house or a mansion, and will guard its home and owner faithfully. It is not a barker, being mostly heard at the chase, in full cry. But, like most other hounds, it has the wanderlust, so care must be taken never to leave the garden gate ajar.

Size

It is desirable that height should neither exceed 16in (40.5cm) nor fall below 13in (33cm). In the United States the height limit is 15in (38cm).

Exercise

Exercise is no problem, because Beagles keep themselves fit as easily in a small garden as on a farm. But, like most dogs, they should be taken for a walk every day. They are notoriously healthy and robust, so you rarely need the services of a veterinarian.

Grooming

The short coat of the Beagle is tough and weatherproof, and needs no grooming. It is recommended that after a muddy walk the Beagle is left in its bed for an hour to clean itself.

Left: The affectionate 'Beardie' makes an ideal family pet and is excellent at obedience work.

BEARDED COLLIE

The Bearded Collie is not so well known as other Collies in Britain, and was almost extinct after the Second World War. Now, however, numbers of this delightful breed are increasing. It is a lovable dog, ideally suited for family life, but retaining its herding capabilities. It is easily trained and reliable with children, and proves a willing, lively playmate.

Size
Ideal height: dog 21-22in (53-56cm); bitch 20-21in (51-53cm).

Exercise
Not suitable for a confined existence. Needs plenty of exercise, including off-the-lead runs.

Grooming
Daily brushing is required. Bathing and chalking are necessary for a show dog.

BEDLINGTON TERRIER

The Bedlington Terrier is an attractive, hardy little dog that resembles a shorn lamb in appearance. It is a dog whose dainty appearance and love of children belies its first-rate watchdog qualities, and it makes a formidable fighter if provoked. It is also a breed that trains easily, and a number have been used successfully in obedience competitions.

Size
Height: about 16in (40.5cm), allowing slight variation below in the case of a bitch and above in the case of a dog. Weight: 18-23lb (8.2-10.4kg).

Exercise
The Bedlington, like most terriers, is a lively, inquisitive breed and will enjoy an off-the-lead run or energetic ball game. It will, however, adapt very happily to apartment life as long as it is given regular adequate walks.

Grooming
This breed's coat does not shed, which makes it a boon for the house-proud, the dead hairs staying in the coat until they are combed out. The breed should be trimmed regularly (otherwise the coat will become tangly) and given a good brushing every day with a fairly stiff brush. Do not bath the animal too often or this may weaken its coat.

Left: The Bedlington Terrier is a trainable breed which will double as a guard and children's pet; it is not so reliable with other dogs.

complete, should be of an elegant white 'powder puff', the head and body trimmed to give a rounded effect, but showing the eyes. Hair around the feet should also be trimmed. Ask the breeder for a showing and grooming chart, and for a demonstration.

BLACK AND TAN COONHOUND

The Black and Tan Coonhound is a fast, hardy, strong working hound that, like the Bloodhound, does not kill its prey. It is similar to the Bloodhound in appearance, but you can detect the Coonhound by its lack of wrinkles, characteristic of the Bloodhound. It is essentially an American breed, one of six types of Coonhound recognized in America, where it is used for hunting opossum and racoon.

Size
Height: dog 25-27in (63.5-68.5cm); bitch 23-25in (58.5-63.5cm).

Exercise
It is a working dog and needs plenty of vigorous exercise.

Grooming
Daily grooming with a hound glove required. Regular ear inspection is advocated.

BLOODHOUND

The Bloodhound is a delightful animal with a nose that is second to none. It follows its quarry, but does not kill. Indeed, it is loved by children, who can accompany it on the lead, and is often kept as a family pet. Bloodhounds are popular show dogs, but individuals are still often called in by the police for tracking purposes.

Size
Height: dog 25-27in (63.5-68.5cm); bitch 23-25in (58.5-63.5cm). Weight: dog 90lb (40.8kg); bitch 80lb (36.3kg).

Exercise
These dogs need plenty of exercise, and have to gallop. Best to join a Bloodhound club if you become an owner, and take part in organized events.

Grooming
Daily grooming with a hound glove is required, plus a regular ear inspection.

Health care
Bloodhounds are subject to torsion (stomach gases building into a bloat). A large proportion are affected and it can prove fatal if not treated by a veterinarian within minutes. It is best to be aware of this so that you know to seek immediate help.

Hair should be removed from inside the dog's ears fairly regularly, which can be done quite simply by pulling the hair with finger and thumb or a pair of tweezers.

BELGIAN SHEPHERD DOG

There are four types of Belgian Shepherd Dog—the Groenendaal, Tervueren, Laekenois and Malinois—all of which are similar to the German Shepherd Dog. The first two breeds, also known as the Belgian Sheepdog and the Belgian Tervuren respectively, are by far the more popular of the four types.

Belgian Shepherd Dogs are basically hunting and herding dogs, but they also make vigilant guards and are kindly protectors of children. Alert, intelligent and agile, these dogs require firm but kind handling.

Size
The desired height for the dog is 24-26in (61-66cm) and for the bitch 22-24in (56-61cm). This applies to all four types.

Exercise
The Belgian Shepherd Dog is a working dog that excels in defending master and property. It is oblivious to bad weather, and enjoys being out of doors, so adequate exercise is very important.

The breed has done well in working trials and in various obedience competitions; a Belgian Shepherd Dog, in the hands of an experienced trainer, will soon learn all that is required of it. Conversely, rough handling will benefit neither owner nor dog, but may turn a forthcoming, eager pup into a nervous animal.

Grooming
Little grooming is needed other than a good surface brushing. Bathing is not recommended, even for exhibition, unless the dog has got its coat into a filthy condition. As it has a double coat, combing out the under-coat will result in a dog with only half a coat.

BERNESE MOUNTAIN DOG
(Bernese Sennenhund)

The Bernese Mountain Dog is the most internationally known of the four Swiss Mountain Dogs, the others being the Great Swiss Sennenhund (or Mountain Dog), the Appenzell Sennenhund and the Entlebuch Sennenhund. It is used as both draught dog and companion in its country of origin, but elsewhere it is gaining popularity as pet and show dog, being easy to train despite its size and strength, loyal, affectionate and docile with both other animals and humans. It is a beautiful dog, with something of the collie in its appearance.

Size
Height: dog 25-27½in (63.5-70cm); bitch 23-26in (58.5-66cm).

Above: The Bichon Frise makes an affectionate pet and an elegant show dog for those who have time to devote to its elaborate presentation.

Exercise
Needs a reasonable amount of exercise and is not ideally suited to town life.

Grooming
Regular brushing will keep the coat in good condition.

BICHON FRISE

The Bichon Frise has been recognized by the British and American Kennel Clubs only in recent years. It is a most appealing and happy little dog, which is becoming increasingly popular as the public becomes acquainted with the breed. It has an attractive, lamb-like appearance and makes an ideal pet.

Size
Height: less than 12in (30cm), smallness being highly desirable.

Exercise
It will fit well into town living and regular walks, but will enjoy the occasional off-the-lead country run and a game in the garden.

Grooming
This is not the breed for novice exhibitors, or for those who are not prepared to spend time in meticulous grooming, bathing, trimming and scissoring. The effect, when

BORDER COLLIE

The Border Collie is a first-class, everyday working dog, famed for herding cattle and rounding up sheep. This is the star of sheepdog trials, the persistent winner of obedience competitions, and the breed favoured by those who want a 'working' dog.

The Border Collie (the name refers to the English-Scottish border) was bred for speed, stamina and brains. It makes a first-class companion and is good with children.

Size
Dog about 21in (53cm); bitch slightly less.

Exercise
This is essentially a working dog that enjoys being out of doors, whether trotting at its master's heels on a routine walk, doing exercises at a dog training class, or working on a farm. It will adapt to whatever role you have for it, but is not ideally suited to town life.

Grooming
Brush regularly with a good pony dandy brush and comb. Inspect the ears for signs of canker, and the ears and feet for foreign matter. Dead fur should be removed when grooming.

BORDER TERRIER

The Border Terrier is the smallest of the working terriers. It is a natural breed that evolved in the border counties of England and Scotland, where its task was to worry foxes from their lair.

It is a sporty working breed and should be able to follow a horse. Hardy and unspoilt, with an equable temperament, it also makes a fine family pet.

Size
Weight: dog 13-15½lb (5.9-7kg); bitch 11½-14lb (5.2-6.4kg).

Exercise
The Border Terrier has immense vitality and is able to keep pace with a horse. It is unfair to keep one unless you can give it adequate exercise.

Grooming
The coat needs a little trimming to tidy up for the show ring, but otherwise requires the minimum of grooming.

Above: The Borzoi is a graceful, aristocratic and elegant dog that possesses courage, muscular power and great speed. Unfortunately, it is a breed that is all too frequently kept as a status symbol.

BORZOI

The Borzoi is an animal of great beauty and grace used in Russia from the 17th century for wolf hunting and coursing. Today it is often regarded more as a fashion accessory.

They are dignified, good-natured animals, but are somewhat aloof and do not make suitable playmates for children.

Size
Height: dog from 29in (73.5cm); bitch from 27in (68.5cm) upwards.

exercising and training. It has served in the armed forces and as a guide dog for the blind (seeing eye dog). Its tail is docked, and when pleased it tends to wag its whole body with pleasure.

Size
Height: dog 22-24in (56-61cm); bitch 21-23in (53-58.5cm). Weight: dogs around 23in (58.5cm) should weigh about 66lb (30kg); and bitches of about 22in (56cm) should weigh about 62lb (28.1kg).

Exercise
Good daily walks and off-the-lead runs are recommended.

Grooming
Daily brushing will keep the coat in good condition.

BRIARD

The Briard is the best-known of the four French sheepdogs—the others being the Beauceron, the Picardy and the Pyrenean Mountain Dog. Briards are good-natured, and can be kept happily either as an affectionate family pet, or for work around the farm; quite a number are finding their way into the show ring.

Size
Height: dog 23-27in (58.5-68.5cm); bitch 22-25½in (56-65cm).

Exercise
Regular exercise is needed, preferably not just a walk around the park.

Grooming
Regular brushing required. The Briard takes pride in cleaning itself.

Below: The Briard takes its name from the Brie area of France. It is a versatile breed that makes a good watchdog or show dog.

Exercise
The Borzoi needs a great deal of exercise, but remember that the dog is a hunter; it is essential that it should be allowed to run only when far from livestock.

Grooming
Daily grooming required to keep the coat silky and free of tangles.

BOSTON TERRIER
(Formerly American Bull Terrier)

The Boston Terrier is a lively and attractive American breed. It is intelligent and trainable, and makes a delightful companion, always ready for a walk or a game. However, achieving the desired markings can be a show aspirant's nightmare, and bitches frequently require caesarean section in whelping.

Size
Weight: not more than 25lb (11.3kg).

Exercise
This breed will happily settle for an on-the-lead walk if you do not have a garden to offer it more freedom of movement. It is essentially a pet dog and should not be confined in an outside kennel.

Grooming
Daily brushing is needed. In the United States ears are cropped in some states according to state law. This practice is illegal in the United Kingdom. The coat rarely sheds.

Health care
The Boston is robust but, as in the case of the Pekingese and other round-eyed breeds, watch that dust and foreign bodies do not penetrate the eyes as this can cause problems.

Above: The Boston Terrier is a delightful little dog that is good with children and makes an effective household guard.

BOUVIER DES FLANDRES

The Bouvier des Flandres is a Belgian cattle dog, hardy, trustworthy, and—when its ears are cropped, as in its country of origin—looking the epitome of ferocity. It can be kept as a pet, but tends to be a one-person dog, though that means guarding their family as well!

Size
Height: dog 24½-27in (62-68.5cm); bitch 23-25½in (58.5-65cm). Weight: dog 77-88lb (34.9-39.9kg); bitch 59½-77lb (27-34.9kg).

Exercise
Needs plenty of exercise. Not ideally suited to town life.

Grooming
Regular brushing will keep the coat in good condition.

BOXER

The Boxer is a delightful animal that takes longer than most to grow up. It loves children and is a faithful protector of the family. However, it is an exuberant, fairly powerful dog, deserving a reasonable-sized home and garden and owners prepared to spend the necessary time on

Above: The Brittany Spaniel is a sensitive dog that needs kind handling. It has boundless energy and combines hunting and pointing abilities with complete devotion to its master.

BRITTANY SPANIEL

The Brittany Spaniel combines well the roles of hunter and companion. It has a natural talent for pointing and has been described as more like a setter than a spaniel. It has an excellent nose, and can cope with difficult terrain. It is, however, a sensitive animal that expects, and deserves, every consideration from its master. It is easily distinguishable by its short, stumpy tail. This breed is relatively unknown in the United Kingdom, but is popular in the United States where it has been successful in field trials.

Size
Height: maximum 20½in (52cm), minimum 18¼in (46.5cm); ideal for dog 19¼-20in (49-51cm), for bitch 18¾-19¾in (47.5-50cm).

Exercise
Relishes plenty of exercise.

Grooming
Daily brushing. Take care that foreign bodies do not lodge in ears, eyes or paws.

BULLDOG

The Bulldog, despite its somewhat ferocious appearance, has a docile temperament and generally adores children. It is quick to learn and will enjoy taking part in games. However, its build precludes any fast running, and it must never be allowed to rush about in hot weather, as its nose does not equip it for rapid breathing. It should never be shut in a car or other confined space unless plenty of fresh air is available.

This breed is not renowned for longevity. It can, however, be warmly recommended as a loyal guard dog and lovable family pet.

Size
Weight: dog 55lb (25kg); bitch 50lb (22.7kg).

Exercise
The Bulldog will benefit from a good daily walk on a loose lead. If the owner lives in a safe, rural area, or has a nearby enclosed park, the dog will enjoy being allowed off the lead so that it may amble at its own pace. But it should not be dragged, or allowed to over-exert itself as a pup. Experience will show just how much exercise it enjoys without tiring. It is definitely not the breed for anyone with a penchant for all-day hiking.

Grooming
A daily brushing with a fairly stiff brush and a rub-down with a hound glove will keep the Bulldog in good condition. Choose a warm summer's day for its annual bath!

BULLMASTIFF

The Bullmastiff is an extremely strong breed, obtained through crossing the Mastiff with the Bulldog. At one time it had an almost unequalled reputation for ferocity, but today's specimens tend to be lovable and trustworthy, despite their power and size.

Size
Height: dog 25-27in (63.5-68.5cm); bitch 24-26in (61-66cm). Weight: dog 110-130lb (49.9-59kg); bitch 90-110lb (40.8-49.9kg).

Exercise
Needs regular exercise. A child or lightweight adult would not be able to hold on to the lead.

Grooming
Regular brushing will keep the coat in good condition.

BULL TERRIER

The Bull Terrier, despite its somewhat fierce appearance, is a gentle dog and utterly reliable with children, especially the bitch, which will literally let them climb all over her. However, if provoked by another dog, this terrier will happily fight to the death. The Bull Terrier never lets go! It is also a fine guard. It may let an intruder into your house, but one thing is certain: it won't let him out again! No one could call this a beautiful breed, but it has an attraction all of its own, and is both healthy and hardy.

Size
The standard has no height or weight limits: the Bull Terrier could be 70lb (31.75kg) in weight, or half that.

Exercise
The Bull Terrier is a powerful dog, with boundless energy, and should not be confined to apartment life, with a run in the back garden. More suitable would be a happily controlled country life with plenty of opportunity to run free. Anyone taking this dog for a walk on the lead must be sure that they are strong enough to hold on to it.

Grooming
Normal daily brushing required.

CAIRN TERRIER

The game little Cairn Terrier comes from Inverness in Scotland and, although a popular show dog elsewhere, and drawing large entries in terrier classes, it is still in Scotland that the Cairn really comes into its own as a family pet.

The Gaelic word 'cairn' means a heap of stones, and is therefore a most suitable name for a terrier that goes to ground. It is an affectionate, sporty little dog, very active, and rarely stubborn, and it makes an ideal family companion. Its almost rain-resistant coat makes it well equipped for life outdoors.

Size
Weight: 14lb (6.4kg).

Exercise
The Cairn is an energetic dog and also an expert killer of rodents. It is in its element trotting with its owner across the fields, or playing a lively game with children. It will adapt to controlled walks on the lead and sedate town living, as long as it has a good-sized garden to romp in.

Below: A fine guard, the Bullmastiff is generally trustworthy and gentle, though, in buying one, you must be sure to get a specimen that is temperamentally sound.

Grooming
The Cairn is an easy dog to groom or, indeed, to prepare for the show ring, as it is presented in a 'natural' condition. It should be brushed and combed, and have any excess feathering removed from behind the front legs and the tail. Any long hairs about the ears and on the underside should also be removed for tidiness.

CARDIGAN WELSH CORGI

The Cardigan Welsh Corgi has been known and worked in South Wales for centuries. It is hardy, fond of children, and tireless, and, despite its original task of nipping the heels of cattle to bring them into line, has a more equable temperament than the Pembroke, and is consequently less likely to nip the heels of unsuspecting visitors.

Size
Height: as near as possible to 12in (30cm). Weight: dog 22-26lb (10-11.8kg); bitch 20-24lb (9-10.9kg).

Exercise
Although traditionally a worker, the Cardigan adapts well to life as a domestic pet, with daily walks of average length. But beware: if you do not give sufficient exercise this breed will soon lose its figure!

Grooming
Daily brushing needed. The breed has a water resistant coat.

Health care
Avoid letting your pet jump from heights, especially if overweight: this could lead to painful spine trouble. This is one of the breeds that may suffer from an eye defect known as progressive retinal atrophy (see page 32), though fortunately this disease has almost been eradicated from Corgis.

CAVALIER KING CHARLES SPANIEL

Many people find it hard to distinguish between the King Charles and the Cavalier King Charles Spaniel; the Cavalier is larger, and there are marked differences in the head formation—the skull is almost flat between the ears and its stop is much shallower than that of the King Charles. However, it has the same characteristics of courage, hardiness and good nature, which makes it a suitable pet for any age group.

Size
Weight: 12-18lb (5.4-8.2kg). A small, well-balanced dog within these weights is desirable.

Exercise
Normal exercise requirement is a daily walk. Will adapt easily to town or country living. It should not, however, be kennelled out of doors.

Grooming
This breed requires daily grooming with a bristle brush and monthly baths (except in cold weather). The paws should be examined for any trace of interdigital cysts, and the ears examined for canker, often detectable by an unpleasant smell. Wipe eyes with cotton wool dipped in a weak saline solution to keep them clear of unsightly 'tear streaks'.

CHESAPEAKE BAY RETRIEVER

The Chesapeake Bay is a favourite with American sportsmen but has to date few devotees in the United Kingdom. It is an excellent swimmer and an unsurpassed retriever of wild duck. It is generally good with children, but can be a little head-strong and difficult to train, and is occasionally aggressive. Distinguishing features are the breed's yellow eyes and web feet. Its coat is water-resistant.

Size
Height: dog 23-26in (58.5-66cm), bitch 21-24in (53-61cm). Weight: dog 65-75lb (29.5-34kg), bitch 55-65lb (25-29.5kg).

Exercise
Needs plenty of hard exercise to stay in good condition.

Grooming
Normal brushing is sufficient.

CHIHUAHUA

The Chihuahua, the world's tiniest dog, is keenly intelligent, fiercely protective and cheap to keep. Its size makes it an ideal pet for town dwellers, though it tends to be strong willed and may even snap at teasing children.

Chihuahuas are not as delicate as one might imagine, but they dislike the cold and appreciate a coat to keep them warm when out of doors in winter. These dogs are definitely not designed for kennel living. They also have a tendency to shiver, a habit that evokes sympathy from onlookers who wrongly imagine that the Chihuahua is terrified or frozen.

There are two varieties: the more popular Long-coated Chihuahua and the Smooth-coated variety. The only difference is in the coat which, in the case of the former, should be long, of soft texture and either flat or slightly wavy.

Size
Weight: between 2-6lb (0.9-2.7kg), (under 4lb (1.8kg) preferred for show). There is no desired height in this breed's standard.

Exercise
Contrary to belief, the Chihuahua is ready, and able, to walk as far as most owners would wish, although it does not object to an occasional ride in a shopping basket. The fact that its exercise requirements are moderate makes this breed an ideal choice of pet for the elderly.

Grooming
The Chihuahua should be groomed with a soft brush. A rub down with a velvet glove, or pad, will make the coat gleam. Nails must be regularly clipped and ears kept free of dust.

Above: Chihuahuas are intelligent pets that become devoted to their owners. Today, the Long-coat (shown here) tends to be more popular than the Smooth-coat.

Below: The most recently introduced of the Dachshund varieties, the Wire-haired Dachshund was bred by crossing the Smooth-haired with the Dandie Dinmont and other terriers.

Health care
Watch out for the molera, a small opening on the top of the skull. The Chihuahua's molera, unlike that of a human baby, may never fill in, so a blow on the head could prove fatal. This breed is prone to hiccups; a spasm can often be cured by lifting the pet purposefully up and down.

CHOW CHOW

The Chow Chow, whose name is perhaps derived from the Chinese Choo Hunting Dog, is a member of the Spitz family known for over 2,000 years, lion-like in appearance and famed for its black tongue. It is odour-free and makes an incredibly loyal companion, tending to devote itself to one member of the family though accepting and returning the affection of other household members. It needs quiet but firm handling: with its aloof temperament it is unlikely to deign to walk at your heel without persuasion. It does not take kindly to strangers and is a fearsome fighter if provoked.

Size
Minimum height for Chows is 18in (46cm), but in every case balance should be the outstanding feature and height left to the discretion of the judges.

Exercise
Most Chow owners seem to manage with regular on-the-lead walks with runs in permitted areas. However, mindful of the Chow's prowess as a hunter of wolves, game and anything that moves, it seems unfair to keep it in confined surroundings or to deprive it of the open spaces that it relishes.

Grooming
About 5 or 10 minutes' brushing a day and about an hour each weekend with a wire brush should keep the Chow gleaming.

CLUMBER SPANIEL

The Clumber is the heaviest of the spaniels and is thought to be of French origin, brought about by crossing the Basset Hound with the Alpine Spaniel (which is now extinct). It is a brave, attractive and reliable dog; a slow but sure worker and an excellent retriever. Hefty in build, it moves with a rolling gait characteristic of the breed.

Size
Weight: dog about 55-70lb (25-32kg); bitch about 45-60lb (20.5-27kg).

Exercise
This is essentially a working dog, best suited to country life and needs plenty of exercise and off-the-lead runs in open spaces.

Grooming
Routine brushing is required. Keep coat tangle-free and take care that mud does not become lodged between the dog's toes.

MINIATURE AND STANDARD
DACHSHUND
(Teckel, Dachel, Dacksel and Badger Hound)

The Dachshund was bred as a badger hound in its native Germany. Badger hunting required a short-legged hound, with a keen sense of smell, coupled with courage and gameness; a dog that could burrow—an ability which if unchecked, today's pet Dachshund will demonstrate in your garden.

Some Dachshunds are still bred as hunting dogs and will bravely tackle opponents larger than themselves, such as badgers. They would also defend their owner until death. However, their role nowadays is mainly as a companion. They like children, but can be a little aggressive with strangers if unchecked. They are affectionate, full of fun and, despite their short legs, can cope with as much exercise as you can give them. They have a large bark for their size and are good watchdogs.

Apart from the size difference, the Miniature Dachshund is in all respects similar to the Standard breed, and both types have three different coat varieties: Long-haired, Smooth-haired and Wire-haired.

Size
Miniature (Long-haired, Smooth-haired and Wire-haired): ideal weight 10lb (4.5kg). It is most important that judges should not award a prize to any dog exceeding 11lb (5kg) in weight.

Standard Long-haired: middle weight up to 18lb (8.2kg) for dogs and 17lb (7.7kg) for bitches. Smooth-haired: dogs should not exceed 25lb (11.3kg); bitches should not exceed 23lb (10.4kg). Wire-haired: dogs should weigh 20-22lb (9-10kg) and bitches 18-20lb (8.2-9kg).

Exercise
Regular exercise is important, as the tendency to put on weight must be discouraged. Short frequent walks are advisable, with plenty of runs in a well-fenced garden.

Grooming
The Dachshund's coat is easy to keep in condition. The Smooth-haired needs only a few minutes' attention every day with a hound glove and soft cloth. A stiff-bristled brush and comb should be used on the Long-haired and Wire-haired varieties.

The Dachshund's teeth are prone to the formation of a hard deposit known as tartar. Regular scaling is recommended, but stains can be removed with a paste of water and cream of tartar, applied with a bit of cotton wool.

Health care
Disc trouble can befall the Dachshund because of its long back and stubby little legs. Anyone who has seen a young dog paralysed, while otherwise in good health, will recognize the need to keep their pet's weight within the breed standard and to prevent it from leaping on and off the furniture. Treatment varies from injections of cortisone to an operation; some owners swear by osteopathy!

DALMATIAN

The Dalmatian has a happy nature, is loyal and devoted to its owners and rarely fights. It is easily trained and fairly simple to present in show. It is generally long-lived, and has a lively youth. Remember that it was bred to run with horse and carriage, and has the need and stamina for plenty of exercise.

Size
Overall balance of prime importance, but the ideal height for a dog is 23-24in (58.5-61cm), for a bitch 22-23in (56-58.5cm).

Exercise
Don't buy a Dalmatian unless you can give it plenty of exercise. It is in its element running behind a horse, but an active, open-air country life will suffice.

Grooming
Daily brushing with occasional bathing required.

Health care
Some Dalmatians suffer from deafness. Check that a pup can hear before buying.

DANDIE DINMONT TERRIER

Although once popular as a badger and fox hunter, the Dandie Dinmont is now kept mainly as a household pet: indeed, it fares better indoors as a single pet than living with its fellows in kennels. Dandie Dinmonts do, however, tend to be a little suspicious of strangers, giving all their devotion to their owner. Despite their size they are excellent guard dogs with a bark that should deter any burglar.

Size
The height should be 8-11in (20-28cm) at the top of the shoulder. Length from top of shoulder to root of tail should be not more than twice the dog's height, but preferably 1-2in (2.5-5cm) less. The ideal weight for a dog in good working condition is as near 18lb (8.2kg) as possible.

Exercise
The Dandie Dinmont is an adaptable dog and will be happy whether put to work killing foxes or enjoying the role of an old lady's pet. It would, however, be unfair to keep this active, inquisitive breed in a home without a garden.

Grooming
Grooming is not a difficult task, the only equipment needed being a stiff brush and comb. Old hairs should be removed with finger and thumb, allowing the undercoat to come through. Incidentally, you should not use a trimming knife, because this will ruin the coat. Brush daily and the coat should always look immaculate.

Below: The Dandie Dinmont Terrier is an active breed that appreciates plenty of exercise and makes a keen watchdog.

DOBERMANN

(Dobermann Pinscher, Doberman)

The Dobermann is a strong, alert guard that will enjoy the comforts of its master's fireside and protect him and his family with its life. It is unlikely to have to give its life, however, for the Dobermann generally gets the better of any opponent and is one of the best guard dogs in the world. It is an aloof animal that takes its responsibilities seriously, is skilled at tracking, and makes a fine police dog. If kennelled outside, it is important that it has a heated, draught-proof kennel.

Size
Ideal height: dog 27in (68.5cm); bitch 25½in (65cm). Considerable

Below: A superb guard, obedience and show dog, the Dobermann requires knowledgeable handling.

deviation from this ideal to be discouraged.

Exercise
Certainly at least 40 minutes each day is needed, which must include a 10-minute off-the-lead run.

Grooming
The Dobermann, with its short coat, needs little grooming other than a daily rub down with Turkish towelling to remove loose hairs.

ELKHOUND

(Norwegian Elkhound)

The Elkhound was bred in Norway to seek out the elk and hold it at bay until its master moved in for the kill. It is a happy breed, loyal and devoted to its master and reliable with children, but it requires firm but gentle discipline in puppyhood. It has a great love of the outdoors, is

energetic, and is not recommended for those unable to provide adequate exercise.

Size
Height: dog 20½in (52cm); bitch 19½in (49.5cm). Weight: dog 50lb (22.7kg); bitch 43lb (19.5kg).

Exercise
Needs plenty of exercise to stay healthy.

Grooming
Daily brushing and combing required.

ENGLISH COCKER SPANIEL

The 'merry' Cocker, as it is called, makes an ideal family pet—a dog for dad to take out shooting, or for the

children to romp with in the garden. It is manageable, intelligent, and a good all-purpose gundog, second to none at flushing out game.

Size
Height: dog 15½-16in (39.5-40.5cm); bitch 15-15½in (38-39.5cm). The weight should be about 28-32lb (12.7-14.5kg).

Exercise
This is an active dog that needs regular exercise. It adores the country and is likely to return from a walk with tail wagging and covered with mud, so it is not perhaps the ideal choice for smart town dwellers; but it does enjoy home comforts, such as a place beside a warm fire.

Grooming
The Cocker requires daily brushing and combing, care being taken that its coat does not become matted. Particular care must be taken that the ears do not become tangled; and watch out that they do not flop into the feeding bowl!

ENGLISH SETTER

The English Setter is the most distinctive of the three Setter varieties: Irish, Gordon and English. It has a gentle nature that makes it the ideal companion for children, at the same time being an excellent gundog. It can be either housed indoors or kennelled outside, and as it needs lots of exercise, it is not a suitable companion for a flat dweller. The English Setter requires a fair amount of grooming.

Size
Height: dog 25½-27in (65-68.5cm); bitch 24-25in (61-63.5cm).
Weight: dog 60-66lb (27.2-30kg); bitch 56-62lb (25.4-28.1kg).

Exercise
Needs at least 10 minutes of exercise a day as a three-month-old pup and an hour in adulthood to keep it in top condition. Trains well to the gun.

Grooming
You will need trimming scissors and a fine steel comb for daily grooming, also a good stiff brush for the coat. Take care that the feathering on the legs does not become tangled. The silky hair under the ears should be removed and also hair under the throat and below the ear down to the breast bone. Care must also be taken to remove hair that forms between the dog's pads. Any straggly hairs have to be plucked from the body before the dog goes into the ring. The English Setter is always bathed before a show, and the coat combed flat when it is dry. American competitors are trimmed more heavily than those exhibited in the United Kingdom.

ENGLISH SPRINGER SPANIEL

The English Springer Spaniel makes an excellent dual-purpose gundog and pet. It is both intelligent and loyal, and excellent with children. It gives a good account of itself in obedience competitions and excels as a happy, efficient retriever.

Size
The approximate height should be 20in (51cm). The approximate weight should be 50lb (22.7kg).

Exercise
This is a breed that needs plenty of exercise, or it is likely to put on weight. Lack of exercise often leads to skin troubles, too.

Grooming
Daily brushing required. Take care that mud does not become caked in the paws, and make sure that the ears are kept clean and tangle-free to prevent infection.

Above: The English Setter is an eye-catching breed, best suited for the country. It admirably combines the role of gundog and family pet and will live indoors or out.

FINNISH SPITZ
(Suomenpystykorva)

The Finnish Spitz is Finland's national dog. It is popular in Scandinavia as both a hunter (mainly of birds) and a show dog. It also has devotees in Great Britain, where it is kept mainly as a pet and show dog. It is a beautiful animal with the habit of cleaning itself like a cat.

Size
Height: dog 17½in (44.5cm); bitch 15½in (39.5cm).

Exercise
This is a real outdoor dog, which likes to run free whenever possible. However, it also relishes its place by the fireside, so it should not be kept kennelled.

Grooming
Normal daily brushing required.

Health care
Although a hardy, healthy dog in adulthood, it can prove delicate as a pup, and this Spitz type is not the easiest to breed.

FLAT-COATED RETRIEVER

The Flat-coated Retriever has enjoyed renewed popularity in Britain since attaining the coveted Best in Show award at Crufts in 1980. It is a natural retriever, used for picking up game, and is hardy and easily trained. It also makes a good household companion if you wish, being very good with children, and may be housed either indoors or out.

Size
Should be 60-70lb (27.2-31.8kg).

Exercise
Thrives on plenty of exercise.

Grooming
Regular brushing and tidying up required.

Below: The attractive English Springer will double as a gundog and family pet. It is good with children and works well in obedience.

FRENCH BULLDOG

The French Bulldog is a devoted animal and makes the ideal family pet. It has a keen, clownish sense of humour, is intelligent, and adapts well to town or country living. It is perhaps the healthiest of the Bull-dogs and does not suffer from the over-developments or nasal diffi-culties of the Boston Terrier and the English Bulldog.

Size
Ideal weight: dog 28lb (12.7kg); bitch 24lb (10.9kg) — but soundness must not be sacrificed to smallness.

Exercise
Short regular walks and off-the-lead scampers are adequate exercise for the French Bulldog.

Grooming
Normal daily brushing required.

Health care
The facial creases should be lubri-cated with petroleum jelly to prevent soreness.

GERMAN SHEPHERD DOG
(Alsatian)

The German Shepherd Dog has one of the largest followings in the world. It is also the breed that rouses the strongest emotions in the public; people either love the German Shepherd or abhor it.

The German Shepherd is one of the most courageous and intelligent of dogs, debatably *the* most intelligent. Breed members have fought bravely, and many lost their lives in two world wars. They have been, and still are, used as guide dogs for the blind ('seeing eye dogs'), police dogs, and military dogs. Certainly they are very popular guards. It is this strong guarding instinct that can be their undoing, however, for a German Shepherd has a strong tendency to be over-protective about its owner's property, and may turn nasty unnecessarily. It could also turn nasty through sheer boredom, if acquired as a mere pet dog. The German Shepherd deserves a job

Above: A devoted pet, the German Shepherd nonetheless needs knowledgeable handling. It is happiest with a job to do and is in its element as an obedience or guard dog.

to do, whether it be in the public service, or competing eagerly in obedience and working trials.

Size
Ideal height: dog 24-26in (61-66cm); bitch 22-24in (56-61cm). The proportion of length to height varies between 10:9 and 10:8.5.

Exercise
Needs plenty of exercise, off-the-lead runs and, if possible, obedience exercises. It will excel at any dog training club in 'scent' and 'retrieve.'

Grooming
Daily brushing is recommended.

Health care
This is a healthy, hardy breed. However, its popularity in recent years has encouraged indiscriminate breeding, resulting in loss of temperament and form. Take care, when purchasing a German

Shepherd Dog, to acquire only from registered HD-free stock. HD (hip dysplasia) is a malformation of the hip joint that can result in the dog being crippled before middle age (see page 32). Reliable vendors do not breed from affected stock. Many people feel this defect came about through over-emphasis on that desired show dog crouch.

GERMAN SHORT-HAIRED POINTER

The German Short-haired Pointer is a good all-round sporting dog, that also makes a charming household pet, being both affectionate and good with children. It is, however, happiest when in the wide open spaces, and is excellent at working wildfowl and most types of game. It is an obedient dog and a first-rate swimmer.

Size
Height: dog 23-25in (58.5-63.5cm); bitch 21-23in (53-58.5cm).

Exercise
Needs plenty of exercise.

Grooming
Brush the coat regularly.

GERMAN WIRE-HAIRED POINTER
(Drahthaar)

In its native country the German Wire-haired Pointer is known as the Drahthaar (literally translated, this means 'wire hair') and is perhaps more spirited and aggressive than its fellow pointers, with stronger guarding instincts and a hardy physique. It is an excellent gundog that is easy to train, and also makes a good household pet, being both even-tempered and good with children.

Size
Height: dog 24-26in (61-66cm); bitch smaller, not less than 22in (56cm).

Exercise
Needs plenty of exerise.

Grooming
Brush the coat regularly.

GOLDEN RETRIEVER

The Golden Retriever cannot be too highly recommended as a breed to suit all the family. It will romp with the children, enjoy a day's shooting,

Above: The German Wire-haired Pointer is an obedient, useful gundog that makes a slightly better watchdog than its relatives.

happily accompany its owner on a shopping trip, or attend a session at the dog training club. This is a trustworthy breed, which can be kennelled, but individuals are happiest sharing the fireside with their family. They love to retrieve and will enjoy nothing better than carrying the newspaper home, or wandering around the house with an old chewed slipper. They are often used as guide dogs for the blind.

Size
Height: dog 22-24in (56-61cm); bitch 20-22in (51-56cm). The average weight should be: dog 70-80lb (31.8-36.3kg); bitch 60-70lb (27.2-31.8kg).

Exercise
Needs at least an hour's exercise every day, and free runs. Also requires ample garden space.

Grooming
Regular brushing will keep the coat in good condition.

GORDON SETTER

The Gordon Setter is a fine gundog, a bird-finding dog, used to silent trekking. It does not fit the role of guard, although it will not accept strangers as readily as the Irish Setter, which could well lick the face of a burglar while presenting him with some item 'retrieved' from its mistress's wardrobe.

The Gordon makes an excellent family pet and is trustworthy with children. It does enjoy an active working life, however, and is not really suitable for apartments.

Size
Height: dog 26in (66cm); bitch 24½in (62cm). Weight: dog about 65lb (29.5kg); bitch 56lb (25.4kg).

Exercise
Ensure that it has plenty of exercise.

Grooming
Regular brushing, and monthly nail clipping.

GREAT DANE

The Great Dane is a wonderful companion, devoted to the family, slow to anger and ready to accept other pets. Despite its size it does not object to apartment life, provided it has plenty of walks. It is easily trained and must always be given warm sleeping quarters. Regrettably this is not a breed renowned for longevity.

Size
Minimum height: dog 30in (76cm); bitch 28in (71cm). Weight: dog 120lb (54.4kg); bitch 100lb (45.4kg).

Exercise
Regular exercise on hard ground recommended.

Grooming
Daily grooming with a body brush required.

Below: The Great Dane is a gentle giant that is generally slow to anger. It is, however, a breed whose presence should deter any burglar.

GREYHOUND

One of the most ancient breeds and, some say, the most misunderstood, for although built for speed and used for racing and coursing, the Greyhound is basically lazy. It adapts well to life as a family pet, and will enjoy nothing better than lazing on a settee or mattress. It is a good-natured, friendly and affectionate dog, and is very gentle with children.

Good pet homes are always needed for ex-racing Greyhounds, so those with a love for the breed may consider making enquiries at their local track, or (in the United Kingdom) to the National Greyhound Racing Club's Retired Greyhound Trust, to discover where dogs are available.

The retired Greyhound racer is not an aged animal; it is unlikely to be more than three or four years old, and may be as little as 18 months if it has proved unsuitable for racing. But remember that it will require a period of de-training. There is no overnight magic formula for preventing the Greyhound from chasing cats and other small moving objects, because this is its natural instinct. And out of doors this dog must be kept on a lead at all times.

Size
Height: dog 28-30in (71-76cm); bitch 27-28in (68.5-71cm). There is no standard desired weight.

Exercise
Three or four short walks every day will be sufficient. Although the Greyhound must never be exercised off the lead in a public place, it will enjoy the opportunity to run free in open country, away from sheep and other livestock. It is a highly sensitive creature, and will learn to respond quickly to the tone of voice, which helps greatly in obedience training.

Speed enthusiasts may like to know that the Greyhound has clocked in at 37 mph (60 km/h)!

Grooming
Daily use of a hound glove will keep the coat shining.

GRIFFON
BRUXELLOIS AND BRABANCON

The Griffon is an attractive, happy little dog that makes a first-class family pet. It has an almost monkey-like face, with a knowing expression, and is hardy, intelligent and terrier-like in temperament. The breed, which is essentially Belgian, was originally used as a guard and catcher of vermin, particularly in stable yards. However, it took the fancy of royalty and became a fashionable pet.

There are two varieties, the only difference being in their coats: the Griffon Bruxellois is a rough-coated variety (known as the Brussels Griffon in America), and the Griffon Brabancon is smooth-coated.

Size
Weight: 5-11lb (2.3-5kg), most desirable 6-10lb (2.7-4.5kg).

Exercise
Like most toy breeds it adapts well to town life and does not need a great deal of exercise, but a romp in the countryside will be greatly appreciated.

Above: The Griffon is a happy, hardy little pet that is obedient and long-lived. The smooth variety (shown here) is known as the Griffon Brabancon.

Grooming
This breed requires twice yearly stripping: best to seek advice, or have this done professionally. You should watch with this and other small breeds that the nails do not grow too long.

HUNGARIAN VIZSLA

The Vizsla is Hungary's national dog and one of the purest breeds in the world. It is an excellent all-purpose gundog, with a keen nose, and well able to point, set and retrieve. Despite its hunting abilities it adapts happily to life as a family pet, and its temperament is sound.

Size
Height: dog 22½-25in (57-63.5cm); bitch 21-23½in (53-60cm). Weight: 48½-66lb (22-30kg).

Exercise
Needs plenty of vigorous exercise.

Grooming
Regular brushing will keep the coat in a healthy condition.

IRISH SETTER
(Red Setter)

The Irish Setter is a first-class gundog that combines this work admirably with the role of family pet, though it does not make a good guard: it loves everybody! It is happiest as a housedog and has great need of affection, which it returns a hundredfold. It is intelligent and utterly reliable with children. It is, however, high spirited and lively and should not be confined in close quarters or kept by those who cannot provide adequate exercise.

Left: The Hungarian Vizsla is a first-class gundog and one of the purest breeds in the world.

dog and even do irreparable harm to its temperament. Some owners resort to clipping which is excusable with an elderly animal, but it causes loss of colour and condition. Normally, a good daily brush will suffice and keep this healthy, hardy dog in smart condition. No doubt you will allow it to keep its thick coat after the show season has finished until the end of the winter months.

IRISH WATER SPANIEL

The Irish Water Spaniel is a most attractive animal, loyal, intelligent and with a deeply affectionate nature. It is an excellent retriever and a strong, fearless swimmer, most useful for wild-fowling.

Size
Height: dog 21-23in (53-58.5cm); bitch 20-22in (51-56cm).

Exercise
Needs plenty of exercise.

Grooming
Needs daily brushing and weekly combing. Seek advice on stripping of unwanted hair and ensure mud does not become caked in the toes.

IRISH WOLFHOUND

The Irish Wolfhound, variously known as the Wolfdog, the Irish Greyhound and the Great Dog of Ireland, is a gentle giant, fierce only when provoked. It is intelligent, intensely loyal and slow to show anger. Irish Wolfhounds do, none-theless, have a mind of their own, so firm, gentle discipline is advocated in puppyhood.

Size
The minimum height and weight of dogs should be 31in (78.5cm) and 120lb (54.4kg); of bitches 28in (71cm) and 90lb (40.8kg). Anything below this should be heavily penalised. Great size, including height at shoulder and proportionate length of body, is the target to be aimed for, and ideally the breed should average 32-34in (81-86cm) in dogs, showing the requisite power, activity, courage and symmetry.

Exercise
Despite its size, the Irish Wolfhound does not require more exercise than smaller breeds, but it should have ample space in which to gambol. Let it have unrestricted play during puppyhood, but do not force it to take lengthy walks, rather allowing it to 'muscle up' by its own joyful activity. Irish Wolfhounds are usually taught both to walk and to move at the trot while being led; as they are so powerful, obedience is essential.

Grooming
Brush regularly, and remove long straggly hairs from ears, neck and underside with finger and thumb. This is a natural-looking breed, which is not difficult to groom.

Below: 'Gentle when stroked, fierce when provoked', the Irish Wolfhound is a loyal and majestic beast that is happiest living as a house dog.

Size
The Americans look for a tall dog, 25-27in (63.5-68.5cm) high, but in Britain no height is specified.

Exercise
An exuberant dog that needs lots of exercise, either working as a gundog or running free in the wide open spaces.

Grooming
Regular brushing, claw clipping, and inspection of ears required.

Above: The Irish Terrier makes an ideal companion, obedience and show dog. It is good with children but enjoys a scrap with other dogs.

Grooming
Like the Airedale, the Irish Terrier will need hand stripping several times a year and it is best to have this done professionally—at least until you have learned the knack. An inexperienced attempt at stripping could prove a painful experience for the

IRISH TERRIER

The Irish Terrier is a sporty little dog, which has been trained successfully to the gun and is first-class at destroying vermin. It has also been a creditable performer in obedience competitions.

To describe it as a dog that looks like a small Airedale with a self-coloured yellow coat would be far from satisfy the many lovers of this ancient and most attractive breed. We have today in the Irish Terrier a fine watchdog, a loyal protector and a most excellent family pet, the only drawback being its somewhat ex-aggerated reputation for fighting other dogs. True to its terrier blood it is tremendously courageous, and stories of faithfulness to its master are legion.

Size
Ideal weight: dog 27lb (12.3kg); bitch 25lb (11.3kg). Height should be approximately 18in (46cm).

Exercise
The Irish Terrier will adapt happily to life as a household pet provided it has a garden to romp in and is taken for regular walks and given plentiful off-the-lead runs.

ITALIAN GREYHOUND

The Italian Greyhound is the perfect Greyhound in miniature, a graceful dainty animal that makes an ideal house pet. It does, however, need plenty of exercise and will enjoy a day's rabbiting, should the opportunity arise. It is odourless and rarely moults, and is both affectionate and easy to train.

Size
The most desirable weight is 6-8lb (2.7-3.6kg), and not exceeding 10lb (4.5kg).

Exercise
Certainly not the dog to keep shut up indoors all day. It thrives on plenty of exercise, but adapts well to town living provided adequate walks and off-the-lead runs are possible.

Grooming
The Greyhound needs little more than a rub down with a silk handkerchief. But remember that this breed feels the cold, hates the wind and rain, and needs a coat. Care must be taken of the teeth. Regular scaling by a veterinarian is recommended (this applies to all toy breeds), but cream of tartar — mixed into a paste on a saucer with a little water, and applied with cotton wool — will often remove unsightly stains.

JACK RUSSELL TERRIER

Named after a sporting parson who developed the strain for hunting, in Devon, England, during the 19th century, the Jack Russell Terrier has become immensely popular in recent years. Unfortunately, the

Above: An affectionate, obedient little dog, the Italian Greyhound appreciates a coat in cold weather as harsh winds can be harmful.

breed cannot be registered with the British Kennel Club, for it is not as yet a pedigreed dog. The British Kennel Club is aware of efforts to standardize the breed, but unable to accept it while there is so much variation in colour, size and form.

Size
The Jack Russell Terrier Club of the United Kingdom has drawn up a provisional breed standard aiming to produce a uniform type of Jack Russell Terrier allowing for two different heights: 11-15in (28-38cm) at the shoulder, and under 11in (28cm) at the shoulder.

Exercise
The Jack Russell Terrier will adapt well to life as a household pet provided regular walks are given. However, it is really in its element in the countryside, ferreting and chasing after foxes.

Grooming
A daily brushing with a stiff brush required.

JAPANESE AKITA

The Japanese Akita, the best-known of the Japanese Spitz breeds, is becoming increasingly popular outside Japan, particularly in the United States. The breed has been exhibited in recent years in the United Kingdom and America, and the Japanese are doing all possible to improve their purebred stock. Bred as a hunter of wild boar, deer and even black bear, the Akita is undoubtedly capable of ferocity, but it is easily trained and generally has an equable temperament. It makes a first-class guard.

Above: The popular Jack Russell can be jealous of rival dogs in the family but is otherwise kindly by nature and rarely looks for trouble.

Size
Height: dog 21-24in (53-61cm), some bigger; bitch 19-21in (48-53cm). Weight: 85-110lb (38.6-49.9kg).

Exercise
Does not require a great deal of exercise. Incidentally, it has webbed feet and is a fine swimmer and a good water dog.

Grooming
Normal daily brushing required.

JAPANESE CHIN
(Japanese Spaniel)

The Japanese Chin might, at first glance, be mistaken for the Pekingese, and it is possible that the two breeds may have evolved from a common stock. It is however, a high-stepping, graceful dog that is taller in the leg and has a much lighter body than the Pekingese.

The Japanese Chin, it must be remembered, is a spaniel and there are some similarities with the King Charles Spaniel, whose origin can also be traced to Japan. However, it has much more of the perky confidence of the tinier breeds than the slower-moving spaniel, and is a lively but dignified little oriental that likes nothing better than to be the centre of attention and is miserable if its advances are thwarted.

Size
Weight: 4-7lb (1.8-3.2kg). (The daintier the better, providing type, quality and soundness are not sacrificed.)

Exercise
This is a happy little dog that will delight in going for walks and

playing games with all the family. It will walk as far as its owners wish, or be happy with a run in the park. The Japanese Chin is quite tough, despite its delicate structure, and will enjoy careful handling by youngsters. But it does like to climb, so be careful it does not fall and injure itself! Guard against vigorous exertion and overheating in warm weather due to breathing difficulties.

Grooming
Daily grooming with pure bristle brush will maintain the Chin's luxurious silky coat in good condition. Always give this breed a bath before a show.

KEESHOND

The Keeshond, Holland's national dog, began life as a barge dog, and still has the knack of finding an out-of-the-way corner for itself. It is a loyal dog, and of sound temperament, but needs a lot of grooming and tends to favour one member of the family. It is an excellent watchdog and generally has a very long life.

Size
Height: dog 18in (46cm); bitch 17in (43cm).

Exercise
Average requirements.

Grooming
Regular attention with a stiff brush required. A check chain should not be used as it will spoil the ruff.

KERRY BLUE TERRIER
(Irish Blue Terrier)

The Kerry Blue Terrier is a good sporting dog, but is kept mainly as a

pet. It loves children but does, however, have a temper when aroused, and needs firm but gentle training when young.

Size
Weight: 33-37lb (15-16.8kg); greater tolerance in America.

Exercise
Bred as a working dog, it needs and deserves plenty of exercise.

Grooming
Daily brushing with a stiff brush and metal comb required. You can easily learn to scissor trim the pet yourself. If you plan to show, however, there is a lot of work involved in preparation.

KING CHARLES SPANIEL
(English Toy Spaniel)

The King Charles Spaniel (Black and Tan variety) is known in America as the English Toy Spaniel, the varieties of which are Prince Charles, King Charles, Ruby and Blenheim. In 1903 an attempt was made in the United Kingdom to change the breed name to Toy Spaniel. However,

Above: The Kerry Blue Terrier makes a fine show dog but needs meticulous preparation. An excellent guard, it loves children but is not averse to fighting its fellows.

Below: The King Charles Spaniel makes an excellent choice of pet, being reliable with children, intelligent and playful. It should always be housed indoors.

the change was opposed by King Edward VII, a devotee of the breed, and it has retained the name, probably attributed to it because of Van Dyck's 17th century paintings, which frequently showed King Charles with these pets.

The King Charles is an ideal choice of pet. It is a good mixer, marvellous with children and — despite its small stature — very hardy, though it is not suited to outdoor kennels.

Size
The most desirable weight is 8-14lb (3.6-6.4kg).

Exercise
The King Charles will look forward to its daily outings, whether accompanying its owner on a shopping trip or going for a scamper in the park. It will be quick to learn how to carry its lead or a newspaper. Don't forget to rub it down with a towel after it has been out in the rain.

Grooming
Daily brushing with a bristle brush is essential. Examine paws for any trace of interdigital cysts, and ears for canker, often detected by an unpleasant smell. Wipe eyes with cotton wool dipped in a weak saline solution to keep them clear of unsightly 'tear streaks', and, except in cold weather, give the dog a monthly bath.

Above: The Labrador Retriever is an excellent gundog and an ideal family pet. The Yellow variety is now more popular than the Black.

LABRADOR RETRIEVER

Like the Golden Retriever, the Labrador Retriever cannot be too highly recommended as a breed tailor-made to suit the whole family. It is an excellent retriever, can be trusted with the children and will give a good account of itself in obedience training competitions. The Labrador Retriever is a breed much favoured as a guide dog (seeing eye dog) for the blind.

Size
Height: dog 22-22½in (56-57cm); bitch 21½-22in (54.5-56cm).

Exercise
Needs an hour a day at least, with free runs, also an ample garden.

Grooming
Regular brushing will keep the coat in good condition.

LAKELAND TERRIER

The Lakeland Terrier is similar in appearance to the Welsh and Airedale Terriers. It makes a first-class family pet, being of sound temperament and convenient size, and is also a fine guard with its strong warning bark. It has been used in the past for both fox and badger hunting, but nowadays is kept mainly as a pet and has, in recent years, been a very successful contender in the show ring. It might be too lively for the elderly.

Size
The height should not exceed 14½in (37cm) at the shoulder. The average weight of a dog is 17lb (7.7kg); bitch 15lb (6.8kg).

Exercise
Unless they choose a toy breed, like the Yorkshire Terrier, nobody should choose a terrier unless they want a pet with plenty of zip. The Lakeland Terrier, true to its breed, is gay and fearless, always ready for a walk or a game. It is suitable for apartment living as long as its owner can provide regular exercise and, hopefully, those much loved days out in the country for off-the-lead runs.

Grooming
Trimming the Lakeland for the show ring requires some skill. Daily brushing will help keep the coat tidy but, even for a pet, professional stripping in the spring, summer and autumn is recommended.

LHASA APSO

The Lhasa Apso comes from the mountains of Tibet. It is a shaggy little dog, rather like an Old English Sheepdog in miniature, and makes an excellent pet, the only possible drawback being its natural suspicion of strangers. It is affectionate and good with children, and is suitable for both town and country living.

Size
Ideal height: dogs 10in (25cm); bitches slightly smaller.

Exercise
This lively breed needs plenty of walks and off-the-lead runs.

Grooming
Needs daily brushing and combing.

LOWCHEN

The Lowchen is a member of the Bichon family, sharing with the imperial Pekingese the title of 'little lion dog', because of the practice of clipping it in the traditional poodle exhibition cut, the lion clip, which, complete with mane and tufted tail, gives it the appearance of a lion in miniature. It is an affectionate, happy, healthy little dog, known in Europe for several centuries.

Size
Height: 10-13in (25-33cm).
Weight: 4-9lb (1.8-4.1kg).

Exercise
This breed adapts well to town or country; although usually presented more suitably for decoration than for sporting activity, it will enjoy regular walks in the park, or a run in the countryside. But many of the exotic breeds are kept in breeding and exhibition kennels where, although extremely well looked after, they never have the chance of a muddy scamper.

Grooming
Clipping is best left to the expert, at any rate until a pattern has been studied and absorbed. Meanwhile, a daily brushing will keep the Lowchen looking handsome.

MALTESE TERRIER

The Maltese Terrier is a good-tempered dog that makes the ideal family pet. It is reliable with children, adaptable about exercise, and usually healthy. It generally remains playful throughout its long life.

Size
Not over 10in (25cm).

Exercise
Can manage a long walk or be content with a stroll in the park.

Grooming
Most important: use a bristle brush every day from puppyhood and use baby powder on legs and underside to keep the animal clean between baths. Obtain advice from the breeder about show preparation.

MANCHESTER TERRIER

The Manchester Terrier is an ideal choice for those seeking a small, hardy dog that causes no trouble and makes a good sporting companion. It will fit well into family life, but does tend to attach itself to one person.

It is long-lived and seldom ill. It can live indoors or outside in a heated kennel, but will be happiest if given a place by the fireside.

Size
Desired height: dog 16in (40.5cm); bitch 15in (38cm).

Exercise
The Manchester is in its element running free in the countryside. Town dwellers need not rule out this breed, however, if they can offer regular walks, off-the-lead runs and a garden.

Above: Long-lived and good with children, the Maltese Terrier needs fastidious grooming and much time spent on show preparation.

Below: The Lakeland Terrier is a lively breed that needs plenty of vigorous exercise. It is now a firm favourite in the show ring.

Grooming
Manchesters do not like rain, and should be rubbed with a towel if they get wet. Otherwise, a daily brushing will keep this essentially clean animal looking smart. Its coat condition is always an indication of health.

MASTIFF

The Mastiff is a large, powerful dog that makes a formidable guard and loyal companion, becoming devoted to its owners. It is suspicious of strangers, and happiest when given a job to do.

Size
Height: dog 30in (76cm); bitch 27½in (70cm).

Exercise
Regular normal exercise required, but preferably with a purpose.

Grooming
Daily brushing will keep the coat in good condition.

Health care
Their size can contribute to limb joint problems. Check with your veterinarian if you suspect trouble.

MINIATURE PINSCHER

The Miniature Pinscher (or Min Pin), sometimes called the 'King of the Toys', makes an ideal pet for the town dweller who, nonetheless, wants a lively sporting companion, not averse to an occasional day's rabbiting. It will follow a scent and give a good account of itself in obedience competitions. The breed's hackney gait is a delight to watch, as it trots along like a dainty little horse. It has the added advantages of rarely moulting and of requiring the minimum of attention to keep its coat in fine condition.

Size
Height: 10-12in (25-30cm). (There are some slight differences in the US standard as regards acceptable colour and size.)

Exercise
The Min Pin will exercise itself in a reasonable-sized garden or accompany its owner on a day-long trek. This adaptable dog will be happy living in an apartment and being taken for walks around the park, or living a free country life.

Grooming
A daily brush and rub down with a

Below: The Newfoundland is a gentle giant, good with children and an instinctive swimmer.

chamois leather will keep the Min Pin in gleaming condition.

NEWFOUND-LAND

The Newfoundland is the traditional life-saving dog, an animal with the over-powering instinct to carry anything in the water safely ashore. It is a gentle giant, a protector of children and the family, and makes a thoroughly reliable companion and guard. It is slow to attack unless provoked.

Size
Average height: dog 28in (71cm); bitch 26in (66cm). Weight: dog 140-150lb (63.5-68kg); bitch 110-120lb (49.9-54.4kg).

Exercise
Regular exercise on hard ground recommended.

Grooming
Daily brushing with a hard brush.

NORFOLK TERRIER

The Norfolk Terrier co-existed with the Norwich Terrier for more than a century until, in 1932, it gained recognition by the British Kennel

Club. There were two types, those with drop ears and those with erect ears. However, in 1964 the British Kennel Club agreed to separate the types, the breed with drop ears becoming the Norfolk Terrier, the prick-eared variety henceforth being known as the Norwich Terrier. The appearance and size of the breed is otherwise the same.

The Norfolk Terrier is a gay, hardy little dog with an equable temperament. It adapts well to almost any life-style, and is fearless and sporty.

Size
Ideal height: 10in (25cm).

Exercise
The Norfolk Terrier will settle for regular walks in a town, but is in its element enjoying off-the-lead runs in the countryside, and is adept at ratting and rabbiting.

Grooming
Little grooming or trimming is required.

NORWEGIAN BUHUND

(Norsk Buhund)

The Buhund is one of Norway's national dogs and was developed as an all-purpose farm dog to control sheep and cattle. It is, however, only since the 1920s that the breed has

become known and appreciated outside its homeland, particularly in the United Kingdom, where it is gaining in popularity.

It is a lively and alert dog, but a natural herder that will, like the Border Collie, round up anything, be it poultry, cattle or people. It needs lots of exercise and makes the ideal playmate for children.

Size
Height: dog not more than 17¾in (45cm); bitch somewhat less.

Exercise
Needs plenty of exercise to unleash its boundless energy.

Grooming
Regular brushing and combing required. It is an easy breed to prepare for showing.

NORWICH TERRIER

Prior to 1964 the Norwich Terrier and the Norfolk Terrier were recognized as one breed by the British Kennel Club. In 1964 the Norwich gained independent status as the prick-eared variety of the two. Its appearance and characteristics are otherwise identical with its Norfolk kin. In the United States both prick-eared and drop-eared varieties were known as the Norwich Terrier until 1 January 1979, when separate breeds were recognized.

Above: The Norfolk Terrier is identical to the Norwich except for its drop ears. A sporty little dog, it loves ratting and rabbiting.

Size

Ideal height 10in (25cm) at the withers; this ideal height must not be attained by excessive length of leg.

Exercise

The Norwich Terrier will settle for regular walks if living in a town, but is happiest when allowed off-the-lead runs in the countryside. It is adept at ratting and rabbiting.

Grooming

Little grooming or trimming is required.

OLD ENGLISH SHEEPDOG
(Bobtail)

The Old English Sheepdog, or Bobtail, is an extremely popular breed with a sound, sensible temperament, though it can be very boisterous in youth. It will live contentedly in a fairly small house despite its bulky appearance.

Size

Height: dog 22in (56cm) and upwards; bitch slightly less.

Exercise

Regular walks of average length — perhaps two good walks of 20 minutes duration per day; and, of course, you need a garden.

Grooming

Daily brushing and weekly combing with a steel comb is required. The hair is brushed forward to cover the eyes — a style which does not appear to affect the dog's vision. White parts are powdered for showing.

Health care

Check the ears for canker, and take care that dead, matted hair does not accumulate around the feet. Some Bobtails are born with a stumpy tail; otherwise the tail is docked.

PAPILLON
(Butterfly Dog)

The Papillon is a toy spaniel that takes its name from the French word for 'butterfly'. The breed is often referred to as the 'Butterfly Dog' because of the manner in which its ears are set on the head, fringed like a butterfly's wings.

The Papillon is an affectionate, lively little dog. It is resilient, whelps easily, is a good walker, and can adapt to extremes of climate. Its attractive appearance and friendly nature make it the ideal family pet.

But, like many toy breeds, it has a tendency to be possessive towards its owners and often resents visitors to the home.

Size

The ideal height is 8-11in (20-28cm). The dog will appear to be slightly longer than high when properly furnished with ruff and hind fringes.

Exercise

Like quite a number of toy breeds, the Papillon will happily walk its owner off his feet, or be content with a walk around the park. One thing is sure: you won't tire it!

Grooming

Daily grooming is required to keep this breed in good condition.

Below: The Papillon is a delightful little dog that has proved an able obedience performer.

PEKINGESE

The Pekingese likes to remind its owners of its regal background, and expects to be petted and pampered. It is not, however, a delicate creature; in fact, it is fearless and fun-loving and enjoys having toys to play with.

It is good with children, but comes into its own as an adult's sole companion, being the centre of attention and preferably having the run of the house. The restricted and neglected Peke is apt to become destructive through boredom. The Peke has a mind of its own and is condescending by nature. But when it decides to offer you its affection, you could not wish for a more loyal and loving companion.

Size
Weight: dog 7-11lb (3.2-5kg); bitch 8-12lb (3.6-5.4kg). There is not, as is often supposed a miniature Pekingese, but within a litter may be found 'sleeve' specimens weighing no more than 6lb (2.7kg). Sleeve Pekes are so called because they could be concealed in the flowing sleeves of the Chinese mandarins.

Exercise
The Peke will happily trudge across fields with its owner, or be content with a sedate walk in the park.

Grooming
The Pekingese needs daily brushing with a brush of soft bristles. The grooming of the underside is usually carried out with the Peke lying on its back, the rest of the job being tackled with the pet standing on a table, or on the owner's lap. Grooming a dog on a table is good preparation for a possible show career. It is not necessary to bath a Peke frequently; as an alternative talcum powder can be applied and brushed through the coat.

PEMBROKE WELSH CORGI

The Pembroke Welsh Corgi has, like the Cardigan, been worked in South Wales for many centuries, but has evolved as a popular and affectionate pet, particularly because it is a breed much favoured by the British royal family. It is hardy and tireless, and makes a devoted companion, but it has an inherent tendency to nip people's ankles, a bad habit which must be discouraged from an early age.

Size
Weight: dog 20-24lb (9-10.9kg); bitch 18-22lb (8.2-10kg). Height: 10-12in (25-30cm) at the shoulder.

Exercise
Although traditionally a worker, the Pembroke adapts well to life as a domestic pet, with daily walks of average length. But beware: if you do not give sufficient exercise this breed will soon lose its figure!

Above: The Pembroke Welsh Corgi is an excellent companion and guard, fond of children but not averse to taking a nip at the ankles of unwanted visitors or burglars.

Grooming
Daily brushing needed. The breed has a water-resistant coat.

POINTER

The Pointer is famed for its classic 'pointing' pose, with its nose and tail in the direction of the game that has been shot. It is a friendly dog, and makes an ideal household pet, getting on well with other animals and children. But it does need a generous amount of exercise.

Size
Desirable height: dog 25-27in (63.5-68.5cm); bitch 24-26in (61-66cm).

Exercise
Needs plenty of exercise.

Grooming
Brush the coat regularly.

POMERANIAN

The Pomeranian is a happy, active little dog that will adapt cheerfully to life either in a one-roomed apartment or a spacious dwelling, revelling in the role of lap dog or enjoying walks with its owner. Alternatively, it will amuse itself adequately in a garden. It makes a faithful and devoted companion.

Size
Weight: dog 4-4½lb (1.8-2kg); bitch 4½-5½lb (2-2.5kg).

Exercise
It is wrong to think that toy breeds are of use for little else except sitting decoratively on their owner's knees, and the Pomeranian is no exception. True, they adore being pampered and petted, but they are also lively little dogs, quite able to walk as far as their owner would wish — often further. Alternatively, they will exercise themselves quite happily in a garden.

Grooming
This is not the breed for those who cannot spare the time for daily grooming. Indeed, the Pomeranian has two coats to care for: a short fluffy under-coat, and a long straight top-coat covering the whole of the body. Daily brushing with a stiff brush is a must. The coat should be dampened with cold water, and the moisture rubbed in with the finger-tips; finally the dog is rubbed down with a towel.

Working from the head, you should then proceed to part the coat and brush it forward from the roots to the tips. Make a further parting and repeat this procedure until the dog's coat has been covered.

The Pomeranian requires regular trimming; obtain advice from a breeder or breed club as to how this should be carried out.

MINIATURE, TOY AND STANDARD POODLE

The Poodle was originally a guard, retriever and protector of sheep, and it still retains its strong retrieving instincts and enjoys water. It has a character full of fun, and is intelligent and obedient.

In the United Kingdom, Poodles have proved good competitors in obedience competitions, but they are far more popular in the show ring, exhibited in the traditional lion clip and a beauty to behold. Poodles are considered by some to be the most difficult dogs to prepare for the ring, requiring nearly a day's pre-show preparation.

There are three varieties of Poodle: Toy, Miniature and Standard. The two smaller varieties make ideal apartment dwellers, whereas the Standard Poodle, which is a robust dog with plenty of stamina, needs more space.

Size
Toy: height should be under 11in (28cm). (There is a slight reduction in the height requirements in the United States.)

Miniature: height should be between 15in (38cm) and 11in (28cm).

Standard: height should be 15in (38cm) and over.

Exercise
Poodles will enjoy a ball game in the garden, practising obedience exercises or trotting beside you in the park. The Standard Poodle requires more exercise than the two smaller varieties.

Grooming
Use a wire-pin pneumatic brush and a wire-toothed metal comb for daily grooming. The lion clip is an essential for the show ring, but pet owners generally resort to the more natural lamb clip, with the hair a short uniform length. It is possible to clip your own dog with a pair of hairdresser's scissors. However, if,

Left: An adaptable, attractive toy breed, the Pomeranian will as readily settle for apartment life as for country living, and will happily walk for miles.

Above: The lion cut is obligatory for the Miniature Poodle in the show ring but not in obedience, at which the breed can excel.

Below: Good-natured and intelligent, the Standard Poodle makes a splendid retriever and show dog if you have time for its preparation.

Above: The Pug tends to experience breathing difficulties in warm weather and during vigorous exercise, and is prone to snoring.

despite the help which is usually available from the breeder, you find the task tedious, there are numerous pet and poodle parlours to which you should take your dog every six weeks. Regular bathing is also essential.

Health care
Fanciers will confirm that the Standard Poodle is the soundest of the varieties. It is possible to acquire healthy Toy and Miniature stock, but care should be taken to purchase from a breeder who puts quality ahead of daintiness. Watch out for signs of ear trouble, nervousness or joint malformations. Nonetheless, a 16-year-old Poodle is not a rarity.

PUG

The Pug is a gay little dog, which looks extremely elegant if not allowed to indulge its inherent greed. Over-eating can result in it becoming gross and short-lived. It makes a charming family pet, provided care is taken that it does not develop respiratory trouble through over-heating or vigorous exercise, for with its flat, squashed-looking face it can encounter breathing difficulties.

Size
The weight should be 14-18lb (6.4-8.2kg). But if allowed to over-indulge it will eat itself out of the Toy Dog category!

Exercise
An energetic dog, the Pug will relish more exercise than many breeds of similar size. The Pug will do best walking on the lead, and should not indulge in vigorous exercise for fear of respiratory trouble.

Grooming
A good daily brushing should be sufficient.

PYRENEAN MOUNTAIN DOG

(Great Pyrenees)

The Pyrenean Mountain Dog is a natural shepherd dog bred to guard flocks in the Pyrenees. Nonetheless, it has become a popular household pet with those who have the space to keep such a large dog. It is hardy and good-natured and will become devoted to the entire family. It also gets on well with other animals and is easy to train. As a working breed, it is happiest with a job to do.

Size
Height: dog at least 28in (71cm); bitch at least 26in (66cm). Weight: dog at least 110lb (49.9kg); bitch at least 90lb (40.8kg).

Exercise
Strangely, for such a big dog, the Pyrenean will adapt to town or country, and be content with walks of average length.

Grooming
Regular brushing will keep the coat in good condition.

RHODESIAN RIDGEBACK

The Rhodesian Ridgeback is a handsome, muscular, medium-sized dog of the hound group, with a short tan-coloured coat, pendulous ears and a long, uncropped tail. The breed is named after the line of hair, shaped like the blade of a broad-sword, that grows in the reverse direction along the back, with two crowns at the shoulder and the point towards the tail. This ridge is a very distinctive marking that is not found in any other breed of dog.

The Rhodesian Ridgeback is of a quiet temperament and rarely barks; it enjoys spending hours curled up lazily in the corner of a room, stretched out in the summer sun, or basking in front of an open fireplace. Although its exploits as a hunter of African game first brought it recognition, the breed was developed as a dual-purpose dog, as a hunter and a gentle guardian of the families of the early white settlers. More and more people are discovering the tranquil temperament of this breed, its affectionate disposition and desire for human companionship—it likes nothing better than to lean against you, or to sit on your feet.

Size
A mature Ridgeback should be a handsome, upstanding animal, dogs being 25-27in (63.5-68.5cm) and bitches 24-26in (61-66cm) in height. Desirable weight: dog 80lb (36.3kg); bitch 70lb (31.75kg), with a permissable variation of 5lb (2.3kg) above and below these weights.

Above: The Rhodesian Ridgeback is an obedient dog which admirably combines the role of family pet and watchdog.

Below: A splendid guard, obedience and show dog, the Rottweiler is fast gaining popularity. It is a powerful dog that needs firm handling.

Exercise
This large, sleepy and apparently slow-moving animal with its characteristic love of lazing, contrasts sharply with its action when alerted. In a flash, it is converted into a graceful streak of rhythmic motion, a pleasure to watch as it quickly overtakes a rabbit or a squirrel in full flight. This is a pet that should have a large garden to run in, and deserves a master able to give it a good walk every day.

Grooming
Daily grooming with a hound glove, coupled with correct feeding and plenty of exercise, will keep the Ridgeback in healthy and gleaming condition.

ROTTWEILER

The Rottweiler is a German working dog of high intelligence and good temperament. It has been a draught dog and herder, and is still used as a guard, police dog, sled dog and mountain rescue dog. In many countries it is sought after as a combination of companion, pet and guard. It responds best to kind but firm handling, and should not be left chained or kennelled in a back yard. It is a popular contender in the show ring and does well in obedience.

Size
Height: dog 25-27in (63.5-68.5cm); bitch 23-25in (58.5-63.5cm).

Exercise
Requires regular walks and runs.

Grooming
Daily brushing will keep the coat in good condition.

ROUGH COLLIE

(Rough-haired Collie)

No breed causes so much consternation to buyers and those giving breed information as the Collie. People tend to have a fixed idea of the type of Collie they want—be it Rough, Smooth, Border, Old English or Bearded—even though they are not necessarily sure of the correct name. If it's a dog like the film star 'Lassie' that you want, you *are* thinking of a Rough Collie, sometimes erroneously called a Scottish Collie; the Sheltie, or Shetland is a 'Lassie' in miniature.

The Rough Collie makes an ideal family pet, being biddable, affectionate and loyal. It is hardy and, despite its thick coat, relatively simple to groom.

Size
Height: dog 22-24in (56-61cm); bitch 20-22in (51-56cm). Weight: dog 45-65lb (20.5-29.5kg); bitch 40-55lb (18.1-25kg).

Exercise
Normal daily exercise required, with off-the-lead runs when possible.

Above: The St Bernard is a gentle giant that is intelligent and trainable, and loves children. It is not, alas, very long-lived.

Grooming

Needs daily brushing. With the right appliance you can vacuum clean the coat with the smallest brush if it gets muddy, but get the dog accustomed to the noise of the machine first.

ST BERNARD

The St Bernard is named after the St Bernard hospice in the Swiss Alps, to which it was introduced between 1660 and 1670, where it became famed for rescuing climbers. It is a powerful, but gentle dog. It adores children and is loyal and affectionate, coupled with which it is supremely intelligent and proves very easy to train. Unfortunately, it is not renowned for its longevity.

Size

The taller the better, provided that symmetry is maintained; it should be thoroughly well proportioned, and of great substance.

Exercise

Do not give the young St Bernard too much exercise. Short, regular walks are advocated, rather than long, tiring ones.

Grooming

Daily brushing will keep the coat in good condition.

SALUKI
(Gazelle Hound)

The Saluki and the horse are prized Arab possessions, the Saluki being capable of great speed and able to keep pace with the fleet-footed Arab stallions. It is still used in the Middle East for hunting the gazelle, but in the West it is kept mainly as an

Below: The Saluki has strong hunting instincts and needs plenty of exercise. Reliable with children, it also makes an excellent guard.

elegant companion, pet and show dog. It is intelligent and somewhat aloof, but is a faithful, gentle companion and trustworthy with children. Care must be taken, particularly in country areas, that the Saluki is kept under control; despite its domestic role, it retains very strong hunting instincts.

Size

Average height: dog 23-28in (58.5-71cm); bitch slightly smaller.

Exercise

Salukis need plenty of exercise, and ownership should not be contemplated by those without a large garden or other exercise area.

Grooming

Brush daily with a soft brush, and use a hound glove. Combing of ear and tail fringes may be necessary.

SAMOYED

The Samoyed is a beautiful Spitz-type that takes its name from the Siberian tribe of the Samoyedes. It is a sled dog in its native country, and is also used as a guard and herder of reindeer. The 'Sammy', as it is often called, is a beautiful, somewhat independent breed that should, according to its standard, show 'marked affection for all mankind'. These dogs adore the snow and are happiest in wide open spaces. But having said that, some can live just as happily in a semi-detached house.

Size

Height: dog 20-22in (51-56cm); bitch 18-20in (46-51cm). Weight in proportion to size.

Exercise

Needs a liberal amount of exercise and, if possible, some obedience work, even if this is only weekly attendance at a dog training club.

Grooming

Regular brushing and combing and a towelling after getting wet. The under-coat sheds once a year; at such times it is best to comb out as much surplus hair as one can. Bathing helps, as this tends to loosen the hair.

SCHIPPERKE

The Schipperke is a delightful breed that originated in Belgium, where its job was to guard canal barges when they had been tied up for the night. The name Schipperke is, in fact, Flemmish for 'little captain'. Apart from being an excellent guard dog, the Schipperke is a most affectionate animal, and particularly good with children. It is also hardy and long-lived. However, it needs individual attention and likes to be treated as a member of the family; it also takes a while to accept strangers.

Size
The weight should be about 12-16lb (5.4-7.3kg).

Exercise
A Schipperke can walk up to 6 miles (10km) or more without any sign of fatigue; but it can manage with a great deal less exercise if its owner lives in a town.

Grooming
The Schipperke has a dense hard coat that needs very little regular grooming.

MINIATURE, STANDARD AND GIANT
SCHNAUZER

The Schnauzers are intelligent, lively and good-natured dogs that love both children and games. They do not, however, trust strangers. Of the three varieties, the Miniature Schnauzer is the most popular. It is

Above: The Schipperke is a hardy, affectionate little dog that makes a first-class guard, but it essentially needs plenty of affection and home comforts.

an attractive little dog that is happiest living with the family indoors. It is long-lived and easy to train. The Standard and less popular Giant Schnauzers both make good guards, and all three varieties do well in obedience competitions.

Size
Miniature: ideal height for dog is 14in (35.5cm); for bitch, 13in (33cm).
Standard: ideal height for dog is 19in (48cm); bitch, 18in (46cm). Any variations of more than 1in (2.5cm) will be penalised.
Giant: height for dog is 25½-27½in (65-70cm), for bitch, 23½-25½in (60-65cm).

Exercise
Schnauzers enjoy regular walks and ball games, and ideally a garden to romp in, though the Miniature and Standard varieties will happily adapt to apartment or country living. The Giant Schnauzer, on the other hand, requires plenty of vigorous exercise and is not recommended for anyone living in an apartment.

Grooming
These dogs require a certain amount of care to keep their coats in prime condition. Daily grooming with a wire brush or glove is necesary and those quizzical whiskers have to be combed. The coat should be stripped at least twice a year and dead hair should be plucked out with finger and thumb. Ask the breeder for more specific advice on grooming the variety you have purchased.

Below: The Giant Schnauzer is a good-natured dog that is nonetheless fearless and ready to defend. It is the least popular of the Schnauzers.

SCOTTISH DEERHOUND

The Scottish Deerhound is a creature of grace and beauty, mentioned frequently in the novels of Sir Walter Scott. It is strong and healthy, anxious to please and asks no more than to be its owner's devoted companion. It is said that once you have owned a Deerhound, never again do you wish to own another breed.

Size
Height: dog not less than 30in (76cm); bitch 28in (71cm). Weight: dog 85-105lb (38.5-47.6kg); bitch 65-80lb (29.5-36.3kg).

Exercise
Needs a great deal of exercise.

Grooming
Requires very little trimming, just removal of extra shaggy hairs for show, and regular brushing. Its coat is weather-resistant, and this breed rarely feels the cold — in fact, it seems to prefer it.

SCOTTISH TERRIER

The Scottish Terrier or Scottie has been aptly described as a gentleman. It is an honest dog, that will not look for trouble but on finding it will always fight fairly. It is a devoted companion to its owner, but has little time for strangers and is not the most suitable of dogs for a family with children or a couple intending to add to their family. It will fight fox or badger, but enjoys itself just as much in an energetic ball game, and likes nothing better than carrying a stick or a ball in its mouth. Altogether an attractive and sporty little animal.

Size
Height: 10-11in (25-28cm). Weight: 19-23lb (8.6-10.4kg).

Exercise
The Scottie loves nothing more than being out of doors and it would be wrong to deprive it of romps in the garden or regular walks several times a day. It can live happily either indoors or in an outside kennel, heated in winter.

Grooming
The Scottie needs daily brushing and combing, particularly its fine beard, and should be trimmed in spring and autumn.

SHETLAND SHEEPDOG

The Shetland Sheepdog is the perfect Rough Collie in miiniature, a

Above: The Scottish Terrier is a dignified but playful little dog that attaches itself to one person.

handy size for the owner who feels, perhaps, that the Rough Collie is too large for his home.

The Sheltie is a good family dog, but a little wary of strangers. It does not take kindly to being petted by those it does not know. It is faithful, supremely intelligent, and generally gives a good account of itself at training classes and in obedience competitions. It is good with horses, and a few are still used as sheepdogs.

Size

Ideal height: dog 14½in (37cm); bitch 14in (35.5cm). Anything more than 1in (2.5cm) above these heights is considered a serious fault. A rather larger dog is preferred in America.

Exercise

Provided the Sheltie has a largish garden in which to expend its

Below: The Shetland Sheepdog is a good choice for competitive obedience as well as the show ring. It makes a faithful family pet but may be distrustful of strangers.

energy, and receives regular daily walks, it will be happy.

Grooming

Not so difficult to keep well-groomed as might be believed. Brush regularly with a stiff-bristled brush and use a comb to avoid tangles, particularly behind the ears. Frequent bathing is unnecessary, but is advisable when the bitch loses her winter coat. The Sheltie is meticulous about its appearance and you will often find this breed cleaning itself.

SHIH TZU

(Chrysanthemum Dog)

The Shih Tzu is a happy and attractive little house-pet which adores human company and hates to be neglected. It is extremely intelligent and arrogant, and looks forward to the long, daily grooming sessions for which time must be allocated if you decide to buy this delightful breed.

Size

Height: not more than 10½in (26.5cm). Weight: 10-18lb (4.5-8.2kg); ideally 10-16lb (4.5-7.3kg).

Exercise

Short, regular walks, and off-the-lead runs required.

Grooming

Needs daily brushing with a pure bristle brush. Do not neglect this task or combing out tangles will be painful. Keep the topknot from getting into the eyes and take care that the ears are free of matted hair or other objects.

SIBERIAN HUSKY

The Siberian Husky is perhaps the most friendly of all Arctic Spitz breeds, having a long history of friendship with man, combining the roles of household companion with work-mate, hauling the sled or herding. It is faithful and reliable.

Size

Height: dog 21-23½in (53-60cm); bitch 20-22in (51-56cm). Weight: dog 45-60lb (20.5-27.2kg); bitch 35-50lb (15.9-22.7kg). Weight should be in proportion to height.

Exercise

Famed for sled racing, remarkable endurance and great powers of speed, this is not a dog to keep confined in a small back yard; it requires a good deal of exercise.

Grooming

Regular brushing will keep the coat in good condition.

SKYE TERRIER

The Skye Terrier is a legend — not only in Scotland where it originated but also throughout the world — because of the touching story of Greyfriars Bobby, whose statue stands near Greyfriars churchyard in Edinburgh. Following his master's death, little Bobby remained by the graveside for the next 14 years, until his own death, deserting his post only to make a daily visit to the café which he used to frequent with his master, where he would be given food to sustain him.

The Skye Terrier originated on the Isle of Skye in the Hebrides and is, despite its beautiful appearance, a relentless fighter if aroused. It is not a vicious dog, but tends to give total trust and devotion to its owner and has little time for strangers. Considerable care has to be given to the grooming of this breed. If given the chance they are valiant hunters, having been bred to hunt fox, otter and badger.

Size
Height: 10in (25cm): Weight: dog 25lb (11.3kg); bitch slightly less.

Exercise
It would be unfair to buy this gay little breed purely as a fashionable accessory, for they are tireless and enjoy nothing better than a long country walk and romp in fresh air.

Grooming
The Skye should be brushed daily and combed once a week with a wide-toothed comb. Incidentally, the coat does not reach its full beauty until the third year.

SMOOTH COLLIE
(Smooth-haired Collie)

Except for its short coat, the Smooth Collie is identical to the Rough Collie, both in temperament and build, yet it is a far less popular breed. It is an affectionate and loyal dog that is easy to train and to groom, and makes an excellent family pet.

Size
Height: dog 22-24in (56-61cm); bitch 20-22in (51-56cm). Weight: dog 45-65lb (20.5-29.5kg); bitch 40-55lb (18.1-25kg).

Exercise
Normal daily exercise required, with off-the-lead runs when possible.

Grooming
Daily brushing will keep the coat in good condition.

SMOOTH FOX TERRIER

The word terrier comes from the Latin word 'terra' meaning 'earth', the job of the terrier being to kill vermin and to worry or 'boot' the fox from its lair.

The Smooth Fox Terrier is arguably the smartest terrier bred for this purpose. It enjoyed almost unrivalled popularity just before and after the Second World War, and is always a popular contender in the show ring, though it has been said that the elegance of this terrier has been attained at the expense of its former hunting ability. It makes an ideal family pet.

Size
Weight: about 16-18lb (7.3-8.2kg) for a dog and 15-17lb (6.8-7.7kg) for a bitch.

Exercise
The terrier once called 'the little athlete of the dog world' deserves a chance to live up to that title. It will

Below: The Smooth Fox Terrier was at the peak of its popularity in the '30s and '40s but it still remains a popular show dog. It also makes a first-class pet.

adjust to a regular trot around the park—on a lead—but deserves the opportunity for frequent off-the-lead runs, preferably in the country.

Grooming
Daily brushing with a stiff brush is recommended. Trimming is required a few weeks before a show, paying particular attention to the inside and outside of ears, jaw, and muzzle. Usually a chalk block is used to ensure that the coat is snowy white.

SOFT-COATED WHEATEN TERRIER

The Soft-coated Wheaten Terrier is an exceptionally intelligent, medium-sized dog, which is defensive without being aggressive. It is an excellent house guard, but gentle with children. The Wheaten has strong sporting instincts, and some have been trained, with success, for the gun.

Size
Weight: dog approximately 35-45lb (15.9-20.5kg). Height: dog approximately 18-19½in (46-49.5cm); bitch slightly less.

Exercise
The Wheaten will relish plenty of exercise. It has excelled in the past as a hunter of rats, rabbits, otters and badgers, and will work any kind of covert, its soft coat being ample

Below: The Soft-coated Wheaten Terrier is recorded as being the oldest Irish breed of terrier. It is a devoted family pet but should not be kennelled out of doors.

protection against the densest undergrowth.

Grooming
The Wheaten's coat does not shed. Daily combing should start from puppyhood, as regular grooming will keep the coat clean and tangle-free. Fuzziness, not natural to the breed, can be aggravated by the use of a wire or plastic brush, and a medium-toothed metal comb should be used instead.

Bathing should be carried out as necessary, if showing, bathing the dog about three days before the event is recommended to avoid a fly-away appearance. Ears, tail and feet need to be tidied, also any long, straggly hairs underneath the body.

STAFFORDSHIRE BULL TERRIER

The Staffordshire Bull Terrier is a sound breed and excellent family dog derived from the crossing of a Bulldog with a terrier breed sometime in the 1800s. Probably the partner of the Old English Bulldog in this match was the Old English Black and Tan Terrier, which preceded the Manchester Terrier. It is, of course, an English breed, recognized by the British Kennel Club in 1935.

The Staffordshire Bull Terrier, in common with its close relation, the Bull Terrier, is a surprisingly gentle dog beneath a somewhat fearsome exterior. It is a good guard dog but adores its family and is utterly reliable with young children.

Size
Height: 14-16in (35.5-40.5cm). Weight: 28-38lb (12.7-17.2kg); bitch 24-34lb (11-15.4kg).

Above: The Staffordshire Bull Terrier has a fearless and lovable character, its only possible drawback being that it has a propensity to fight other dogs.

Exercise
The Staffordshire Bull Terrier cannot resist a fight with another dog if given the chance, so keep this breed on the lead unless walking in wide open spaces. It is a first-class ratter and a good companion in the field but will adapt to life in a normal-sized house and garden as long as regular walks are given.

Grooming
This breed requires little attention other than a good daily brushing.

SWEDISH VALLHUND
(Västgötaspets)

The Västgötaspets, to give this breed its Swedish name, looks something like a Cardigan/Pembroke Corgi cross. There is certainly a connection between the Corgi and this attractive breed, but it is impossible to determine whether it evolved as the result of Vikings taking Corgis to Sweden, or if Swedish dogs brought to Britain developed the Corgi. Bred as a cattle dog, it is an active, intelligent worker that is rapidly gaining popularity world-wide.

Size
Height: dog 13in (33cm); bitch 12.3in (31.2cm).

Exercise
Fares best if given plenty of exercise.

Grooming
Normal daily brushing required.

TIBETAN SPANIEL

The Tibetan Spaniel is an attractive small dog, with a happy, if independent, nature. It is easily trained and makes an ideal family pet, being reliable with children. In appearance it resembles a rather large Pekingese.

Size
Height about 10in (25cm). Weight: 9-15lb (4-6.8kg) is ideal.

Exercise
This dog requires average walks and off-the-lead runs.

Grooming
Needs daily brushing.

TIBETAN TERRIER

In appearance the Tibetan Terrier resembles a small Old English Sheepdog, and is in truth not a terrier at all, having no history of going to earth. It has a charming shaggy appearance and a happy disposition, and makes a delightful pet.

Size
Height: dog should be 14-16in (35.5-40-5cm); bitches should be slightly smaller.

Exercise
The Tibetan Terrier enjoys an off-the-lead scamper and the freedom of a garden; otherwise normal, regular walks will suffice.

Grooming
Needs thorough brushing daily.

WEIMARANER

(Silver Ghost)

Although bred in Germany in the 18th century, the Weimaraner only burst upon the British scene in the early 1950s, since when it has become popular as a family pet, show dog and contender in obedience competitions. Also called the Silver Ghost, is an excellent gundog which originally hunted big game. It is obedient and eminently trainable, excelling in obedience competitions, and has been used as both police dog and guard. It makes

Left: The Whippet was designed for racing and coursing, and is now also popular in the show ring.

a good pet, but is happiest when given a job to do.

Size
Height: dog 24-27in (61-68.5cm); bitch 22-25in (56-63.5cm).

Exercise
Needs plenty of exercise and has boundless energy. No need to rule out town living, but it is essential that the Weimaraner has lots of supervised freedom.

Grooming
Needs very little brushing, if any, for its sleek coat will naturally free itself of mud. Clip nails when necessary.

Below: The Weimaraner is an appealing breed which has proved itself in agility, obedience and the show ring. It has also been used in police work.

WELSH SPRINGER SPANIEL

The Welsh Springer Spaniel is a lively dog with plenty of enthusiasm and endurance. It is somewhere between the little Cocker Spaniel and the English Springer in stature. It is a tireless breed, and, in common with most spaniels, provided it is given plenty of exercise and correct feeding, it will live to a ripe old age.

Size
Height: dog up to 19in (48cm); bitch approximately 18in (46cm).

Exercise
Like most spaniels the Welsh Springer is essentially a working animal and is not ideally suited for apartment life or for those with insufficient time to take it for lengthy walks.

Grooming
Similar to other spaniels, with regular brushing and combing.

WELSH TERRIER

The Welsh Terrier has much in common with the Airedale, Irish and Lakeland Terriers and resembles a small Airedale in appearance. It makes a good household pet, generally has a good temperament, and is affectionate, obedient and great fun.

Size
The height should not exceed 15½in (39.5cm). In working condition, 20-21lb (9-9.5kg) is a fair average weight.

Exercise
Regular daily walks and a romp in the garden will suffice, but like most terriers it will appreciate a run in wide open spaces.

Grooming
The Welsh Terrier's coat needs stripping twice yearly and regular brushing to maintain it in show condition, but many pet owners resort to clipping their terriers. The coat is usually left on in winter to provide extra warmth.

WEST HIGHLAND WHITE TERRIER

The West Highland White Terrier, or Westie as it is commonly called, is a game, hardy little dog that originated in Argyle, Scotland. In recent years it has gained tremendous popularity because of its attractive appearance, sporting instincts and handy size. It gets on well with children and other dogs and makes an ideal family pet.

Size
Height: about 11in (28cm).

Exercise
The Westie will adapt to town or country, and will live either indoors or in a kennel. However, it will be happiest as a family pet allowed to share the comfort of the fireside, but given adequate free runs in the countryside. Remember that it was originally used as a working terrier, and its job was to hunt fox and badger. It is also, of course, a good ratter. This breed will enjoy an energetic ball game.

Grooming
Although the Westie may be the ideal choice for someone who wants a healthy active dog, it is perhaps not so ideal for the show aspirant who does not want to spend much time on grooming. The Westie's coat must be brushed and combed every day, and have surplus hair stripped twice a year. The neckline is particularly important, and straggly hairs should be removed from ears and tail. Ideally, the Westie's coat should be approximately 2in (5cm) in length, with the neck and throat hair shorter. It is probably wise to ask the breeder to demonstrate what is required before you make your purchase, and let you have a grooming chart with full instructions.

WHIPPET

The Whippet is an excellent choice for those who want a dog that will combine the role of an affectionate and gentle pet with performance on the track and/or in the show ring. It has a peaceful temperament, but can be a little nervous in strange surroundings.

Size
Ideal height: dog 18½in (47cm); bitch 17½in (44.5cm). Judges should use their discretion and not unduly penalize an otherwise good specimen.

Exercise
The Whippet is a racer, capable of 35-40 miles (56-64km) an hour. It will adapt to life away from the excitement of a track, but make sure that you give it plenty of exercise.

Right: Though similar in most respects, the Wire Fox Terrier is more popular than the Smooth.

Grooming
Needs little grooming, but tail usually needs tidying up for show. Teeth should be scaled regularly. Nails will need clipping.

Health care
Whippets are hardy, despite their delicate appearance, but should sleep indoors and be kept out of draughts.

WIRE FOX TERRIER

The Wire-haired Fox Terrier is, when well turned out, a delightful sight to see. It is intelligent, cheerful, and easily trained; a first-rate children's companion, with the typical terrier's 'get up and go'.

Above: The West Highland White Terrier is a sporty little dog which makes an ideal pet but a time-consuming breed to show.

Size
A full-size well-balanced dog should not exceed 15½in (39cm); the bitch being slightly lower, nor should the length of back from withers to root of tail exceed 12in (30cm). Weight: 18lb (8.2kg) in show condition; a bitch about 2lb (0.9kg) less, with a margin of 1lb (0.45g) either way.

Exercise
The Wire-haired Fox Terrier will enjoy nothing more than going rabbiting with its master. It adores sniffing out vermin and is not afraid of a fight, despite its usual good nature. It adapts well to life as a household pet, but needs a country home rather than apartment life.

Grooming
Hand stripping is required in spring, summer and autumn—more frequently if it is the intention to show. Normally a daily brushing will suffice, but watch the coat carefully as terriers are susceptible to eczema. Chalking is usual for a show.

YORKSHIRE TERRIER

The Yorkshire Terrier, or Yorkie as it is frequently called, is a popular little dog which rivals the Chihuahua for the title of the world's smallest dog, though it has been described as a big dog inhabiting a small dog's body. It is unlikely to be over-awed by larger animals and wants to make friends with everybody. It is a healthy and fearless little dog and makes an affectionate pet.

Size
Weight: up to 7lb (3.2kg).

Exercise
The Yorkie is well suited to town and apartment life, but proves a tireless companion on a country walk.

Grooming
Many Yorkie owners are content for their pet to have a somewhat scruffy 'shaggy dog' look as long as they know it is clean and healthy. The show aspirant, however, has a busy time ahead, for to achieve an immaculate coat, the Yorkshire Terrier requires endless grooming, shampooing and oiling. The show Yorkie spends much of its life, away from the ring, wearing curlers!

4

Caring for Your Dog

S hould your dog live indoors or spend its life in an outside kennel? What happens when you go on holiday or have to take a business trip? What is the best equipment to buy for a pup, and the least likely to be chewed? These are but a few of the considerations to be discussed in the following chapter, which also contains standard advice on feeding, grooming and exercising.

Of course, dogs, like people, are individuals whose requirements differ according to their circumstances: the working dog, for instance, needs more sustenance than its lazier fellows, the pregnant bitch should have extra rations as her whelping draws near, and an ageing dog should have its daily ration of food split into two portions. It is therefore vitally important when caring for your dog to be aware of its individual requirements.

Right: Regular grooming should involve special attention to eyes, ears, teeth and nails.

Below: Puppies need a special feeding programme to help them grow properly.

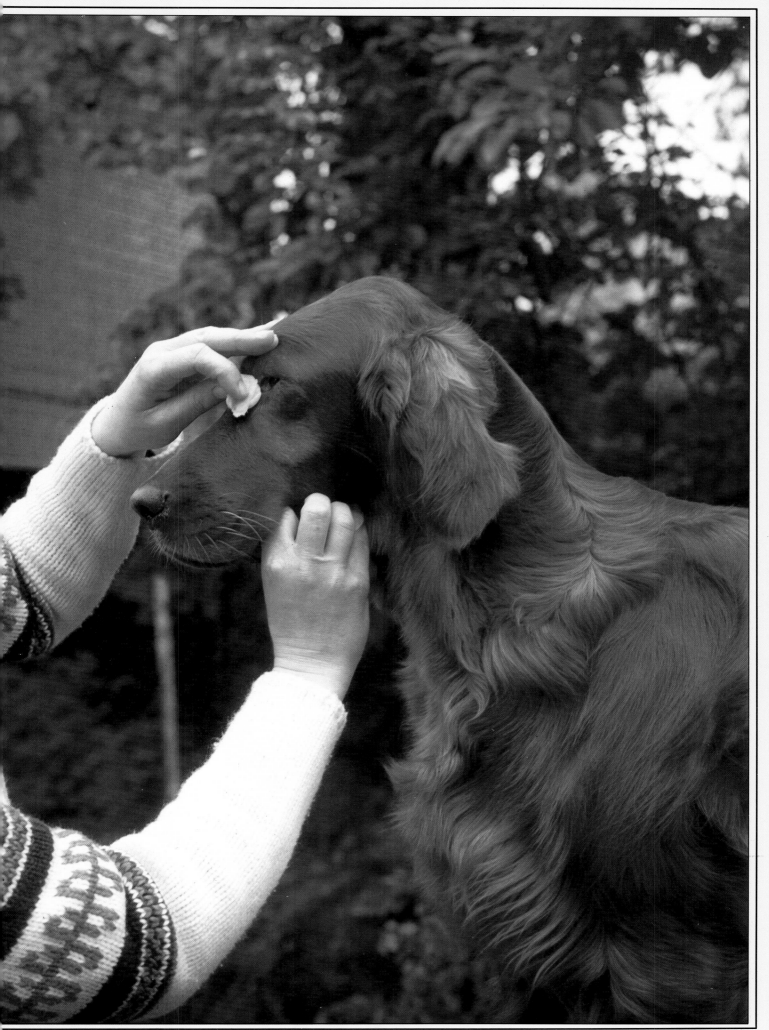

In order to maintain a healthy and happy pet you must be aware of your dog's basic needs. Puppies, like babies, need special care and attention, and it is important to provide them with the right diet and the correct amount of exercise for their growing bodies. Similarly, adult dogs need the right care; it is estimated that up to 50% of pets in the United Kingdom are overweight which is mostly the result of poor diet and inadequate exercise. Dogs also require regular grooming to keep their coats and various other parts of their body in good condition.

Your dog's requirements with regards to accommodation and equipment are equally important, and today there is an increasingly wide and confusing range of manufactured goods from which to choose.

ACCOMMODATION

Before bringing home a puppy you must first decide whether the dog is to live indoors or be kennelled outside in the garden or yard. Although most people usually decide to keep a family pet inside the home, many hardy breeds, and in particular those with weather-resistant coats such as the Scottish Deerhound, seem actually to prefer the cold and will certainly come to no harm kennelled outside. Small short-coated breeds, however, do not do well out of doors, and toy breeds, which have a particular need for warmth, should never be kept under such conditions.

Where a number of dogs are to be kept, as with dog breeding, it is often impractical for them all to live indoors, so breeders often keep one indoor companion, such as an ageing dog or bitch, and accommodate the others outside. Most working dogs are also kept outside.

Having installed a dog in the house, you should not then reallocate it an outside billet. Once the dog has become accustomed to companionship and household warmth it would be unkind to transfer it to the isolation and lower temperatures of outdoor life.

You should always bear in mind that a kennelled dog cannot, like its indoor counterpart, draw your attention to its empty water bowl, or make its presence felt at its regular mealtime. It is therefore important not to neglect the animal; a kennelled dog needs companionship and affection, daily exercise, grooming and regular feeding just as does a house dog.

Beds and bedding

A dog, like ourselves, welcomes a place to call its own, a familiar place to which it can retreat when it feels like a quiet sleep, or where it can gnaw its bone in peace, away from the noise of the children or out of the way of adult feet. You should, therefore, select a warm draught-free corner in which to put your pet's bedding, such as in the kitchen, and having done so allow it to remain there permanently. In time your dog's presence in its own corner will become a reassuring and familiar sight to you.

It is wise not to invest in an expensive basket, or a traditional wicker one, for a puppy. The animal will soon chew it to pieces. If you wish to buy such a basket it is better to wait until the pup is past the teething stage. Initially, it is more sensible to use a canvas bed, slightly raised off the floor, or a basket made of heavy-duty plastic, a type which is particularly hardwearing, and simple both to disinfect and clean. Alternatively, you can simply use a cardboard box, suitably adapted, which can be destroyed if chewed and readily replaced.

Make the pup comfortable by placing in its bed something soft such as an old cushion, blanket or shawl. Some people prefer to use synthetic sheepskin bedding which is washable, ideal for whelping and readily available through most pet accessory outlets. A hot water bottle well wrapped up, or a piece of material smelling of a pup's mother, may help to console a puppy during its first lonely nights away from its family.

A welcome innovation to canine comfort is the bean-bag bed, made from tough canvas and filled with fire-retardant polystyrene beads. There are a number of advantages

Left: A Labrador puppy in a lined wooden bed, confined by a portable mesh run to prevent wandering. The newspaper floor-cover is easily replaced if soiled.

Below: This Whippet is comfortably accommodated in a fibreglass bed lined with artificial sheepskin. Other accessories shown include its leash and whippet collar.

Above: A spaniel puppy sits by its bed. This plastic covered flexible bed is not expensive to buy but is all too readily chewed by pups till they replace their baby teeth.

to this type of bed. It is sufficiently attractive to be left in a sitting-room, is easily transportable, usually waterproof and in some cases, has removable zip covers to aid washing. New beads are also available to replace the old ones when the bed begins to sag.

Most owners rely on the warmth remaining from the fireside or the central heating system to give their pet heat throughout the night. It is possible to buy baskets with low-voltage electrical fitments, or slim metal heating pads, which, when placed under a blanket and plugged into an electric point, provide just sufficient heat.

Indoor kennelling

Today, there are an enormous range of items manufactured for dogs, such as carrying cases, portable indoor kennels and pens, which make suitable indoor living quarters.

Sturdy travelling boxes are not only ideal for transporting tiny breeds but can also double up as

the ideal home. 'Boxing' or 'crating' a small dog is not, as some people may think, cruel. Tiny dogs, such as Chihuahuas, like nothing better than the security of being shut up in a warm secure box, the door of which can be left open during the daytime. Such housing methods also aid house-training: a dog will rarely wet its own bed.

Indoor wooden kennels, not unlike rabbit hutches, or wire-mesh pens are frequently seen in the homes of breeders of the small varieties, particularly where both dogs and bitches are kept and it is necessary temporarily to put a bitch in season into isolation.

Above: A fibreglass travelling cage as used by airlines and shipping lines. It is light and strong and is easily cleaned. Such cages are used to transport dogs to quarantine.

Below: A dog shelters from the sun in a conventional wooden kennel, with its water readily accessible. Outdoor dogs must always be protected from extremes of weather.

Outdoor kennelling

Before buying an outdoor kennel you should give some thought to the size of the occupant. Most reputable kennel manufacturers and retailers are familiar with the breeds and will be able to advise on the best buy for your requirements.

A dog kennel must be large enough for the occupant to stand, stretch and curl up to go to sleep in with comfort; but if it is too large the dog's body heat will be lost. The kennel must be watertight and should be raised so that the floor is not in contact with the ground. It should be positioned to face southwest in winter and northwest in summer, and you must ensure there is sufficient shade in warm weather. Bedding may comprise of clean straw, wood-wool or sacking, or you may prefer to put down old carpeting.

If the dog is not thick-coated or a working breed, some thought should be given to heating. But a word of

warning: you must not underestimate the curiosity or the chewing capacity of a young or bored dog. Never put a calor gas paraffin heater in a kennel, nor any other form of heating, that is not well out of the reach of the dog.

Electric fan heaters which can be thermostatically controlled are probably the best and safest means of kennel heating. Tubular heaters and heat bulbs are also worth consideration, but for safety's sake, unless you are a competent electrician, you should engage a professional to do the installation.

The interior of the kennel should be painted with a quick-drying paint such as emulsion, which will help to keep it watertight and make it easier to clean. But be careful not to use paints containing lead or wood preservatives which could result in your dog being poisoned. Some people choose to nail a flap of carpet over the kennel opening, which keeps out draughts yet allows the dog to move freely in and out. The kennel should be cleaned out daily, for which purpose a hinged roof is a great advantage.

Exercising the kennelled dog

An animal which is confined to an outside kennel should be provided with either a wired-in run (many kennels are offered with complementary runs in varying sizes) or a running chain. The latter may be constructed by driving two posts

Above: Unless on a running leash dogs should not be tied up outside.

Right: Even for luxury kennels the same rules of positioning and weatherproofing apply as to others.

into the ground a few yards apart; a length of stout wire is then fixed between them, to which is attached a chain via a large ring or clip, leaving the chain free to travel along the wire. A device of this type permits the dog a certain amount of freedom, and enables it to patrol a fairly large area.

Garden safety

Before the pup arrives, garden fencing should be checked for any possible escape routes. If you have to put up new fencing, panelled wood or chain link fencing is probably the most dog-proof. It should be higher than you might at first think necessary; even toy breeds can jump remarkably high. Unless the garden gate hangs almost at ground level, it would be advisable to tack some netting around the bottom.

Any fish ponds should be covered over and all traces of weedkiller, slug pellets or rat poison removed from the garden. If in the future it is necessary to use weedkillers or insecticides your pets must be kept away from the treated area for at least 24 hours.

Boarding kennels

There are times when, because of business trips, holidays or emergencies such as illness, your dog has to be put into boarding kennels. It is as well to sound out facilities in your area early on, in case such an eventuality should suddenly arise. Bookings for peak periods such as Christmas, Easter and the summer months have, in any case, to be made well in advance.

In some countries, such as the United Kingdom and the United States, boarding kennels are licensed by the local authority and as such are subject to inspection by the health and sanitation departments. In the United States such establishments must belong to the American Boarding Kennel Association. Standards of boarding kennels can, however, vary enormously, some establishments offering individual kennels with sophisticated heating systems and exclusive outdoor runs, even piped music, others offering perhaps no heat at all with the inmates being exercised in groups. Also, some kennels that may be eminently suitable for large, tough breeds are unsuitable for smaller, more delicate varieties.

If you have a toy breed it is sensible to seek out a boarding kennel which specializes in small dogs, or one that is run by a breeder of small varieties. Small dogs require particular care and it is better to entrust them to someone who is familiar with their needs.

You should always check where your dog is being accommodated rather than just leaving it at reception.

It is not desirable for dogs to be exercised with other boarders and if possible, they should have individual kennels (though several from one household may be kennelled together). Most importantly, for their health's sake, they should be kennelled in a draught-free area.

An indication of a good boarding kennel is one that asks for proof of inoculation, and takes a note of the dog's usual diet, its age, the name of your veterinarian and a contact address for yourself. It is not unknown for dogs accustomed to a household environment to come out of kennels with medical problems due to unsuitable accommodation or inadequate supervision, so it is well worth ensuring that you have left your pet in capable hands.

Some kennels dissuade owners from bringing along the pet's basket, bedding and toys, preferring to provide all the necessary items themselves. However, the dog that is allowed to sleep in its own basket with familiar objects is often more likely to settle in happily than a dog that is deprived of all the things to which it is accustomed.

Bad kennels tend to be in the minority, as kennel owners rely on their good reputation to maintain their business. Although the occasional boarder may pine for its owners, most canine guests are so interested in everything going on around them that they seem hardly

Left: A home for unwanted dogs. The sleeping quarters connect directly onto the mesh runs, which are of the highest quality. Many boarding kennels are designed this way.

Above: An ultra-luxury kennels for pampered pets. Such places are expensive, yet boarders will get the same amount of care and kindness as found in any good premises.

Below: Quarantine establishments are built to special standards to prevent cross-infection. Their inmates have special scrutiny during their stay of several months.

to notice their owner's absence. It is advisable, however, to make the pet's first stay in a boarding kennel a short one—perhaps a weekend—in preparation for some longer absence being planned. In this way the dog will be familiar with its new surroundings and will know that its owner is coming back for it.

It should be noted that puppies under six months of age may not be accepted for boarding because of the time involved in preparing extra feeds.

EQUIPMENT

Apart from a bed or kennel, there are various other items you need to invest in when you buy a dog. You will need a food bowl and a drinking

bowl, both of which should be
washed separately from other dishes,
and used for no other purpose than
providing food and water for your
dog. The bowls may be of earthenware, plastic, stainless steel or
vitreous enamel. All types are
acceptable. Plastic bowls, however,
although less expensive than the
others are not suitable for puppies
because they will be chewed.
Earthenware utensils are a good
choice because they are the least
likely to be overturned and are very
easy to clean.

Leads and collars

In many countries dogs are required
by law to wear collars, plus some
form of identification (see Dogs and
the Law, pages 186-189). Many
breeds traditionally wear distinctive
collars, such as the broad, bejewelled
collar of the poodle, or the bespiked
and buckled collars which adorn
Bull Terriers and Mastiffs.

A dog's collar should be neither
too slack, so that the animal may slip
out of it, nor too tight for comfort. A
simple check for size is to ensure
that you can slip two fingers
between the collar and the dog's
neck. Leather collars are very
popular in conjunction with a 5ft
(1.5m) stitched bridle leather lead
(or leash) with a comfortable handle
at one end and a quality trigger at
the other.

Nylon leads and collars are less
expensive than leather ones and as
a pup will quickly outgrow its first
outfit such a set could initially be
more suitable.

Many exhibitors will denounce
mention of the puppy harness on
the grounds that its use will spoil the
animal's action. But, although it is
advisable not to use one for a
prolonged period of time, the
harness, which enables you to pull
and lift the pup up bodily rather than
from the neck, is of undoubted help
when a pup is proving hard to lead
train, and fights in terror the
restriction of a collar. A fortnight
with a harness can, in many cases,
work wonders.

The check chain (see page 119) is
most commonly used for training
and obedience work. However, a
new type of canvas check collar
from America, used in conjunction
with a fairly broad canvas leash
similar to an equine show lead, is
fast gaining devotees.

Also finding favour is a recent
British design by an internationally
renowned canine behaviourist, Dr
Roger Mugford. The nylon head-
collar works on the simple principle
of guiding the dog from the head,
and is made in a selection of sizes.
Another innovation often used in
conjunction with this headwear is a
retractable leash which has a 16ft
(5m) length for normal exercising
and expands up to 32ft (10m)
for tracking or security work. The
leash retracts automatically with
instant stop and brake control. Such
a leash is of undoubted benefit for
exercising a bitch in season, for
controlling an aggressive dog while

permitting it ample freedom, and for
use by nervous owners who are
fearful of letting their dogs off
the leash.

Name tags

As already mentioned, in certain
countries including the United
Kingdom and much of the United
States, a dog is required by law to
wear a name tag or some other
form of identification. The simplest
type is a metal disc engraved with
the owner's address and telephone
number which can be attached to
the dog's collar.

Many owners also have the dog's
name engraved on the reverse of
the disc so that if the dog becomes
lost, whoever finds it can soothe the
possibly frightened animal with the
familiar sound of its name. There
are, however, those who prefer not
to give this information, believing
that it could make it easier for
an unscrupulous person to steal
their pet.

An alternative method of identification is a small screw-topped
capsule into which the necessary
information, written on a piece of
paper, can be inserted.

An additional precaution against loss or theft becoming increasingly popular in the United States is tatooing. The dog can be tatooed on the inside of the ear flap or inner thigh with the owner's Social Security number which is then registered with one of several identification registering agencies in the country. The agencies will then help to locate a lost or stolen pet. The system is not, as yet, popular in the United Kingdom and there is no national dog registry. Dog-napping is not uncommon these days, with stolen animals frequently being sold to pet stores or research laboratories. Tatooing provides a permanent form of identification which can help avoid such practices. A veterinarian or local kennel club should be able to give you further information on this form of identification.

Chews and toys

It is always important to give a puppy chews and toys. Some pets may discard a rubber ring or squeaky toy before they are one year old but others will take pleasure in keeping such objects throughout life.

Throwing a ball, bone or chew for your pet may well be the start of teaching your dog to retrieve. But although training should be fun for a dog, you should not make the mistake of turning every game into an obedience lesson. Your dog must be allowed to enjoy itself for enjoyment's sake or it could turn into a rather sober animal.

Rawhide chews are a firm favourite with dogs of all ages but are of particular help through the teething stage. A recent warning, however, has been issued by the Californian Veterinary Medical Association against rawhide chew bones made in Korea. They are said to be producing bizarre neurological behaviour problems in dogs, some of which include hysterical barking, screaming and running in circles. The chew bones may also be originating in Malaysia and Taiwan.

Below: Most dogs will get freat fun and good exercise chasing and retrieving toys such as this ring.

Below: This retractible lead allows good control over dogs and can be adjusted to any appropriate length.

Above: Dr Mugford's nylon head-collar is designed for comfortable but positive head control.

FEEDING AND NUTRITION

Conscientious dog owners no longer speak in disparaging terms of those who feed their pets commercial products. Indeed, it is now widely recognized that nutritional deficiencies are more often found in dogs fed on home-prepared diets than in those that receive commercial foods. Such foods are scientifically prepared to provide a balanced diet with all the nutrients the animal needs given in the correct proportions.

At one time it was believed that a dog would fare well on an all-meat diet. In fact, such a diet could result in the animal developing lameness or other problems because meat contains insufficient calcium and phosphorus.

This is one of the reasons why, if it is your intention to feed your pet with home cooking, or with anything other than commercial products, it would be wise to discuss the matter first with a veterinarian or nutritionist, so that you can be sure of providing your pet with the basic essential requirements of proteins, carbohydrates, vitamins, minerals and roughage.

The nutritional requirements of the dog are not so very different from our own. The dog derives energy from foods that are rich in carbohydrate or fat. However, its energy requirements, and therefore the amount of carbohydrates or fats needed, will depend on the amount of exercise or work undertaken by the animal. A town dog, for example, that exercises in the local park will not have the same energy food requirements as a working country dog.

The minerals calcium and phosphorus are vital for healthy teeth and bones. If a puppy has an inbalance of minerals in its diet, this may result in permanent bone damage. Bones and bonemeal should be added to any diet as they have a high calcium content. Liver is a good source of certain vitamins, and high roughage foods such as rolled oats, wholegrain wheat biscuits, toasted wholemeal bread, bran, brown rice, finely grated raw carrot, chopped celery tops, parsley and watercress are sensible addition to a home-prepared diet.

— **Commercially prepared foods** —
Feeding with commercial products is not only far less time-consuming than preparing food yourself but also ensures that the dog is receiving the correct food for its size and lifestyle. The chart opposite provides a guide to a healthy diet, according to the size of dog; more detailed advice is readily available from your veterinarian or the manufacturers.

If you decide to feed your dog with commercially prepared foods it is vital to ascertain whether the can or package you take from the shelf is in itself a complete balanced diet or whether another substance must be added. A balanced diet will contain the vitamins A, B and D, together with essential minerals. Dogs, unlike humans, can make their own Vitamin C provided that they have

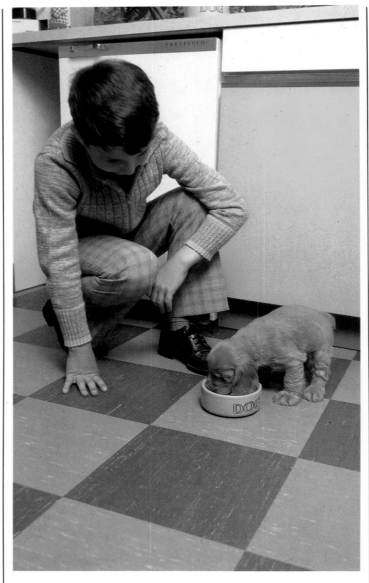

Above: Pups must be fed several small meals a day in the same place, such as the kitchen where spillages are easily cleaned.

Right: Most adult dogs are fed once daily — usually in the early evening — and water should be available at all times.

the necessary precursor in their diet. A balanced diet will supply a dog's average needs but, where Vitamin C supplementation is required, the advice of a veterinary surgeon is advisable regarding dosage. (Vitamin C is now widely recognized as being beneficial to dogs suffering from stress and in particular those recovering from a prolonged illness or surgery.)

Commercial foods come in three main types: canned foods, dry foods and semi-moist foods. Sales of frozen foods for dogs are relatively small, such rations usually being purchased from a pet shop or supplied by direct household delivery in the form of large blocks of meat and meal mixture.

Canned foods have a moisture content of around 75%, dry foods, including biscuits, meal and rehydratable food of about 10%, and semi-moist foods, which constitute a relatively new sector of the pet food market, have a moisture content of 15-50%.

It is vital that a dog always has free access to fresh water to enable it to adjust its fluid intake according to the moisture content of its food. This is especially important for dogs feeding on dry diets that have not been pre-soaked. Dogs enjoy rainwater, and they may be given some as an alternative to tap water provided it is collected from an uncontaminated source.

— **Types of dog food** —
The following is a list of the various dog foods available.

Plain biscuit meal Ideal to mix with any type of meat or fish to provide essential carbohydrate.

Large dog biscuits Provide good jaw exercise for medium and large dogs. Ensure biscuits are fresh and uncontaminated.

SPECIMEN FEEDING CHART FOR ADULT DOGS		
Type & body weight	Daily quantities of fresh or canned meat	Daily quantities of biscuit meal and cereals
Toy dogs up to 10lb (4·5kg)	4-8oz (110-225g)	1-1½cups (40-60g)
Small dogs 10-20lb (4·5-9kg)	8-13½oz (225-380g)	1½-3 cups (60-120g)
Medium dogs 20-50lb (9-23kg)	13½oz-1lb 7oz (380-650g)	3-5cups (120-200g)
Large dogs 50-110lb (23-50kg)	1lb 7oz-2lb 7oz (650g-1·1kg)	5-10 cups (200-400g)

Right: Various types of dog foods (from top right, clockwise): fresh meat; canned dog food with mixer; semi-moist food; dry mixer; dry complete food; dog bscuits.

Bone-shaped biscuits Ideal for dogs to carry about, and not so hard as large ones. Useful to satisfy fast-growing dogs between meals.

Small dog biscuits Available in various shapes and flavours. Good for rewards and retrieving games.

Meaty canned dog food Made with animal products not in demand for human diet, together with 'meat-like' chunks made from vegetable protein. Feed with equal volume of biscuit. No extra vitamins needed.

Meat and cereal canned food Costs less initially, but you will need to feed twice as much as meaty canned food. Do not add more biscuit. No extra vitamins needed.

Canned puppy food Formulated for puppies and gives them an excellent start in life. No extra vitamins needed.

Semi-moist complete food Made of partly dehydrated chunks of meat substitute. Feed straight from the sachet in which it is packed. Easy to carry and convenient when you and your dog are away from home.

Dry complete food Dry chunks containing all essential nutrients. Can be fed mixed with milk, water or broth, or dry with water available.

Dry flaked complete food Good for soaking in gravy, milk or hot water. Do not allow dry diets to go rancid in storage: you should buy little and often.

Feeding a puppy

It is advisable to adhere strictly to the diet sheet provided by the breeder or your veterinarian for the first 1-2 weeks, after which many changes may be gradually introduced. However, the following recommendations should be helpful.

Until a puppy is three months of age it needs four meals a day — breakast, lunch, tea and supper — because at this stage it cannot digest its total food requirement in one ration. Once you have fixed the mealtimes you should keep them to roughly the same time each day.

Breakfast and supper should consist of 1-2 teaspoonfuls of a dry branded baby food mixed with milk and a little sugar. Lunch and tea should be a meat meal, for example, a saucerful of lean minced beef, preferably slightly cooked, supplemented with puppy meal or biscuit in the proportion of three parts meat to two parts biscuit.

When the pup reaches four months of age, the evening feed can be omitted, and at six months breakfast can also be discontinued so that the pup is receiving just two meat and biscuit meals a day. A

Above: Only large unsplinterable knuckle bones should be fed to dogs — even puppies. The gnawing is good for teeth and provides minerals.

Below: Retrieving dogs especially get natural pleasure chasing and fetching sticks. This keeps them fit and active and prevents obesity.

Right: Many game dogs like this Gordon Setter are good swimmers and are keen on water. Swimming is an excellent, natural exercise.

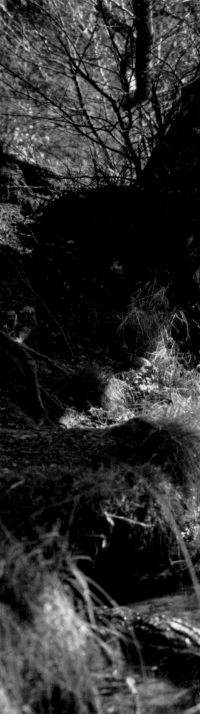

dog is considered to be an adult by the age of one year, by which time most dogs should be fed once a day only, with the exception of toy breeds and elderly dogs which fare better if their ration is divided into two smaller meals.

Dogs soon recognize the approach of feeding time and look forward to it. Obviously this must be a time that will fit in with your own commitments. Generally, however, early evening is considered the best time to feed a dog.

Feeding a pregnant bitch

A bitch in whelp will need extra food during the last four weeks of her pregnancy and during lactation. The food intake should be gradually increased so that, by the time of giving birth, the bitch is receiving approximately one third more food than normal. While nursing her puppies, she should continue to have more than her normal food intake; if the litter is large, her rations may be supplemented by 10-15% more meat.

Obesity

A fat dog, like a fat human, is prone to many ailments which may result in a decreased lifespan. It is easy to determine whether your dog is overweight. The ribs of a fit, active dog are not visible, but you should be able to feel them when the fingers are moved gently over the dog's sides.

If careful reduction in food intake does not result in weight loss, consult your veterinarian who may well arrange for your dog to be put on a specially formulated obesity diet.

Bones

The only type of bones you should give to a dog are marrow bones. You must never give it bones that

splinter, such as chicken, rabbit or chop bones, as the splinters can easily become lodged in the throat or pierce the stomach wall, causing great discomfort and injury to the animal.

Exercise

It is important that you give your dog adequate exercise, the amount required depending not only on the size of the animal but also on its breeding. The largest dogs do not necessarily need the most exercise; for instance, the Border Collie, bred for a highly-active working life, requires more exercise than the larger Great Dane.

Puppies should not be exercised while too young, and certainly not in public places before they have had their preliminary inoculations. Nor should they be taken out on the lead before they have had the necessary

Left: Playing 'retrieve' in the garden is a good form of exercise.

lead training indoors.

At the same time, a young animal should become accustomed to traffic noise and people, otherwise, if it encounters them at a later date it might be unduly distressed. Therefore, while a puppy is too young to be walked in the street, it is sensible to carry it about with you occasionally for short trips out of doors.

Puppies under six months of age should not be taken for long walks, nor should elderly dogs. If, however, your elderly companion has been taken for a walk at a certain time all its life you should not discontinue the practice, but simply reduce the length of the walk and its duration.

Most dogs benefit from a good 20 minutes walk twice daily. Toy breeds enjoy walks too; some can even outwalk their owners. There are some breeds of dog, however, such as the Bulldog, which want only a sedate walk in the park.

Ideally, dogs should be given a short burst of freedom every day and they will get much pleasure out of retrieving a stick or ball.

Swimming, whenever possible, is a good form of exercise, particularly for bitches who have recently been whelped, as it helps to restore their figures. Any form of play in the garden also helps to keep a dog fit, and much pleasure can be had from devising agility tests; for example, the dog can be taught to jump through a suspended tyre, crawl under a low object or run up a short ladder. If your dog is kept in a fenced garden it is advisable not to encourage it to jump.

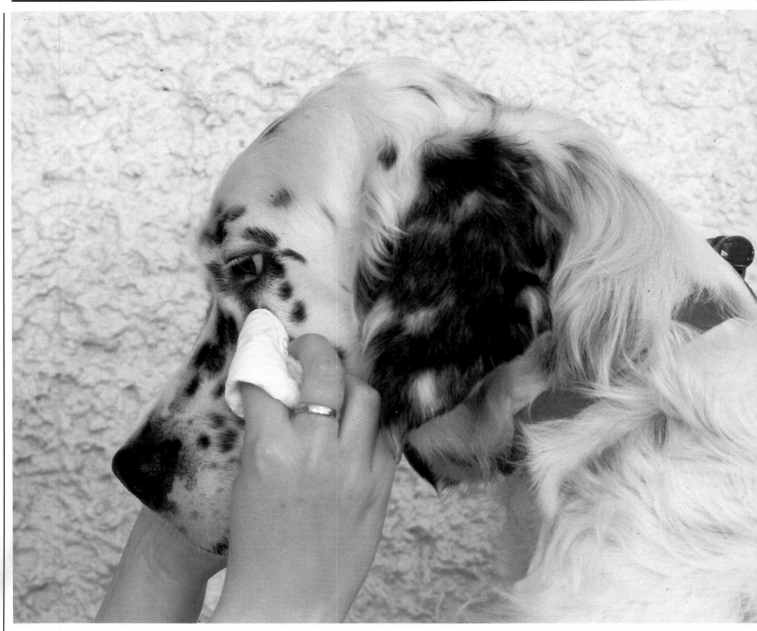

GROOMING

The pet dog, in common with the show dog, requires daily grooming for its general well-being. Baths, however, can usually be restricted to sunny days when, after a good towelling, your dog can run around out of doors and dry off.

Short-coated dogs should be brushed, with a brush of short stiff bristles or with a hound glove. A silk scarf or velvet pad may be used to make the coat shine. Long-coated dogs should be brushed using a nylon bristled brush.

As well as daily grooming, routine care should be taken of eyes, ears, teeth and nails. During grooming, you should inspect the skin for parasites, keep eyes and ears clean, remove hair growing inside the ears (as is often necessary with poodles), clean the teeth, check paws for interdigital cysts and, particularly in the case of dogs that do not get much exercise on hard ground, clip the toe-nails at regular intervals.

Eyes Wipe away any stains with cotton wool (known simply as cotton in the United States) dipped in luke-warm water or cold tea.

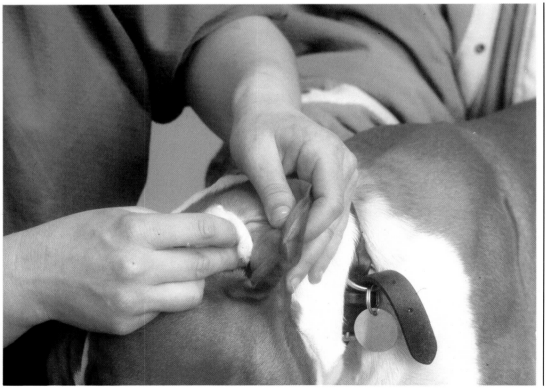

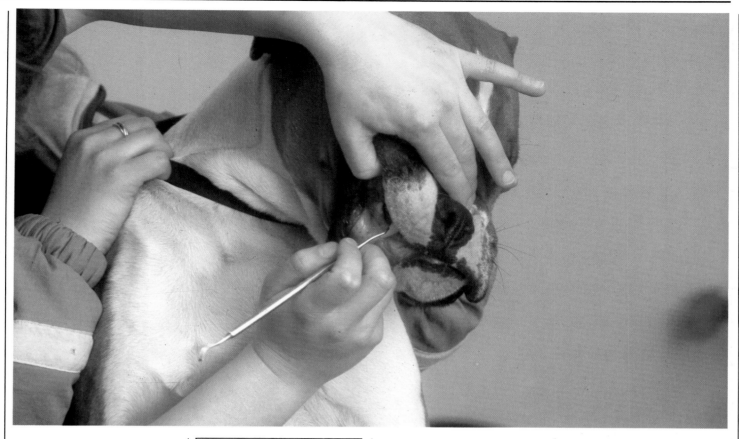

Left: This English Setter is having its eye gently bathed using cotton wool to remove any matter. A fresh pad must be used for each eye.

Ears Ears that are heavily weighted with hair block off the ear canal and induce disease, so daily combing is essential. Clean inside the dog's ears with cotton wool moistened with olive oil, being careful not to probe too deeply. Cotton buds for baby use are also acceptable.

Teeth Small breeds, in particular, may need to have their teeth scaled at regular intervals by a veterinarian. Members of some breeds may show signs of tooth decay as early as three years of age. Correct feeding and avoidance of sugary titbits will help avoid tooth decay. There are a number of canine toothpastes on the market. Alternatively, you can remove unsightly stains with a mixture of human toothpowder and water.

Nails Dogs that are regularly exercised on hard ground may wear their nails down naturally to an acceptable length. Those that do not get much road work, and in particular toy breeds, need their nails clipped about every two months using a pair of nail clippers. It goes without saying that the dog accustomed to nail clipping from puppyhood is likely to accept the operation more gracefully than the frightened adult. However, some dogs detest nail clipping and hide whenever the clippers appear. In this

Left: A Boxer is having its ears cleaned with moistened cotton wool. Only visible parts should be cleaned; deep probing must be left to a vet.

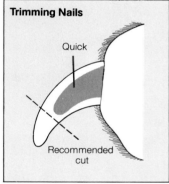

Trimming Nails

Quick

Recommended cut

Above and below: Cutting nails. Hold foot firmly and cut below the quick to avoid bleeding and pain. The quick can be seen in white nails but is masked in black.

instance it may be necessary to ask the breeder or your veterinarian to undertake the task for you.

Clipping beyond the quick (the white nail growth) can cause intense bleeding and pain. If in doubt as to where to clip, you should seek advice. Filing the nails of larger breeds may prove more satisfactory.

Grooming the show dog

The show dog, especially if it is long-coated, may need a considerable amount of pre-show preparation. Whereas some breeds should be bathed the day before each show, others should be bathed several days beforehand to allow the natural oils to return to the coat.

One of the first things to discover is the skin condition of your chosen breed. This can best be discovered

Above: A docile dog will let you clean its teeth using a dental scaler. Anaesthetics are needed for extensive cases of dental treatment.

by talking with those who have been successful in exhibiting the variety.

A good coat is largely the result of correct feeding and exercise and, consequently, good health. However, you can improve and maintain it by proper shampooing and rinsing. If you are in the slightest doubt about the product you are using, dilute it so that it is half water, half shampoo; and never forget that the best way to ensure a gleaming coat is to rinse thoroughly until no trace of shampoo remains.

Any conditioner used should go on the dog's coat and not on its skin.

Above top: A large sink is necessary to bath this large breed indoors. A shower attachment greatly eases the wetting and rinsing of the back.

Above: Shampoo is applied after a thorough wetting, taking care to avoid the eyes and ears. All traces must be rinsed off meticulously.

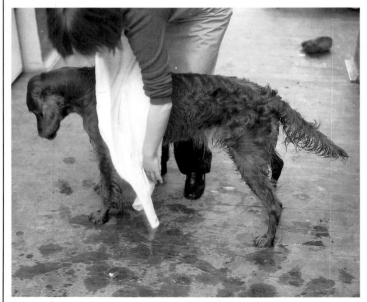

Above: A thorough towelling, particularly to the legs, chest and tail, precedes a blow-dry or a brisk sunny walk to dry the coat.

Right: After its bath, the Irish Setter is groomed using a variety of brushes and combs until its beautiful coat is gleaming.

If more weight of coat is required you should put a little conditioner over the outside layers of the coat and rinse in cool water. If, however, you wish to add more height and volume to a fine coat you should rinse off the conditioner using warm water rather than cool.

The presentation of a short-coated breed should present as great a challenge to an exhibitor as that of a long-coated breed. You must ensure that your dog stands out in the ring because of its gleaming coat and obvious good health, and to do that your dog's coat must be worked on. A harsh coat that lacks vitality will almost certainly keep an animal out of the winning line, and muzzles should be kept especially clean. Whereas the owners of long-coated breeds are sometimes able to detract attention from their dogs' flaws, everything about a short-coated breed is visible and, therefore, nothing short of perfection is acceptable.

If you are entering a short-coated breed for a show a good tip is to work on its coat every day during the week preceeding the show using a silk scarf or a velvet pad, so that the coat becomes particularly shiny.

The length of time involved in preparing a dog for showing differs from one breed to another, and it is therefore sensible to find out what you are letting yourself in for before deciding on the type of dog you wish to show.

For instance, the poodle makes a marvellous pet, but if you buy one for exhibition you must be prepared to spend two or three hours of every day, every week, in preparation. This applies similarly to breeds such as the American Cocker Spaniel, the Bichon Frise and the Old English Sheepdog, to name but a few

The lion clip is obligatory for the show poodle, though most owners of pet poodles prefer the lamb clip, with the hair a uniform length. There are also a number of glamorous, if outrageous, clips, which some poodle parlours may be prepared to carry out for you. But if you wish to do the job yourself, it would be well worth enrolling in a grooming course, following which you will certainly need to acquire some clippers, blades, nail clippers, scissors, a metal comb, a brush and a hair drier.

The Yorkshire Terrier is a breed that almost rivals the poodle in the time that must be spent in show preparation. After bathing, rinsing and oiling, its coat must be wrapped in paper curlers to avoid any damage or breakage of its long tresses.

The Bichon Frise has to be carefully scissored. It has a longish coat, which must not be scissored too short, but it is necessary to achieve a teddy bear look on the face: something that is not easily achieved by the novice. The American cocker is equally difficult to prepare; the skull and muzzle hair must be trimmed with electric clippers, it shoulders carefully scissored, and feathering should be left on its ears, legs and belly.

Terriers have to be stripped with a stripping knife (a cutting implement with a serrated edge). Alternatively, some people use a cut-throat razor. The terrier is worked down with the knife so that the dead coat is pulled out. This takes a long time, and can prove painful for the dog if carried out by an inexperienced person.

The owner of a pet terrier who takes it to a salon is generally asked whether the dog is to be clipped or stripped. Unless stripping is specifically requested the animal will normally be clipped with the use of a number four blade. This leaves the dog looking as if it has been stripped, with the coat neat and tidy and not too close to the skin. A show terrier should never be clipped though because it causes the coat to curl.

Stripping must be carried out methodically over a period of several weeks, and to produce a dog in show condition can take up to five or six months.

Top left: A Standard Poodle is being brushed and blow-dried, in preparation for being trimmed. This is always preceded by a bath.

Bottom left: The Poodle is then given a show clip, using a pair of hairdressers' scissors.

Below top: A coarse-toothed metal comb is used for a semi-long-coated breed such as this Schnauzer.

Below bottom: Wire-coated breeds need regular stripping, using a special tool, as well as combing.

Below right: The Schnauzer is groomed daily with a wire brush, a useful general purpose tool for most breeds.

1 Dual-purpose (double-sided) brush for general use.
2 Dematting comb. Use with care to prevent laceration.
3 Metal comb—fine teeth for short coats, coarse for long.
4 Glove brush (hound glove), worn on hand to follow body.
5 Nail cutters—human toe-nail type for curled nails.
6 Double-sided comb combines coarse and fine teeth.
7 Insecticidal dusting powder, from veterinarian or pet store. Follow instructions.
8 Aerosol insecticides are long-acting and penetrate even dense coats without actually wetting the dog much.
9 Talcum powder (French chalk) for general cleansing.
10 Soap—cosmetic for cleansing, insecticidal against fleas.
11 Shampoo-like soap, for cleansing or anti-parasitic use. Follow instructions.
12 Nail cutters (guillotine type), for comfortable cutting.
13 Thinning scissors, used to thin coats with minimal cutting.
14 Trimming scissors for general coat shortening.
15 Bristle grooming brush for general use, with strap.
16 Medicated skin dressings, supplied by a veterinarian. Use does not de-oil coat.
17 Curved (Mayo) scissors for trimming, especially feet.
18 Stripping knife for terrier coats. Use 2-3 times per year.
19 Wire brush. Good general tool combining brush/comb.

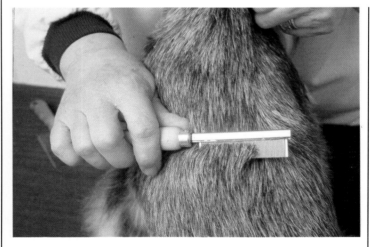

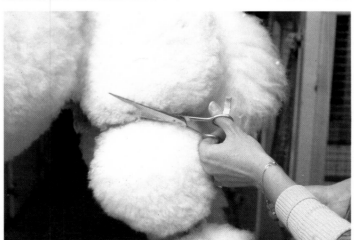

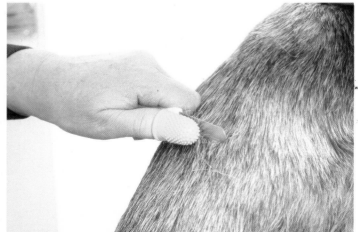

Basic Grooming Equipment

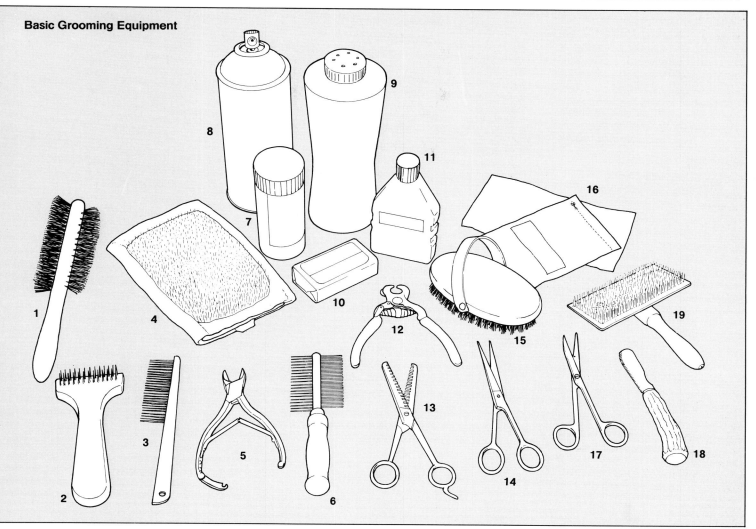

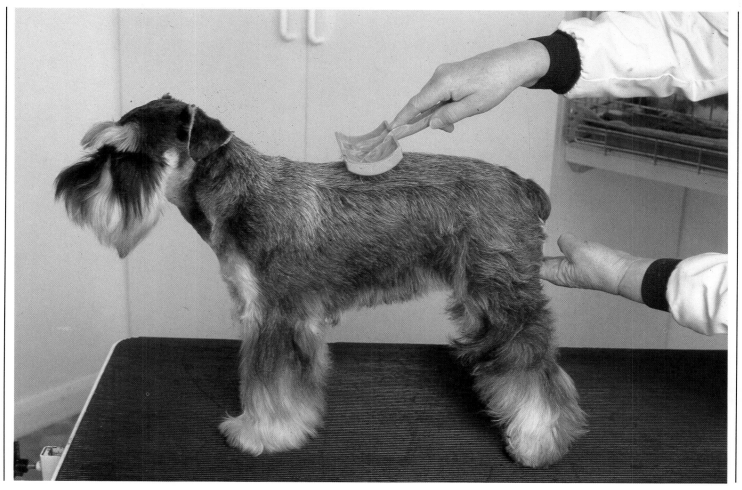

5

Health Care

Prevention is always better than cure, and attention to inoculations and regular health checks should enable dog owners to keep their canine companions for a lengthy span.

The need to consult a veterinarian when troubles occur cannot be over-emphasized. But it is also important that the owner is able to detect signs of ill health, knows how to administer medication once the problem has been diagnosed, and can identify the more common complaints.

With the growing interest in alternative medicine it is appropriate to mention homoeopathic cures, in the knowledge that homoeopathy and other fringe practices are much sought after by the dog owners of today as an adjunct, but not an alternative, to recognized veterinary medicine.

Right: Puppies must be vaccinated and regularly wormed to keep them healthy.

Below: An annual health check by a veterinarian is recommended.

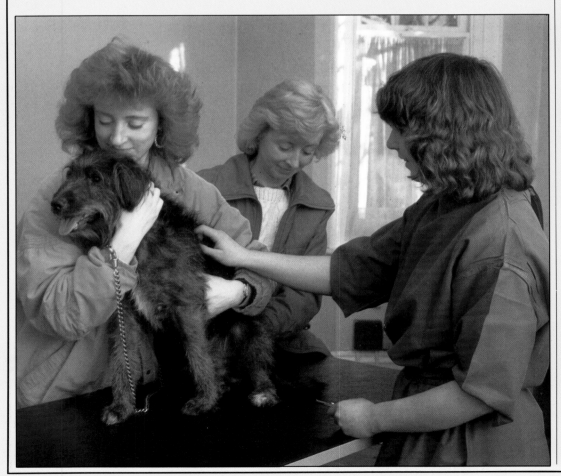

J ust as some children seem to sail through early life into adulthood with little more than the occasional cold and others seem to contract all manner of illnesses, there are some dogs that soldier on for 14 years or more having rarely had an illness, and others which, despite every care, seem always to be in the veterinarian's surgery. However, with modern advances in veterinary science there is no doubt that dogs are living longer and healthier lives, and that owners who take proper care of their pets have a good chance of their dog's company for many years.

Vaccinations and worming

As a matter of course, all dogs should be vaccinated against disease and wormed, not just as puppies but at regular intervals thereafter.

Highly effective vaccines, free from side effects, are available to protect a dog from distemper, infectious hepatitis (liver inflammation), two forms of leptospirosis (diseases of the liver and kidneys), and canine parvovirus (a recently identified cause of fatal enteritis in puppies and infertility in breeding bitches). All these diseases are described in further detail on pages 100-106. Vaccination against these diseases can be combined and is usually given at about 9-10 weeks of age, consisting of two injections with a 2-3 week interval between. As no two dogs develop the same degree of immunity following vaccination, and vaccines rarely provide lifelong protection, it is important that booster inoculations are given at regular intervals. This usually involves a yearly trip to your veterinarian, which also provides an opportunity to give the dog a general check-up.

There is also a vaccine against rabies which is recommended for dogs living in countries where the disease is prevalent. In fact, in some countries, such as the United States, dogs are required by law to have rabies vaccinations. In rabies-free areas, such as Australasia and the United Kingdom, such precautions are not necessary.

Regular worming is also an

important part of health care. There are various types of worms that infect dogs, most of which can be cheaply and effectively controlled by means of medication from a veterinary surgeon. For the various types of worms and their recommended treatments see pages 106/7.

Health checks

It is a good idea to give your dog regular health checks, a function which is easily combined with grooming. When cleaning the teeth, check for broken or loose teeth, holes in the teeth, and receding or inflamed gums. But bear in mind that puppies of up to six months of age may have loose teeth anyway as they are still losing their milk teeth.

The eyes should be checked for inflammation or cloudiness in the cornea (the transparent layer which forms the front of the eyeball). A badly inflamed eye will be kept half closed and will water profusely, the dog frequently rubbing at it in discomfort. Ears should be checked for excessive wax or an unpleasant

Below: Keep your dog under firm control at the vets. A small dog or pup is best kept on your lap.

Above: Newly acquired puppies and adult dogs should have a vet examine them as soon as possible for signs of illness or disease.

smell, also for signs of squelching when rubbed around the base.

The general condition of the coat should be noted and signs of baldness or external parasites looked for.

Signs of ill-health

A rapid change in weight can be an indication of a sick animal. It is as well to weigh a dog at regular intervals to monitor its weight, an operation that is easily carried out by first weighing yourself on the bathroom scales and then reweighing yourself with the dog in your arms. The difference between the two weights will equal the weight of the dog. Alternatively, with small dogs, you can weigh them on the kitchen scales. It may be necessary to take a large, heavy dog to a public weighing machine in order to find a base large enough for it to sit on.

Right: Puppyhood vaccination and booster injections take only one moment and are usually pain-free.

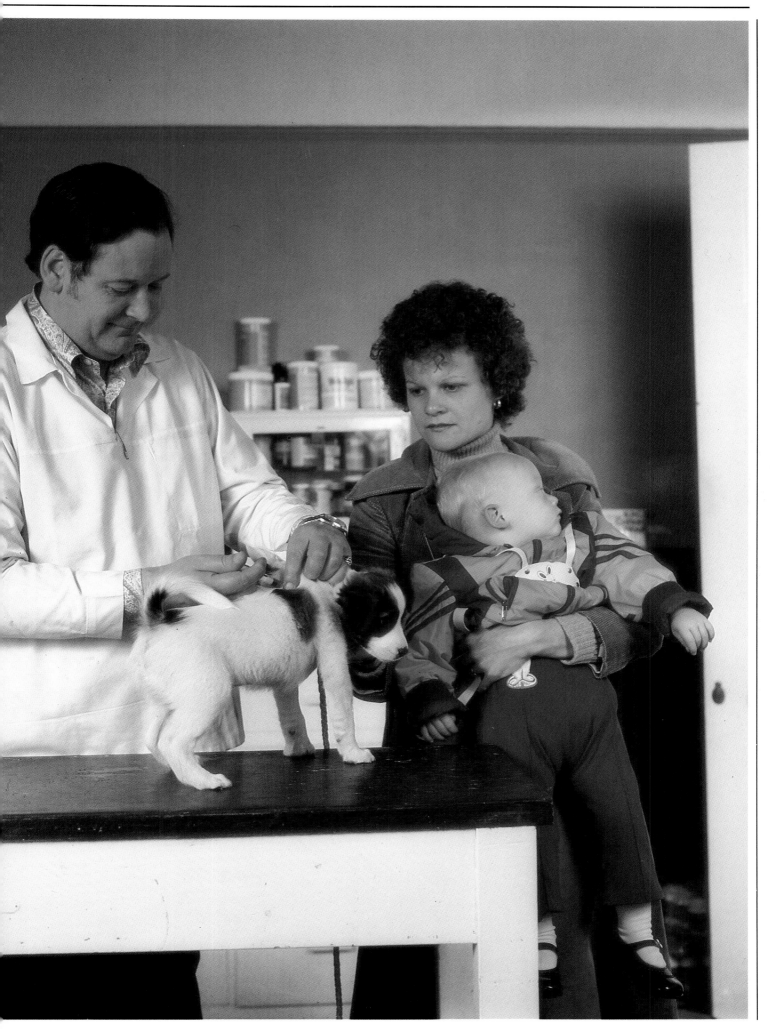

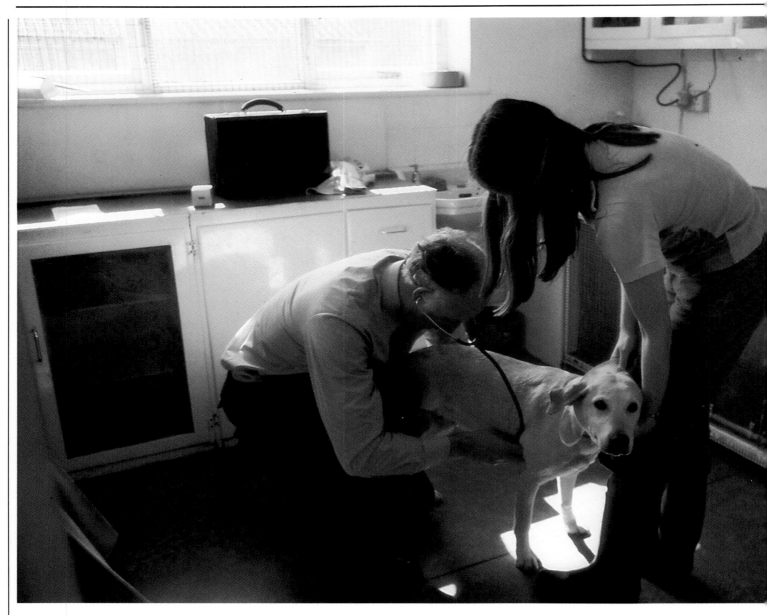

Change in temperature is also a good indication that your dog is unwell. The normal temperature of a dog is about 101·5°F (38·6°C), with the exception of hairless dogs whose normal temperature is rather higher. The temperature can be taken by gently inserting a lubricated thermometer for about two-thirds of its length into the rectum of the dog. It should be left there for about a minute to get an accurate reading. If the temperature has risen in excess of 103°F (39·5°C) then professional advice should be sought. Large dogs may need to be held by a second person while their temperature is being taken, and in some cases it might be wise to muzzle them if they are aggressive.

Other indications of ill-health include any unusual behaviour such as lethargy and an unwillingness to take exercise, or changes in appetite or thirst. Generally speaking, if a dog goes off its food for one day there is no need to be concerned: occasional fasting does no harm. But if a dog refuses food and appears off colour a second day an owner should not delay in seeking veterinary advice. Vomiting and diarrhoea are more obvious signs of sickness, though these may simply be the result of a temporary upset.

Above: Larger dogs are often examined on the floor. The owner is only required to steady the patient.

Below: Temperature-taking is quick and easy. The thermometer is inserted in the rectum.

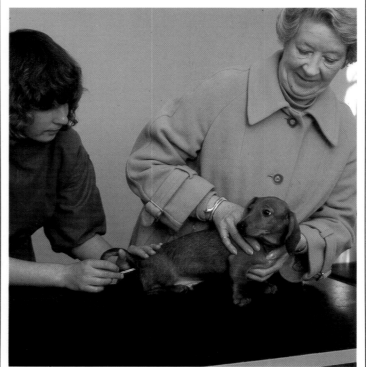

You should not be afraid of worrying a veterinarian unnecessarily if you think your dog may be unwell. A veterinarian would much rather have the opportunity of examining a dog, and putting its owner's mind at rest if there is nothing to worry about, than have the owner wait until the animal is, perhaps, irretrievably ill.

—— **Administering medication** ——
Should the veterinarian prescribe pills, the best way of giving them is to conceal each one in a piece of cheese, or some other titbit that your dog usually finds irresistible. If the dog refuses to co-operate, the pill can be administered in the following way: place your left hand on the dog's head, the thumb on the right side and the forefinger on the left; gently squeeze at the hinge of the dog's jaws until the mouth opens; drop the pill at the back of the tongue, and with your index and middle fingers push the pill down the dog's throat until the animal swallows. You may have to repeat this procedure several times; frequently when you release the dog, believing it to have swallowed the pill, it will proceed to spit out the unwanted medication with disdain.

Generally speaking, liquid medications should not exceed one

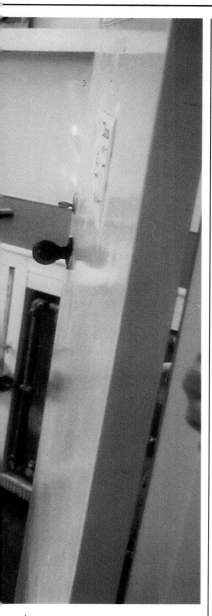

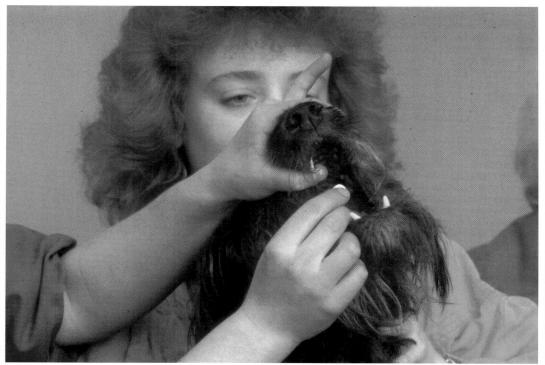

Above: A tablet is given firmly but gently. It is dropped right at the back of the mouth and pushed over the base of the tongue so that it is swallowed.

Right: To administer ear medication the ear flap is raised to show the descending ear canal. The drops or ointment are inserted and the ear is gently massaged to work the medication downwards.

Below: Ointment is applied carefully to the open eye. The head must be steadied to prevent a sudden movement. When released, the dog will blink and spread the medication evenly over the eye.

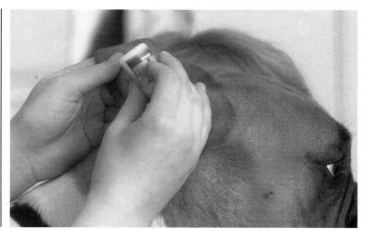

teaspoonful (5ml) per dose. To administer a dose, the dog's jaws should be held firmly closed, with the head tilted well back. A flap of the lip should then be pulled out to one side, forming a natural funnel into which the medicine can be poured. The dog should not be released until it has appeared to swallow.

Ear drops should be administered into the largest visible opening. A gentle massage of the ear afterwards will help to disperse the liquid through the canal. Ear powders should never be used unless prescribed by a veterinarian as they tend to clog the ear and cause irritation.

Eye drops and ointments are slightly more difficult to administer and it is often helpful to get the aid of a second person. The dog should be made to sit with its head slightly raised. Holding the dog's head firmly against your body will help to keep it steady during this delicate operation. Using your thumb and forefinger to keep the eyelids open, with the free hand drip the required number of drops or squeeze the necessary amount of ointment onto the eye, being very careful that the nozzle of the bottle or tube does not touch the eyeball. The dog should be prevented from rubbing its eye for a few minutes after application.

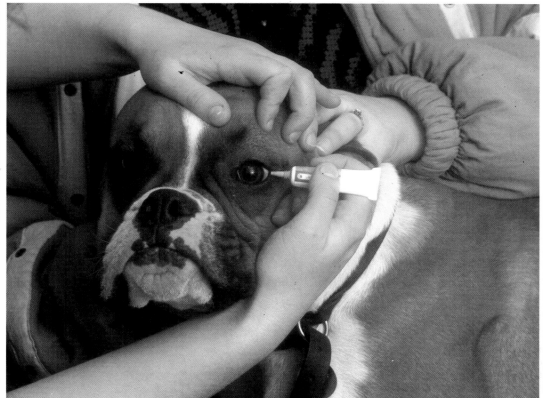

Canine ailments

The following are some of the more common complaints that may afflict your dog, with advice on what to look for and how best to deal with each problem. As a rule, if you feel your dog is unwell you should take it to a veterinary surgeon. On no account should you treat your dog yourself with proprietary products bought over the pet store counter. The remedies could be first class if used correctly, but without professional diagnosis you could be doing your dog more harm than good. If, however, before seeking professional advice you *have* given your pet some unprescribed treatment, it is important that you inform the veterinarian of the fact.

Anal glands, impacted The anal glands, or scent glands, are situated on each side of the anus under the skin. They are about the size of grapes, and excrete a thick coloured liquid which can be emptied into the rectum on sudden movement or upon the dog passing a hard motion. The excretion, which gives off an unpleasant odour, is used for marking territory, and may once have been part of a protective mechanism to discourage enemies, working in the same way as the product of a skunk's scent glands.

It is not unusual for these glands to become impacted (blocked) and cause irritation. In an attempt to relieve the irritation the dog may drag its bottom along the ground, a sight which causes many owners to think that their dog has worms. Should this condition occur, your veterinarian will simply squeeze the glands by pressing upwards and inwards to release the fluid. Many owners undertake this—admittedly rather messy—task themselves, once they have been shown by their veterinarian how it should be done.

Canker See Ear complaints.

Cataracts See Eye complaints.

Cryptorchid An inherited condition in which a dog is born with both testicles absent from the scrotum. A cryptorchid must not be bred from, and is not permitted in the show ring. It is important, however, to point out that often in the case of toy breeds, for example the Chihuahua, one or both testicles may not appear until the puppy is several months old. A dog with only one descended testicle is called a monorchid.

Cysts, inter-digital These are swellings that appear between the toes, usually caused by a blockage of the sweat glands of the feet. Treatment includes placing the affected foot into a bowl of warm salted water, which tends to draw the swellings to a head. When the cysts rupture they should be cleaned with warm salted water three or four times a day. Lancing is sometimes necessary.

Diarrhoea This can be caused by change of diet, a mental upset such as may result from change of ownership or environment, eating unsuitable food or eating from an

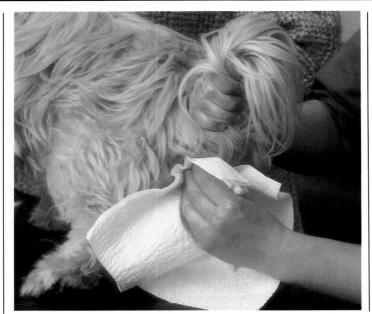

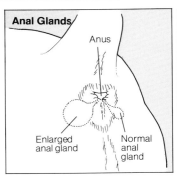

Above: The dog's anal glands lie just under the skin slightly below and on each side of the anus. They normally empty themselves when a motion is passed. They cannot be felt when empty but are grape-sized when full.

Left: The glands can be emptied by applying pressure just below and on either side of the anus.

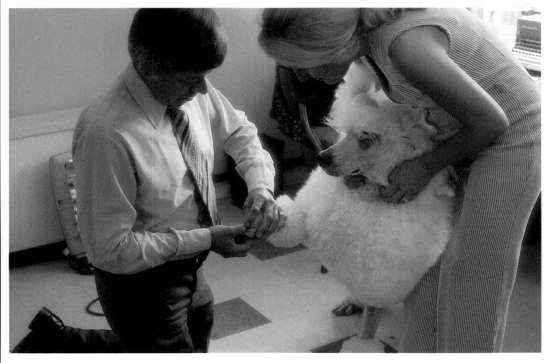

Above: The feet should be checked for overgrown nails, cuts, and foreign bodies such as grass awns.

unclean bowl; alternatively, it may be the first indication of something more serious, such as canine distemper, parvovirus infection, or gastro-enteritis.

To treat the condition you should starve the dog for 24 hours, dosing with a teaspoonful (5ml) of kaolin and liquid paraffin emulsion (or kaopectate concentrate) four hourly. If the dog is not restored to normal health within 24 hours, veterinary advice should be sought.

Distemper Canine distemper was the scourge of the 1930's, when many an owner would sit up through the night with an afflicted puppy only to see it die in the morning. Happily this virus infection, which enters the dog's body particularly through the nose and mouth, has now been virtually wiped out by vaccination. The vaccine ensures

maximum protection against the disease from as early as six weeks of age. The recommended age for vaccination, however, may vary from country to country.

The virus, which spreads easily to unprotected dogs, is present in all countries and may be spread by direct contact with infected dogs, or indirect contact, such as with contaminated pavements, human clothing, bedding or brushes.

Early signs of the virus are a high temperature, which may persist for from 1-2 days, a dry cough, discharge from the eyes and nostrils and diarrhoea with resulting dehydration and weight loss. The dog will appear depressed and thoroughly miserable. Distemper may clear up within 10 days, or it could persist for several weeks, even months, with periods of apparent improvement and set-backs.

Ear complaints A dog with ear trouble is easy to recognize; it will shake its head, paw at its ears, and sometimes push its head along the

ground or into its owner's lap, a gesture which may be misinterpreted as a sign of affection. If this should occur, check the ear to see if anything has become lodged inside it, such as mites, grass seeds, matted hair or an excess of wax. You must be careful not to probe too far though, as this can cause great damage to the ear. If there does appear to be some irritant present, you should not try to dislodge it yourself, though a temporary remedy to relieve the sufferer is to insert a few drops of warm olive oil into the ear. You should then seek professional help, as your veterinarian will be able to rectify the problem safely and effectively to give your pet immense relief.

Canker is a common term for inflammation of the ear. The ear feels hot, looks inflamed, and produces a foul-smelling brown discharge. The best temporary remedy is to clean the ear carefully with a solution comprising one teaspoonful of bicarbonate of soda to one-sixth of a pint (100ml) of

Above: The ears should be checked for excessive wax or discharge, foreign bodies or malodour.

Left: A vet examines the deep ear with a special instrument called an auriscope.

warm water or warm olive oil. Unfortunately, there is a tendency for pet owners to diagnose all ear troubles as canker and to treat it with remedies bought from pet stores. This is inadvisable: you may be treating the dog for a complaint it does not have!

Haematomas are blood-filled swellings that sometimes occur in the ear flap. These could be the result of a sharp blow that has ruptured the blood vessels in the ear, or could be caused by the pet scratching and tossing its head as the result of ear irritation or infection. Surgery is usually required to prevent deformity of the ear flap.

Another condition from which dogs may suffer is otitis media

(inflammation of the middle ear). It is a condition which usually comes from an infection of the external ear passage. The usual symptoms are pain, ear discharge, fever and possibly loss of balance, and treatment should be by veterinary prescription only.

Eczema An inflammatory skin condition that results from a self-inflicted wound such as may be caused by scratching, and bacterial infection. It is characterized by redness and the formation of blisters which burst open, producing a watery discharge. This discharge moistens the skin and causes the development of scales or crusts which mat the hair, irritating the skin and causing further infection. Eczema usually affects the root of the tail, the back, shoulders and neck, and behind the ears. The most common signs are the pet's scratching and the formation of crusting blisters. An afflicted dog should be taken to the veterinarians for treatment.

Eye complaints There are many different eye diseases (including some hereditary complaints, see pages 32/3) and the need to obtain correct diagnosis and treatment, rather than attempt home remedies, cannot be too strongly emphasized. By far the most common problems are the result of injury or infection. Before seeing your veterinarian, try bathing the affected eye with a weak solution of warm boracic lotion. If there is no improvement in 24 hours you should seek veterinary advice immediately.

If the eye appears red and there is a watery discharge, this could be an indication that some foreign matter has become lodged under the eyelid. Your dog may paw the eye in an effort to alleviate the irritation. Such a sign should encourage you to examine the eye closely.

Ask someone to take a firm, but gentle hold of your pet while you carefully spread its eyelids apart. If you find a foreign particle, you may attempt to lift it off the surface of the eye with a strand of sterile cotton wool.

Above: A vet checks the internal structure of the eye using an opthalmoscope, an instrument commonly used to detect disease.

Bathing the eye with warm water may also prove helpful. However, if the object is, for instance, grass seed which has become embedded in the eyeball, veterinary help will be necessary.

If you cannot find an apparent reason for your pet's discomfort, do not assume that there is nothing amiss. The soreness may be the result of a scratched cornea or a general eye infection such as conjunctivitis. Prompt treatment could save your dog's sight. If scratches or other slight injuries to the surface of the eye are neglected, they may result in cloudy, bluish spots on the cornea. These spots are the result of white blood cells invading the cornea to repel any accompanying infection. If the eye is treated properly the infection will recede and the spotting will clear.

Common External Dog Parasites

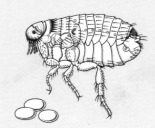

Dog flea (*Ctenocephalides canis*)

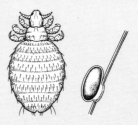

Dog louse (*Linognathus setosus*)

Clouding deeper in the eye, where the lens is becoming opaque, is often found in older dogs. This is the result of ageing, and the dog is unlikely to go blind, though some visual defect may be noticed. True cataracts occur at any age and are often inherited; in many cases, surgery is feasible and restores good sight.

Fits Between the World Wars, bleaching agents in white bread were responsible for fits in many dogs. Infections such as distemper still cause fits, but epileptic-type fits are the commonest kind. First aid treatment is by nursing the dog in a darkened room, but veterinary diagnosis is essential before medication to control the fits effectively can be prescribed.

Fleas (and other external parasites) Dogs often pick up fleas, ticks and other parasites from other animals via, in particular, grass. The treatment for these comes in the form of a shampoo, an aerosol, or a powder puffer. Alternatively, the dog can be made to wear a collar which exudes an insect-killing vapour, although this method has come under criticism because the vapour has been suspected of causing skin irritation. All dogs have fleas at some time or another, and temporary infestation should not cause dog owners to worry.

Right: A flea collar is simply fitted to rid a dog of fleas and other external parasites.

Below right: An exaggerated scratch response to a simple touch may often indicate fleas or the onset of skin disease.

Below: Common skin parasites and their eggs. The mite cannot be seen with the naked eye. The big parasites — fleas, lice and ticks — are removed by insecticides.

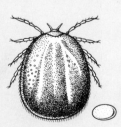

Dog tick *(Ixodes ricinus)*

Follicular mite *(Demodex canis)*

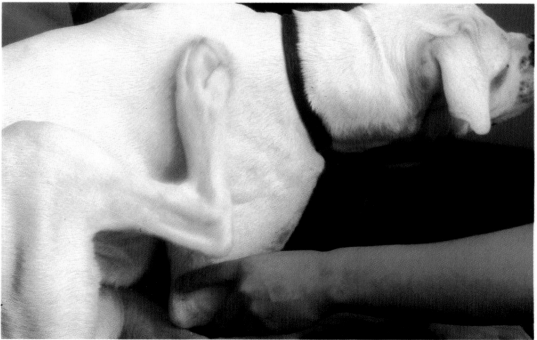

Gastro-enteritis This is inflammation of the stomach and intestines, caused by various agents, such as viruses, bacterial infections or poisons, or by unwholesome scavenging. The dog has diarrhoea, and may vomit and lose its appetite. Primary treatment is to withhold food totally and allow only small quantities of boiled water. If recovery does not occur within 12 hours, or if the condition should worsen, seek veterinary aid immediately. In its severest form, this disease can lead to mortality, especially in young dogs or toy breeds of any age, so care is vital.

Haematomas See Ear complaints.

Heart disease Symptoms of heart ailments are intolerance to exercise and a dry cough. Excess body weight should be controlled by dieting and the amount of exercise given to the dog should be restricted to that recommended by a veterinarian. Digitalis, an ancient drug derived from the foxglove plant, may be one of the recommended treatments as it stabilizes the heart beat. Strict observance to the recommended dose, however, is absolutely essential. Dogs with heart trouble can live for some considerable length of time with the aid of this drug.

Hepatitis, viral Inflammation of the liver which can afflict dogs of any age but is particularly dangerous to puppies. A dog suffering from this disease is very obviously ill, with symptoms including vomiting and lack of appetite. The disease can prove fatal and requires immediate and intensive treatment by a veterinarian. Viral hepatitis is preventable by vaccination, which is highly recommended.

Hip dysplasia See Hereditary complaints, page 32.

Incontinence, urinary There could be any number of reasons for the frequent passing of water, ranging from cystitis (inflammation of the bladder) to bladder stones, tumours or enlarged prostate glands (part of the male reproductive system). The condition must be correctly diagnosed by a veterinarian before treatment can be instituted.

Jaw, overshot or undershot Terms used to describe conditions in which the upper jaw is either too long (overshot) or too short (undershot) for the lower jaw. In the former instance, the teeth of the lower jaw do not touch the inner surface of the upper incisors. Conversely, with an undershot jaw, the lower incisors project beyond those of the upper jaw. Both conditions are show faults in some breeds.

Kennel cough Scientifically known as tracheitis, this is a common complaint in boarding kennels or any other place where dogs are kept in large numbers. The sufferer has a dry, hacking cough that is particularly severe at night. Young dogs and puppies are particularly susceptible and it can take several weeks to clear up. Cough linctuses may help. However, there is now a vaccine available which helps to protect against infection.

Kidney disease This is a fairly common disease in dogs, the cause usually being traced to infection or ageing in the tissues of the kidney. Symptoms may include pain in the back or stiff hind legs, but increased thirst and the frequent passing of urine is more common. It is easily diagnosed by a urine or blood test but the treatment merely alleviates the condition rather than cures it.

Leptospirosis The name given to two distinct infections caused by

Above: A gentle pinch on the windpipe will trigger a persistent cough in a case of kennel cough.

closely related bacteria. Leptospirosis canicola affects the kidneys and is acquired from the urine of other dogs. Leptospirosis icterohaemorrhagia affects the liver and kidneys, and is transmitted by rats. This latter disease is particularly dangerous because it can also affect humans, when it is better known as Weil's disease. Dogs affected by either disease are extremely sick, collapsing, usually with a high fever, and vomiting. The mortality rate is high and treatment

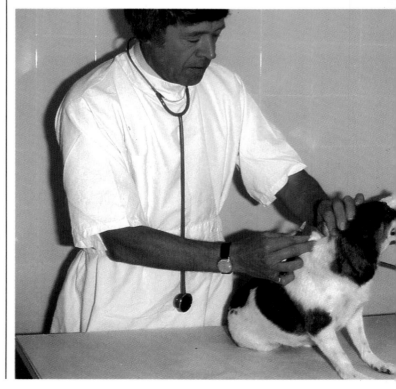

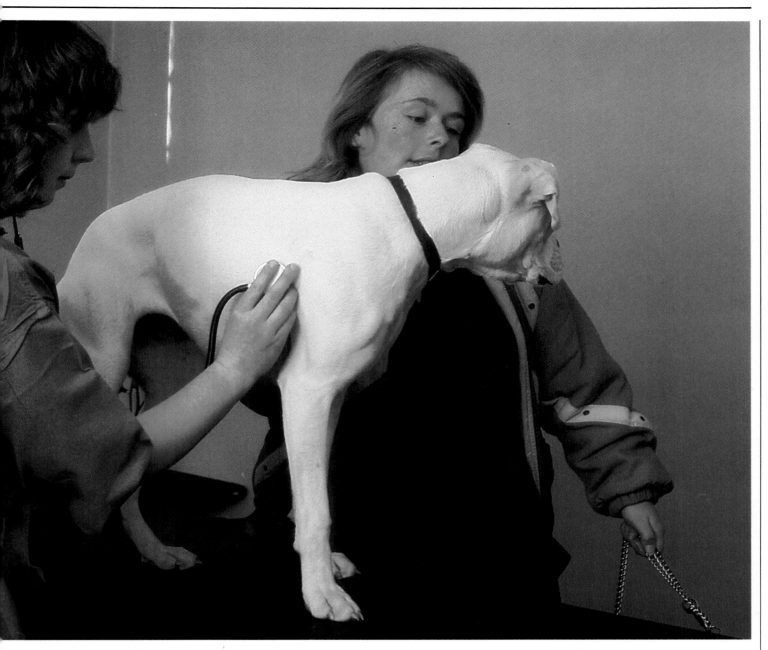

Above: Usually with kennel cough, unlike distemper, the lungs are unaffected and the chest is clear.

Left: Injections like vaccines or antibiotics are usually painless.

requires early diagnosis by a veterinarian and intensive therapy. Vaccines exist to provide protection against both forms and are highly recommended.

Mange A term used to describe a number of highly transmissible skin diseases, and not to be confused with eczema. Mange is caused by tiny mites, invisible to the naked eye, and the condition should be treated without delay. The two commonest types are demodectic (follicular) mange, which shows as bald patches, sometimes with pustules, and sarcoptic mange, which begins with small red spots that cause a great deal of irritation. The latter is, in fact, the canine equivalent to the human skin disease scabies. Follicular mange is the more serious of the two, for there is no guarantee of a cure.

Monorchid A monorchid is a dog with only one testicle descended into the scrotum. There is no reason why a dog of this type cannot sire puppies, but breeding from him is not recommended as the condition is hereditary. The dog may also be ineligible for showing.

Parvovirus, canine (CPV) A new virus disease that first struck the canine population of the United Kingdom in 1978. Since that time cases of the disease, particularly in puppies and young dogs, have been reported almost everywhere. Tens of thousands of dogs have suffered severe illness or died, and several kennel owners have been forced out of business as a result of the disease. Fortunately, vaccines against CPV were quickly developed, providing protection against the disease.

A 'heart' form is common in young pups from the age of about two weeks. In this form, puppies that are apparently fit and healthy will suddenly collapse and die from acute heart failure. This is caused by the destruction of the heart muscle by the CPV infection, resulting in myocarditis (heart muscle inflam-

mation). All breeds are susceptible and the death rate in affected litters may vary from 10-100%. It is believed that the virus can be passed on to puppies during pregnancy as well as shortly after birth.

Survivors of the heart, or myocarditis, form may suffer from varying degrees of impairment of the heart function and may die of progressive heart failure at a later stage.

The most common form of the disease is one which affects older puppies and adult dogs. It is typified by severe enteritis (inflammation of the intestines), with persistent vomiting and diarrhoea. Infectious enteritis can be caused by other viruses and bacteria, but in the case of parvovirus vomiting is usually the first sign, with frequent production of a frothy bile-coloured liquid followed by severe and foul-smelling diarrhoea with grey or greyish-yellow faeces that contain flecks or moderate quantities of blood. Badly affected animals quickly become dehydrated and can die within 48-72 hours of the onset of the disease, despite intensive care and fluid treatment.

Obviously the best way to control this new and serious disease is by use of an effective vaccine. There are several available and your veterinarian will recommend the vaccination programme best suited for your dog.

Poisoning If you think your dog has swallowed poison you should contact a veterinarian without delay. As a temporary measure, if the animal has only just taken the poison, you can give it a simple emetic (medicine that causes vomiting), such as salt and water, which will cause the poison to be vomited. Wherever possible, take the packet or bottle of suspected poison to the veterinarian as this will help in selecting the best treatment.

Rabies A highly infectious disease caused by a virus which attacks the brain, causing nervous symptoms such as 'wild rage' and 'dumb' paralysis, resulting in death. It is spread by the bite of an infected animal and can be satisfactorily vaccinated against in dogs and humans. In the United States, every dog is required by law to have rabies inoculations. The first shot can be given as early as three months and will create immunity for one year. Booster shots must be given every three years thereafter. Hawaii is the only US state where there is a quarantine period (four months) for dogs coming into the state.

The United Kingdom is rabies-free, due to its strict quarantine regulations. Any dog entering the country from overseas must be kept in isolation for six months in a government-approved quarantine establishment. In virtually every other country rabies is present to a greater or lesser degree.

Ringworm A fungal infection of the skin which results in hair loss and exaggerated scurfiness (flaking skin). It is highly infectious and readily transmitted to other animals and humans. Once correctly diagnosed it is easily treated.

Skin complaints The most common skin complaints are caused by external parasites such as fleas, lice and mites. These are dealt with separately under the headings fleas and mange (a disease caused by mites). Other skin complaints include eczema and fungal infections such as ringworm (see above). Cleanliness, regular grooming and sensible diet are the best ways to combat skin problems but veterinary advice should be sought as soon as any infection is suspected.

Vomiting A dog may vomit for any number of reasons, including bolting its food, worm infestation, bowel blockage or parvovirus. The dog should be starved for 24 hours and allowed only small quantities of boiled water. A single case of vomiting is usually nothing to worry about, but if this should happen several times a day it could indicate a more serious problem. The dog should therefore be taken to see a veterinarian if its condition has not improved after 24 hours.

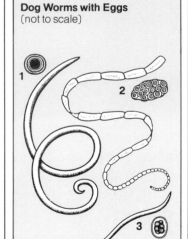

Dog Worms with Eggs
(not to scale)

Above: Three common dog worms.
1 Roundworm *(Toxocara canis)*
2 Tapeworm *(Dipylidium caninum)*
3 Hookworm *(Ancylostoma caninum)*

Worms There are several types of worms that infest the intestines of dogs, the most prevalent being roundworms and tapeworms. Roundworms, called toxocara, generally attack young puppies, and the larvae can attack humans (see page 110). A dog with toxocara worms will usually be in poor condition with a pot-belly, and may suffer from vomiting and diarrhoea. Treatment, known as worming, is ideally prescribed by a veterinarian and, to prevent any infection, puppies should be wormed at intervals of 1-2 weeks from three weeks of age up to six months; thereafter dogs should be wormed at six-monthly intervals. Worming a breeding bitch at two-weekly intervals is also advocated from one week before whelping until one or two weeks after weaning the pups.

The recommended treatment can vary though in different parts of the world. In the United States, for example, once a puppy has been treated for worms at about 3-5 weeks of age, it is given two more treatments at three-weekly intervals and is not treated again unless it is a bitch about to give birth.

Tapeworms are usually found in the adult dog and can be detected in the faeces, where the segments resemble grains of rice. Tablets to clear this parasite should be obtained from your veterinarian. Tapeworms are only contracted from swallowing an infested flea during self-grooming or from eating raw infected meat, particularly sheep offal. Prevention, therefore, is by regular de-fleaing where appropriate, and dogs should never be fed raw offal.

Heartworms are an increasing threat to dogs in certain parts of the world and, though not common in Europe, they do cause a problem in the United States. Prevention currently is the best protection against these parasites. Dogs in areas of heartworm danger must take medication to keep from becoming infected. Treatment after infection is risky. Medicines which kill the heartworm can be dangerous

A Simple First-Aid Kit

1 Bland eye ointment. If in doubt, seek advice from your veterinarian.
2 Suitable cream or balm for grazes and scalds.
3 Sedative tablets (these should be supplied by a veterinarian, with details of dosage).
4 Aspirin tablets, peferably the soluble variety – one tablet treats a 20lb (9kg) dog.
5 Surgical or methylated spirit for cleansing and sterilizing.
6/7 Adhesive plaster rolls.
8 Crepe bandages for sprains and injured limbs.
9 Suitable antiseptic solution, safe for use with dogs – e.g. antiseptics designed for use with babies.
10 Stomach mixture, e.g. kaolin or bismuth for sickness and diarrhoea.
11 Wound powder. Antiseptic powder for cuts and grazes or after operations. Easy to apply from plastic puffer.
12 White open-wove cotton
to bandages for dressing cuts
14 and wounds.
15 Lint or sterile dressings for cuts and grazes.
16 Nail clippers.
17 Blunt-ended tweezers, such as eyebrow tweezers, to remove thorns, ticks, etc., from the skin.
18 Cotton wool for dressings and bandages.
19 Curved, blunt-ended scissors

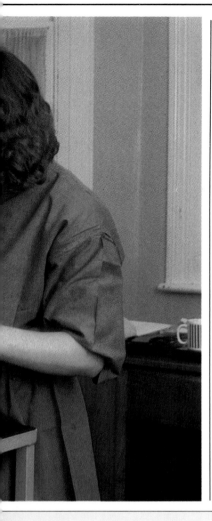

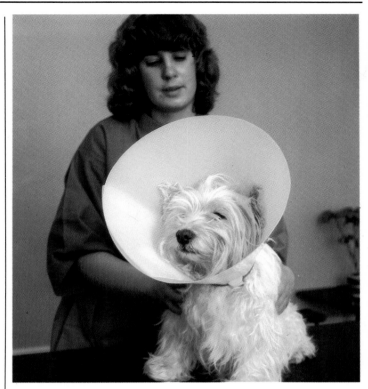

to the dog as well, and if the dog is heavily infected, dead and dying heartworms fill its circulatory system with debris which can be fatal. A veterinarian will know the incidence of heartworm infestation in an area and can recommend preventative measures to help protect a dog.

Hookworms can cause the most harm in puppies. They are not so common in the United Kingdom except in a few infected kennels, but cause a greater problem in other parts of the world, including the United States. The worms may be passed from dam to offspring during pregnancy, and it is therefore extremely important to have a bitch checked before mating and again near the end of gestation. Hookworms attach themselves to the wall of the small intestine and suck blood, causing anaemia and diarrhoea. If untreated or undetected at an early age, puppies will usually die. A routine microscopic check of faeces is advisable to detect infestation. Most breeders will have routine checks done on dogs that have been out on show circuits or boarding with dogs other than their own kennel mates. Treatment of puppies or adults should never be undertaken by the non-professional; effective medication could prove to be dangerous when administered by a well-meaning owner.

Left: Worms are easily and cheaply cleared by administering a course of tablets supplied by your vet.

Above: An 'Elizabethan collar' is easily fitted round the neck and prevents dogs from scratching their ears or licking wounds.

Below: It is useful to build a simple dog's first-aid kit. You may never need some of the items but just

having them handy can be a comfort. Shown here is a basic kit of equipment and materials. The kit excludes splints because they are rarely required. If you ever suspect your dog has a limb fracture you can probably improvise splints from household materials, pending veterinary treatment.

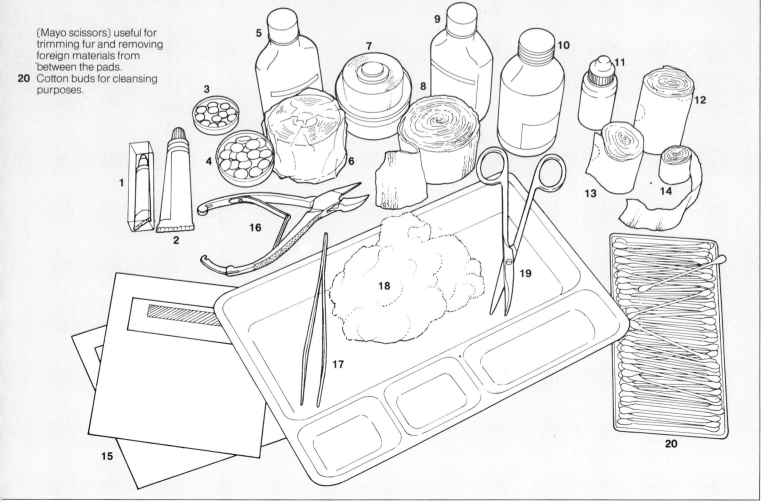

(Mayo scissors) useful for trimming fur and removing foreign materials from between the pads.
20 Cotton buds for cleansing purposes.

HOMOEOPATHY

Homoeopathy is increasingly being used as an adjunct to conventional veterinary medicine. It is important to emphasize the word 'adjunct' because homoeopathy, and other fields of 'alternative' medicine, should not be regarded as a substitute for a routine visit to a veterinarian. If you are interested in this form of treatment, it is as well to discuss it with your veterinarian to get a second, qualified opinion as to its desirability.

Homoeopathy is in general use throughout the world. In Britain it is recognized by an Act of Parliament and, as a system of medicine for humans, is on prescription under the country's National Health Service. However, it is still not universally known that it can be effective in the treatment of animals. The word comes from the Greek word *homoios* meaning 'like', and homoeopathy is the medical practice of treating like with like. It involves

the treatment of an illness with a substance that will, in a healthy person, produce symptoms similar to those displayed by the sick person.

The principle is long-standing, having been used since the time of Hippocrates, the Greek founder of medicine, who lived around 450 BC. More than 1,000 years later, a Swiss alchemist, Paracelsus, used an identical healing system based upon the principle of like curing like. But it was not until the end of the eighteenth century that homoeopathy, as we know it today, came into being, largely due to the efforts of a German physician named Samuel Hahnemann. Appalled by existing medical practices, he decided to use the homoeopathic principle to develop an effective, gentle and safe alternative.

Hahnemann found that by taking small doses of cinchona bark he could produce in himself mild symptoms of malaria. If similar

Above: Homoeopathy must be regarded as an adjunct to veterinary medicine rather than an alternative, and regular veterinary checks should still be carried out.

Above right: Dogs that pine for their master during a stay in boarding kennels can be treated with the homoeopathic remedy ignatia.

doses were administered to those suffering from malaria, a cure was effected, the cinchona triggering a reflex in the body that helped the body to cure itself. From this beginning Hahnemann was eventually to catalogue more than 200 remedies drawn from vegetable, mineral and, more rarely, animal materials, all of which had been proved by Hahnemann and his colleagues to be capable of curing various illnesses.

The three basic principles Hahnemann established were:

A medicine which in large doses produces the symptoms of a disease will in small doses cure that disease.

By extreme dilution the medicine's curative properties are enhanced and the poisonous side effects are lost.

Homoeopathic medicines are prescribed by the study of the whole individual and according to basic temperament.

Homoeopathy is therefore essentially a natural healing process, the remedies assisting the person (or animal) to regain health by stimulating natural healing forces. They appear to trigger off a healing response which results in a cure. As one of the principles of homoeopathy is that people and animals vary in their response to an illness according to their temperament, it follows that a homoeopathic veterinarian will not, as a matter of course, prescribe

HOMOEOPATHIC REMEDIES

Aconite For fright and shock; at the onset of feverish conditions

Arnica For bruising; to help promote rapid healing after accident or injury; for wasp and bee stings; before and after tooth extraction

Arsen alb For vomiting and diarrhoea

Calendula and hypericum mother tincture A combination used as an antiseptic and mouthwash

Gelsemium For timidity and nervousness; for feverish and restless states

Ignatia For pining, for example, when in boarding kennels

Nux vom For poor appetites, for digestive upsets and constipation; for the touchy, irritable animal

Rhus tox For rheumatic conditions, particularly after exposure to damp and cold

Sulphur For skin conditions, such as eczema

a specific remedy for a particular illness, but will try to discover the animal's temperament and responses, so that a prescription can be made on an individual basis.

As far as safety is concerned, homoeopathic remedies are diluted to such an extent during preparation that there are no side effects, and they are non-addictive. A child accidentally using a pet's medication would not be harmed.

Treatments come in the form of tablets, powders, pillules, tinctures, lotions and ointments. These are highly acceptable to animals, and not all internal treatments need be swallowed as some medications are absorbed through the surface of the mouth.

Homoeopathic remedies are produced in different potencies—in other words, the basic or mother tincture is processed in the laboratory to varying concentrations. The '6C' potency is usually recommended for the home treatment of pets.

Potencies of greater than 30C should not be used except under the guidance of a veterinarian, and mother tinctures should never be applied to the eyes in an undiluted form.

Homoeopathy has proved to be effective over the last two centuries, and has often succeeded where other forms of treatment have failed. It has been noticed by many owners of animals which have received homoeopathic treatment that the temperament and general appearance of their pets have improved.

Many pharmacies now stock a wide range of homoeopathic remedies suitable for animals and owners alike. The table lists a number of such remedies and their uses. Further information may also be had from specific bodies, such as the Homoeopathic Development Foundation in London and the Homoeopathic Educational Service in California, which operate comprehensive information services.

CONTROL OF BREEDING

If you do not wish to breed from your bitch—and it is never advisable to do so at her first season—there are a number of options open to you. The bitch comes into season generally every six months, the heat period being approximately three weeks, during which time she is capable of conception. At other times of the year a bitch is unlikely to attract the opposite sex. But during the height of her season she will go to any lengths to escape and find a mate, regardless of the relative size or breed of her prospective suitor.

A veterinarian can prescribe tablets that will delay a bitch's season, or the animal can be given an injection that will eliminate her seasons for a time without ill effect on her health or future ability to produce litters. Both these courses, however, could prove rather expensive.

Alternatively, a bitch on heat can be kept securely confined during her season except for exercise periods, during which she should remain strictly on the lead while the owner keeps a sharp look out for canine suitors. A final option is for the owner to decide to have the bitch spayed (having her ovaries and uterus removed) by a veterinarian.

Spaying is unlikely to have an adverse affect on a bitch's health, though there *could* be a tendency for her to put on weight if diet and exercise are not carefully controlled. Also, spayed bitches may not be accepted for exhibition in the show ring. But with so many unwanted puppies being born, spaying is a practice that is widely advocated.

Mis-mating

If a bitch is inadvertently mated, it is possible for the pregnancy to be terminated by a veterinarian administering an injection within 36 hours. This does not affect the bitch's ability to produce future litters. However, she must not be aborted twice in any one season. Termination usually increases the normal period of the season. Should a bitch of pure breeding produce a mixed litter as a result of mis-mating, there is no truth in the old adage that she is ruined for further planned breeding.

Neutering the dog

Although not so widely practised as spaying, castration of the dog is sometimes carried out, particularly if an animal has a reputation as a fighter, or attempts to mount every visitor's leg—much to the embarrassment of both the dog's owner and the visitor—though this latter activity, which is most prevalent in adolescent dogs, may be eradicated by proper training. (Alternatively, an injection or course of tablets may be advocated by your veterinarian for an aggressive, straying or over-sexed dog.) Castration is sometimes the only answer where a dog that is not wanted for stud purposes is living in the same house or kennel as an unspayed bitch.

HEALTH RISKS TO HUMANS

Health risks associated with the keeping of healthy dogs are minimal. Those that exist have, in recent years, been exaggerated by the anti-dog lobby. Provided that a dog is healthy, wormed and vaccinated, and that its home is run under hygienic conditions, even slight risks should be eliminated. Normal precautions to be taken by owners include the washing of hands after handling a dog, immediate cleaning of soiled premises and the separate cleaning of the animal's feeding bowl. It would be foolish, however, to deny that some risks do exist.

Below: Dogs and humans live together in harmony. Vaccination, worming, good health and hygiene ensure minimal risk to families.

Roundworm infection

Roundworms are usually found in young puppies, and on rare occasions the larvae can infect humans. The infection can only be passed into the body via the mouth; for example, a child who plays in a sand pit where an infected dog has excreted, and who subsequently puts its fingers in its mouth, runs the risk of infection. Symptoms of toxocara infection in humans is highly variable; in children abdominal pain and visual problems can be the first signs. To minimize the risk of infection it is therefore important that dogs are properly wormed. Most puppies become infected inside the womb or when suckling, with the result that, without treatment, they will be passing out worm eggs by the time they are four or five weeks old. The bitch herself may also be excreting eggs during lactation.

Tapeworm infection

Some types of tapeworm infect both dogs and humans, though the incidence of human infection is low. Hydatid disease is the name given to infection with the dog tapeworm *Echinococcus granulosis*. The adult stage of this particular tapeworm is very small, only 0·2in (5mm), but the intermediate stage, found mainly in sheep in the form of cysts in the liver and lungs, can be quite large. Infection in people can be acquired from infected dogs and the condition produces cysts as in sheep. Admittedly the cases are rare, and these mainly in areas where there is a close association between humans, dogs and sheep.

The most common dog tapeworm is *Dipylidium caninum*. However, the cases of human infection are very few indeed. The life cycle of the parasite involves an intermediate stage in a flea, and for humans to become infected, they would literally have to swallow a flea!

Other problems

Despite the disproportionate press coverage given to toxocariasis (infection with toxocara roundworm larvae), by far the more common and harmful disease that humans catch from animals is salmonellosis, caused by the bacterium *Salmonella*. The majority of *Salmonella* infections are food-borne and are not directly attributable to contact with infected animals. Indeed, with an infected dog, the risk of transmission to humans is low and is only likely to occur if sensible hygienic precautions such as the washing of hands are neglected.

Ringworm is a fungal infection that can be contracted from dogs amongst other sources, the most likely species being *Microsporum canis*. Because of the risks involved, it is important that a veterinarian is consulted at the first sign of any skin complaint.

External parasites such as fleas and mites can also cause skin irritation and allergies in humans.

Right: Hospital pens are custombuilt for short-term occupation, and are both compact and easy to clean.

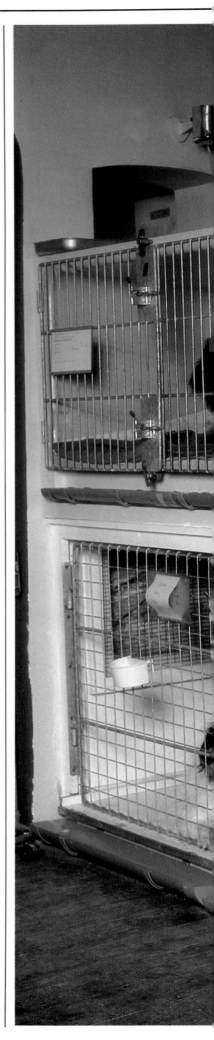

6

Obedience Training

A dog's formal training does not begin until it is six months of age, but prior to this there are many lessons to be learnt. First and foremost a young puppy must be taught to perform its toilet in the correct place. It must also learn to respond to its name and become accustomed to wearing its collar and lead.

Once it is old enough, every dog should be taught to respond to the basic commands: 'sit', 'down', 'come', 'stay' and 'heel'. In certain circumstances, instant obedience to one of these commands may save a dog's life, particularly where a collision with a car seems imminent. But training need not stop there. There are many more advanced exercises which a dog must learn if it is to compete in obedience trials, such as scent discrimination, retrieve, and the 'down-stay' for up to 10 minutes' duration. It is up to the owner to decide how far he or she wishes to progress with the training.

Right: Early lead training is given at home before a pup is taken onto the street.
Below: Dog training classes help to train the handler as well as the dog.

Tempting though it may be to permit a puppy to do as it wishes, training—in easy stages—is essential. Dogs are pack animals accustomed to the dictates of a leader. In any situation where a number of dogs are kept, such as in breeding kennels, it is easy to define the 'boss' dog from which the others take a lead, and to mark out its likely successors. In a domestic environment the companion dog looks to its human master for authority and leadership. A well trained dog is therefore a 'happy' dog, and is not only a pleasure to its handler, but can also be a pleasure to other people who have to share its environment.

Naming your dog

It is important to give your puppy a name before progressing with its training; your dog must be familiar with its name so that it is left in no doubt, when you issue a command prefaced by 'Bob', 'Jet' or 'Nell', that you are referring to it. Try to avoid fancy names containing several syllables and restrict your choice to those such as Ben, Moss, Jill, Red and others which are easy to deliver—and for the dog to recognize. You should then use the chosen name whenever you refer to the dog: 'Good boy Ben', 'Shall we take a walk now, Ben?'.

We have all heard proud owners remark that their dog understands every word they say. Dogs cannot, in fact, understand the meaning of words but they do associate sounds with actions, so that the dog told to get its 'lead', come and have its 'dinner', or go to 'bed', soon associates the emphasized, often repeated, word with an action or event.

House-training

House-training, or house-breaking as it is called in America, should begin almost from the moment the puppy arrives in its new home. It is vital for the owner to understand that some dogs—and indeed certain breeds—have a higher intelligence quotient than others and that, even in the matter of toilet training, one puppy may learn in a fortnight what it could take another several months to grasp. However, the slowest of learners may eventually turn out to be the cleanest of dogs.

You cannot put your puppy in its basket at night and expect it to be clean until morning. Puppies cannot control the urge of nature as long as adult dogs, nor should they be expected to do so. But by carrying out the following steps it should be possible to house-train your puppy as speedily, and with as little upset, as possible.

Having positioned the basket in a draught-free place, cover the surrounding floor area with newspaper. Place the puppy onto the paper after each drink, or meal, praising it lavishly when it performs its toilet. You should also put the puppy onto the paper after each mishap or when it is preparing to evacuate elsewhere. The circling movement of a pup about to squat will soon become easy to recognize.

Once the puppy has learnt what

Above: A sternly voiced reprimand combined with a pointing finger is enough to let this Beagle pup know that it has done something wrong.

Below: This pup should be praised for learning so young to relieve itself outdoors and on the grass border—a first step to kerb training.

Right: A puppy being walked in town must be kept on the lead at all times. It should be given gutter-training and become accustomed to traffic.

the paper is there for, the paper should be moved close to the door which leads into the yard or garden. When the puppy has got into the habit of toddling to the door you can open it and encourage the pup to perform its toilet out of doors. Before long the puppy will stand at the door whenever it wants to be let out. You should also put the puppy out for a few minutes after each meal or drink, and first thing in the morning and at bed-time.

The owner without a garden, or yard, has a more difficult problem, particularly as, on no account, should the pup be allowed to venture out into the street until after its routine inoculations have taken effect. In such circumstances, newspaper should be laid as before, and the pup should be encouraged to perform its toilet in a cat litter tray.

Always praise lavishly when your puppy has performed in the correct place, uttering the words 'Good boy' (or 'girl') and, most importantly, the pup's name. The puppy wants only to learn, and to please you.

An owner should never resort to slaps, or the unhygienic habit of rubbing the pup's nose in its own faeces when there has been a mishap. Tone of voice should be sufficient admonishment.

Bed-time

It is a mistake to allow a small pup to snuggle down at the foot of your bed in the belief that, in a week or two, it can be transferred to its designated quarters. If you take this course of action the pup, once dismissed to the kitchen (or kennel) will constantly endeavour to be reinstated at close proximity to you. You would also be performing a disservice to the pup. If it can attain a degree of independence this will prove beneficial should you, at some future date, have to leave it in the care of another person, or in boarding kennels.

When the time comes to say 'Goodnight', you must do so firmly, but gently. First make sure that there is nothing in the room against which the pup could fall and injure itself, or that it might chew, then lay the puppy gently in its bed and tuck a warm, hot water bottle under the bedding. This will provide comfort and warmth similar to that which the pup derived from its mother and litter brothers and sisters. You may also like to tuck a small alarm clock into the basket—the puppy will associate the ticking with the beating of its mother's heart, and this will help to comfort it. Then, having left a bowl of water within close proximity, say 'Goodnight' firmly, and put out the light.

You may not hear a whimper until morning. More likely, if the puppy has been receiving a lot of attention it will, on finding itself deserted, set up a plaintive howl. If you must rise from your bed, lift a finger to your mouth very sternly as you warn the puppy to 'be quiet'. Do not give in or return a second time. Once a ritual has been established, the puppy will soon reconcile itself and stay peacefully in its own bed until morning.

Early lead training

Although the pup must not be taken out into the street until its inoculations have taken effect, the early weeks present a good opportunity for the owner to accustom it to wearing a collar and lead.

You should start by using a soft collar and lead, making sure you do not fasten the collar too tightly—as a rule there should be enough slack to enable you to slip two fingers beneath the collar. Let the pup toddle about wearing the collar and lead for short periods of time, taking care that is does not trip up or get the lead caught on anything.

Once the puppy has learnt to accept the collar and lead, you can begin to accustom it to positioning itself by your side. You can do this by placing the puppy well in front of you and offering it a treat in your left hand. Then, holding the lead in your right hand you should draw the puppy gently towards you, saying 'Good boy' (or 'girl') as you do so. Once the pup is readily coming to your left hand side, you can move gradually backwards, increasing the space the pup must cover to reach you. Soon you will be able to revert to leading the puppy on your left hand side in preparation for teaching it to walk at heel.

Above: At a training class dogs are made to sit, with their owners in attendance ready to discourage distractions from neighbouring dogs.

Below: Having successfully completed an exercise the dogs are praised and given a rest. Such breaks help to stop them getting bored.

Above right: These dogs are learning to sit-stay. During this exercise they are expected to obey commands without distraction from neighbours.

Below right: Dogs are taught to walk to heel first on the lead and later off the lead, and must stick close to their owners' left knee.

Dog training clubs

Many people decide to enrol their puppy at a dog training class. However, it is unusual for such clubs to accept puppies under six months of age and, as there may be a waiting list, it is a good idea to make contact with a local club as soon as possible and perhaps to attend a training session as a spectator.

It is important when choosing a club to find one which operates in line with your special interest and that you do not enrol at a dog training club if what you are really looking for is a ringcraft class, better known as a showing or handling class in the United States.

Training clubs specialize in teaching basic obedience, in some cases progressing to competitive obedience and agility. The ringcraft class, on the other hand, prepares new entrants for the show ring.

The breed enthusiast who wishes to exhibit in the show ring will usually find the breed society knowledgeable about clubs within a reasonable radius that offer ringcraft training. However, such clubs are not as abundant as dog training clubs. It is sensible to check out the facilities offered by the various local clubs with the local reference library, the veterinarian's surgery or with local dog breeders or boarding kennels, who are generally well informed on such matters.

It is important to note that trying to combine both show ring and obedience training is not always satisfactory. The show dog, for instance, is required to stand for lengthy periods in the ring, whereas the obedience dog is more accustomed to remaining in a sit or down position. Such differences can prove confusing for a young dog.

Some dog training clubs are affiliated to the national kennel club, others are privately owned. Recently, in some countries, such as the

United Kingdom, clubs have been set up under the auspices of the local authorities who are anxious to promote pet owner education and canine care.

Most dog training clubs are, first and foremost, concerned with basic obedience, and teaching a dog to 'sit', 'stay', 'come' and 'heel'. Whether those who take advantage of the facilities will progress to competitive obedience must depend on the extent of their ambition, whether they have the right dog (in terms of breed and capability), on the club facilities, and on the experience of the instructors concerned.

Clubs obviously differ in what they have to offer and the length of the courses, but the following is an indication of what you may expect from an average club.

The club may offer an introductory course (lasting about eight weeks) which concentrates on solving problems, teaching basic exercises and enabling pupils to get to know the temperament of their dog.

The next stage would involve

more heelwork, introduce hand signals, prepare for handling off leash, and teach the retrieve. Following this, the more advanced stage would give instruction on send aways and more serious obedience work. Owner and dog would not be put into a higher class level, simply because they have attended the club for a specific number of weeks, until they have mastered the preliminary exercises.

When pupils attend class for the first time they may be given a problem sheet which lists various difficulties that can be encountered with a new pet, such as jumping up at people, barking excessively, and showing aggression towards other dogs. Attendants would be asked to tick the faults which apply to their dogs, so that individual attention can be given to their needs.

Some clubs have a road safety test after the initial course, during which the dogs are expected to cope with varying distractions similar to those which they might encounter on an everyday outing.

Where to start

You should begin to train your dog in earnest when it is six months old. The following are a few points worth noting before you start.

Who should train? One person should be responsible for training a dog, but all family members should be encouraged to take an interest.

Consistency Being consistent in the issuing of commands is vital. It will confuse the dog if one family member uses the command 'sit', while another uses the words 'sit down'. The table opposite lists the most common words of command and their meanings.

How often and how long? In order to train your dog properly you must be prepared to set aside a certain amount of time. Generally speaking, five-minute sessions given four times a day, or even two 10-minute sessions, are quite sufficient.

Home work Some dog training clubs give their pupils home work, with goals to be attained each week.

Where to train During initial training it is best to practise in an area familiar to the dog, and free from distractions, such as in the garden. Later training can be undertaken with distractions.

How to end the lesson A lesson should always end with a short play session, with the dog on the leash so that the owner still maintains physical control.

Wearing apparel Owners should avoid wearing tight-fitting clothes for dog training, and women should not wear high heeled shoes. Preferably, you should wear comfortable clothes and flat shoes or trainers.

Smoking People should not smoke while training their dogs.

Praise Throughout the lessons, and indeed for the remainder of your dog's life, the animal should be praised, using the word 'good' — 'good boy', 'good girl', 'good dog'. By the tone of voice the words should be made to sound sincere and meaningful.

Petting Verbal praise and encouragement is essential to training, but any physical expression of praise distracts a dog from its lessons. This is better left until after the successful performance of an exercise.

Nagging You should not nag your dog by continually repeating a command, for example, by saying 'sit, sit, sit'. You are virtually asking your dog to sit on the third command. Give a clear command to your dog, once only. If the dog does not obey a first command you should apply correction by repeating the command, and at the same time giving a physical demonstration of what the dog should be doing.

Know your breed Most novice dog owners tend to read up as much as they can on their chosen breeds. They should, therefore, know what their dog was bred for and utilise this knowledge in its training. For example, the Labrador Retriever should be exceptionally good at retrieving, the Shetland Sheepdog at heelwork and the Basset Hound and Beagle at following a scent.

Above: Play is an important adjunct to training as it maintains interest. Fun with a ball or stick is much appreciated by the young pup.

Right: Lavish praise must be given when the pupil has obeyed its orders satisfactorily.

Words of command

Come	Come to me
Down	Lie down
Heel	Walk on my left side
Okay	A release word meaning 'You can move now'
Sit	Sit down
Stand	Stand up
Stay	Remain in position

Just a game

In obedience training the handler must remember from the start that, to the dog, every exercise it is taught is another game. The mind of the dog is such that it is always striving to

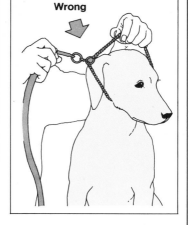

Wrong

Top: To fit a check chain, form a noose with the ring-loop hanging down. With the dog walking on your left, the chain will operate correctly.

Above: A correctly fitted check chain combines comfort for the dog with control for the handler.

Above: This chain is fitted incorrectly; it will not slacken when released and may choke the dog.

please its handler but as soon as the enjoyment factor goes out of training, and the game becomes a bore, the dog will lose its enthusiasm to learn and will start to misbehave.

The dog — rather like the small child who quickly tires of lessons — finds it hard to concentrate for long. Therefore, it is important that initial training sessions do not extend beyond five minutes. You can ensure that the dog has not forgotten what it has been taught by commanding it to sit at various times during the day. And, when it is playing in the garden and brings back its ball, remember that it is actually learning how to retrieve.

Equipment

During training the owner should use a 6ft long (1.8m) lead made either of leather or nylon. A 'safe' collar, usually a check chain, should also be worn by the dog at all times.

A check chain is a length of chain with a small ring at each end. To use it, you must double part of the chain through one of the rings to form a noose. Facing the dog, the noose should be slipped over the dog's head and the free ring attached to the leash. It is important that the noose is correctly positioned on the dog as otherwise it will not be effective. (For correct positioning of the chain see diagram opposite.) The ring through which the chain passes must be free to slide up and down the chain, so that when the leash is raised the noose tightens and when the leasn is lowered the noose immediately slackens. The chain must also be long enough to ensure proper sliding action, but there must be no more than 4in (10cm) spare when the chain is tight around the dog's neck.

To use the chain correctly, you should apply a forward guiding movement as you gently bring the dog up from the sit position and into forward motion. This action must be simultaneous with the word of command 'heel'. The action of the collar tightening round the dog's neck on the forward movement of the lead, and its release upon the dog obeying the command and moving with the handler, teaches the dog to obey commands promptly.

TRAINING YOUR DOG

The following instructions outline simple and effective methods of training your dog to obey your commands. The initial commands ('sit', 'stay', 'heel' and 'down') are an essential part of basic training which all pet owners should teach their dogs to obey. The more advanced obedience exercises are those which a dog must master if ever it is to be entered into obedience trials.

It is important to point out that just as one trainer may prefer to use a nylon collar and canvas lead, and another a traditional check chain and bridle leather leash, there is more than one way of training a dog. The best way is to begin by using a tried and trusted method and then, perhaps, as you advance, start to become a little more adventurous, finally settling on a combination of methods.

One of the things that will quickly be discovered is that most obedience exercises performed in trialling are merely an extension of those learnt in the preliminary stages, the main differences being that, as training progresses, these exercises will be executed with and without distractions, both on and off the lead, and on different surfaces.

It will be appreciated that a handler working a dog off the lead has a far less degree of physical control, therefore, the basic exercises must be completely mastered on lead before proceeding to a higher level.

Obedience training is a logical progression from one exercise to another. Timing is very important. While each exercise must be fully grasped before another is commenced, most exercises can be

Right: In obedience training a dog is always taught to sit on the left hand side of its handler.

broken down into parts and introduced as part of normal play before formal training begins.

Sit

To teach the dog to sit you should start by holding the lead in the right hand. Then, with your left hand, press the dog's hindquarters down, at the same time giving the command 'sit' in a firm voice. You should always keep your back straight while performing this, so as not to bend over the dog in case this intimidates it.

Once the dog has learnt what is required, it should be praised lavishly and may be rewarded with a titbit. In time the dog will learn to sit promptly on command without a lead being used.

Sit-stay

To teach the sit-stay, command the dog to 'sit' and, holding the lead in your right hand, move a pace to the right, watching out for any sign of movement in the dog. If the dog is unsteady, return to it and repeat the command. If it is steady, back away to three-quarters of the length of the lead, giving the command 'sit-stay' as you do so. Under no circumstance should you allow the lead to become tight as this will cause the dog to get up. Remain at a distance for a short period of time, initially perhaps counting up to five, then walk back to the dog and fondle and praise it. Whilst away from the dog you should not speak or move unnecessarily.

As training progresses, you will be able to extend the length of time your dog is required to sit-stay, and eventually the lead will no longer become necessary.

Right: The sit-stay command is given with the dog facing the owner. The dog must not move till commanded.

Teaching the Sit

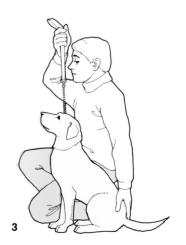

The sit is one of the first commands which all dogs should be taught to obey, whether a household pet or a potential obedience champion.

1 On the command 'sit', press the dog's hindquarters firmly down with your left hand while keeping the dog's head supported in the air.

2 Keep the lead taut in the right hand, giving it a slight upwards pull as you press the hindquarters down to help the dog respond.

3 Crouching down beside, but not over, the dog may prove helpful in teaching more unruly dogs to perform the exercise correctly.

Teaching the Sit-stay

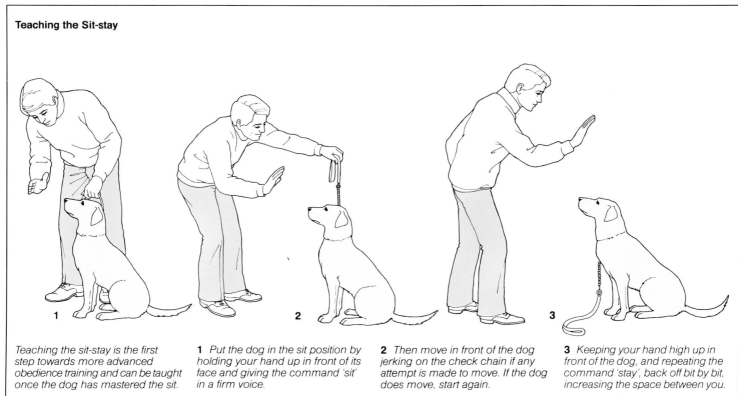

1   2   3

Teaching the sit-stay is the first step towards more advanced obedience training and can be taught once the dog has mastered the sit.

1 *Put the dog in the sit position by holding your hand up in front of its face and giving the command 'sit' in a firm voice.*

2 *Then move in front of the dog jerking on the check chain if any attempt is made to move. If the dog does move, start again.*

3 *Keeping your hand high up in front of the dog, and repeating the command 'stay', back off bit by bit, increasing the space between you.*

Heelwork

With the dog walking beside you on the left hand side, you should give a slight jerk on the check chain and use the command 'heel boy' ('heel girl') whenever the animal gets in front of you. This will have the effect of tightening the collar, causing the dog to fall back into place beside you. The dog must be kept close to your left thigh, and turns should not be attempted until the dog is competent at walking at heel. Nor should the exercise be attempted off the lead until perfected.

During heelwork it is important to give praise or otherwise at the right moment. Encouragement should be given while the dog remains at heel but if you have to correct the animal by use of the check collar, then at that moment your tone of voice should indicate displeasure. It should not be necessary to use more than a dog's name and the command 'heel', the tone of your voice should do the rest.

Down

There are several ways to teach your dog the 'down' command. One is to get it to sit at your side, and then gently slide its front feet forward until it attains the down position, remembering as you do so to give the command 'down' in a clear, positive voice, and praising the dog when it has successfully accomplished the exercise for you.

Another method of getting the dog down is to put it in the sit position at your side, and for you to go down on one knee with your left hand against the dog's shoulder. The right hand then removes the dog's left foot from the ground whilst pressure from the left hand pushes the dog down sideways. This should be performed with the simultaneous command of 'down'.

For many, the easiest way to get the dog down is to pass the lead under the left foot, holding the lead in the right hand. By pulling the lead and pushing down on the dog's back at about shoulder level with the left hand, and giving the command 'down', the dog should go into the required position.

The command 'down' is an extremely important one to teach your dog, as instant observation to this command can sometimes avoid traffic accidents, for example, when a dog is on the point of dashing across the road in front of an oncoming vehicle. Such incidents can not only mortally injure the dog but can also cause loss of human life if the vehicle swerves to avoid the dog and, instead, crashes into another car or pedestrian.

Down-stay

This exercise can be taught once the dog has mastered the 'down'; having achieved the down, emphasis must be placed on the word 'stay', so that the command becomes in effect 'down-stay'.

The procedure is taught in exactly the same manner as the 'sit-stay', the handler backing off a few paces then returning to praise the dog, gradually increasing both the distance and the time spent away from the dog. At first you may perform this exercise with the dog on a long lead laid out on the floor between you. But do remember that you must return to correct the dog each time it moves. Ultimately, the lead will not be required.

Above: When walking to heel on-lead, the dog should pull neither forward nor back, and the lead should hang slack.

Right: Police dogs are seen here in a down-stay exercise. The handlers will leave their dogs' sight and the dogs will 'freeze' until called.

Walking to Heel

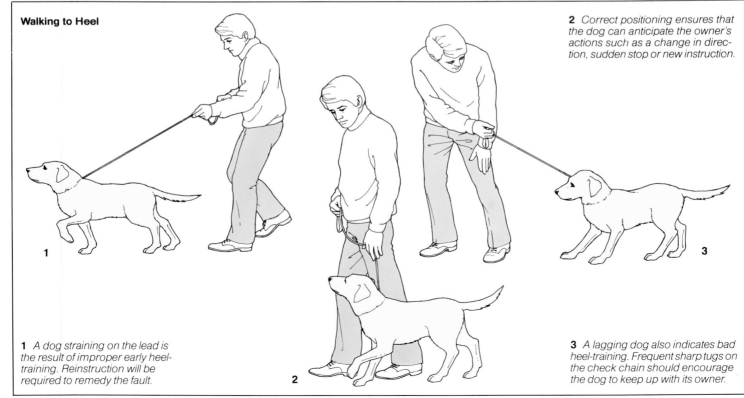

2 Correct positioning ensures that the dog can anticipate the owner's actions such as a change in direction, sudden stop or new instruction.

1 A dog straining on the lead is the result of improper early heel-training. Reinstruction will be required to remedy the fault.

3 A lagging dog also indicates bad heel-training. Frequent sharp tugs on the check chain should encourage the dog to keep up with its owner.

Teaching the Down-stay

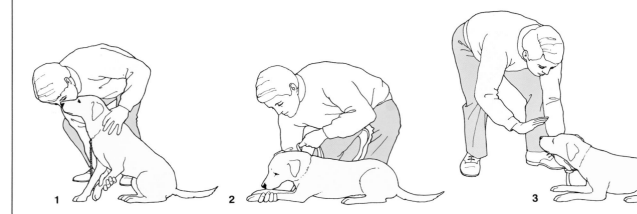

Above: The down-stay sequence is an extension of the sit-stay routine. Practise it till it becomes second-nature — this usually takes 3-4 days.

1 *Teach the dog the down position by sliding the dog's front legs forward and pushing the shoulders firmly down towards the ground.*

2 *The 'down-stay' command is then given to emphasize the position. Keep repeating it and try to avoid too much repetitive pushing down.*

3 *When settled in the down position repeat the command 'stay' and reinforce this by giving a hand signal in front of the dog's face.*

Recall

Most owners of young dogs have witnessed, often with something approaching helplessness, the sight of their puppy chasing round and round in circles after an outing, refusing to be caught or have its lead put on, and frequently making the owner look ridiculous.

When the wayward dog is finally captured the natural reaction may be to reprimand it severely. Yet such treatment, especially if repeated on a number of occasions, is likely to have the reverse effect, for the dog will associate the action of returning to its handler with that of a reprimand. The whole essence of training is based on love, praise and reward. If, when the dog finally returns, it is praised, the action will have a pleasurable association.

To teach this exercise the 'sit' and 'down-stay' must first be mastered. Then, using the command 'sit' followed by the command 'wait' you should back away from the dog to the extent of the lead, being careful not to pull the lead tight until you command the dog to 'come'. The command should be given in an inviting tone encouraging the dog to come quickly to you. The command 'sit' should be given as the dog arrives in front of you and this may be reinforced by pushing the dog into the sit position with the left hand.

Should the dog anticipate the command of 'come', you must not make too much of this otherwise problems may arise later. Take the dog back quietly and give it a firm command of 'sit'.

For competitions emphasis should be made here of the importance of getting the dog to sit straight in front of the handler. Care should be taken not to handle the dog too much in doing so as this is likely to be counter-productive. Instead, you should take half a pace back with one foot and guide the dog into

the space created, the other foot acting as a guide for the dog, thereby encouraging it to sit straight.

Down, out of sight

Once your dog has mastered the 'down-stay' you may like to issue the command while you slip out of sight for a few moments, remembering as you do so not to speak or look directly at your dog, or give any sign or movement similiar to the action of doing the recall.

Your dog will eventually learn to 'down-stay' for considerable periods of time. Indeed, once you begin to take its response for granted you could, if you are not careful, forget that your well trained dog is still 'on command'. On return to your dog you should use a chosen 'release' word to cancel out the command to

stay. Such a word should only be used for the purpose of releasing the dog from a previous 'stay' command, and only given when you return to the dog's side.

Sit-finish

One of the achievements that most impresses the obedience enthusiast is the way in which an obedient dog will, on completion of an exercise, return to its handler on command, do a straight 'sit' in front of him, and go quietly round the handler's legs to the heel position when that command to do so is given.

The dog will already have been taught to sit in front of its handler during the recall. Now it must be taught to go to heel on the handler's command from the sit in front. This can be taught as follows.

Above: To teach the recall, the dog is made to sit-stay on-lead and, on the command 'come', is encouraged to respond by a tug on the lead.

Right: The advanced pupil will respond to its summons without aids. It must recall unerringly and come to a sit finish in front of its handler.

With your dog sitting in front of you and the lead in your right hand, give the command 'heel' and draw the right hand back behind you, gently drawing the dog round. Passing the lead behind you into your left hand, guide the dog round on to your left side and give the command to sit. This must be done gently and with much encouragement.

Teaching the Recall

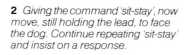

1 *Put the dog in the sit position and hold the lead in the right hand so that it lies slightly taut across your body. The dog must not move.*

2 *Giving the command 'sit-stay', now move, still holding the lead, to face the dog. Continue repeating 'sit-stay' and insist on a response.*

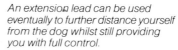

An extension lead can be used eventually to further distance yourself from the dog whilst still providing you with full control.

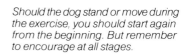

Should the dog stand or move during the exercise, you should start again from the beginning. But remember to encourage at all stages.

3 After a suitable pause, give the command 'come' and if necessary pull the lead towards you. Make a fuss when the dog responds.

If the response is slow, make an even bigger fuss and if all else fails, proffer a titbit as an incentive for extra encouragement.

Crouching down or retreating away often has the effect of hastening the response of the dog. But you should always be in control.

4 The exercise finishes with the dog sitting facing you, close and straight. On command 'heel' the dog must reposition to your left.

Sit on heel

The purpose of this exercise is to teach your dog to sit whenever you stop walking, for instance, when you stop to cross the road. At first your dog will not be accustomed to being commanded to sit while waiting at heel, though it will already have been taught to sit on command at your side. When the sit is incorporated into heelwork there should be little problem, though it may be necessary to go back to guiding the dog for a while, by raising the lead in the right hand and pushing the dog's hindquarters into a sitting position. Soon the dog will be sitting automatically when the handler stops.

Retrieve

Formal training for the retrieve can begin only when the recall is being performed reliably. Preparation can begin in play by getting the dog interested in fetching a variety of articles. Care must be taken to select articles which will build up the dog's confidence. In other words, you should not expect the dog to pick up any item which is too large, too heavy or awkward.

The exercise should be started with the dog sitting by your side.

Offer it a stick, a dumb-bell, or any particular article that the animal has shown interest in fetching and carrying. If the dog takes the article from you, you should praise it lavishly. Keep repeating this part of the exercise. Now hold the article just below the dog's chin and instruct the animal to 'hold'. If the command is obeyed, again praise lavishly before taking the article away from the dog.

Next, you should keep lowering the article until it is picked up from your hand at floor level, then, by stages, from the floor itself at distances of up to a yard away.

If work on the sit-stay and recall has been done thoroughly, you should now be able to command the dog to 'wait' while you throw the article a short distance and then to 'fetch'. On its return the dog should be asked to 'sit' in front of you so that the article can be taken from it. The animal must then be praised for an exercise well done.

Left: You can begin to teach the retrieve during play by throwing toys such as a rubber ball or a stick and encouraging your dog to 'fetch'.

Left: In the retrieve, the dog sits while the dumb-bell is thrown, and is then encouraged to 'fetch' by the handler pointing to the object.

Above: Having fetched the dumb-bell, without chewing it, the dog must sit in front of the handler, offering the article until it is taken.

Above: Awaiting command — scent discrimination is a form of retrieve.

Left: The dog is allowed some time to select the scented item before picking it up and returning.

Soon other articles may be introduced until the dog will retrieve any article on command.

Scent

To perform this exercise a dog must be taught to retrieve an article from amongst other similar articles by means of scent alone. It follows that the retrieve must be well practised before scent discrimination is attempted.

You can start the training by finding an article which is acceptable to the dog, perhaps the same item that you used when teaching the retrieve. Carry this item on your person for about a week, so that it is well scented, then place it on the floor with one or two well-washed, and unscented articles. To avoid scent contamination of the un-scented articles they should be kept in clean polythene bags until the exercise begins, and then tipped straight onto the floor.

Take the dog up to the articles and, starting with those which are unscented, command the dog to 'seek'. Encourage the dog to examine each item, and to pick up that which is scented. Once this has been achieved the item should be taken from the dog, and the animal praised.

Once you are satisfied with the dog's performance 'on-lead', you can proceed to send the dog to seek 'off-lead', making sure, at all times, that the requisite article is well scented. Practice will increase the dog's confidence so that you may gradually increase the number and type of articles displayed. When the exercise is going well you can occasionally practise with cloth articles in preparation for advanced competition work. In such competitions articles provided by the judge will be used. These vary enormously so your practice items must include a wide range of materials.

Advanced scent competitions vary from country to country. Typically, however, the dog must find an article, with the judge's scent on it, from a total of 10 articles. This is not an easy task, especially as false scents by other people will be included.

Send Away

This is an exercise which can be started in play at a fairly early stage; however, you will need a friend to assist you. Ask the friend to walk about 10ft (3m) away and call the dog by name. Now release the dog, giving the command 'away'. The friend should praise the dog for obeying the command, and you should do likewise to boost the dog's confidence.

In formal training the send away is taught by using an article, or marker, with which the dog is familiar, such as a piece of its bedding. Place the article on the ground and, starting from about 6ft (1.8m) away, give the command 'away' and guide the dog, on the lead, to the article. On reaching it, give the command 'down'. The dog should then be praised and the exercise can be repeated. This time you can move back to about 10ft (3m). When the exercise has been successfully repeated, you should start again, at the shorter distance, sending the dog 'away' off the lead. You must always set the dog facing towards its ultimate destination using both hands to point the dog's head towards the area where the article lies.

The distance can be lengthened by stages, moving the marker to different locations, all the while building up the dog's confidence in going away until eventually you are able to add the command 'down' subsequent to recall.

Distant Control

This is a fairly advanced exercise which, in competition work, typically consists of the dog obeying six commands given by the handler at the judge's instruction.

To perform the exercise the dog must obey the commands 'down', 'sit', and 'stand' promptly. The exercise has to be carried out from a distance of not less than 10 paces and the dog must not move forward in the carrying out of the commands. Therefore, the dog must be taught to obey the various commands while remaining on the spot.

Training should start by teaching the 'sit to the down', as already described on page 122. It is important to get the dog doing this movement without stepping forward or shuffling to one side, and the best teaching method to use is the one in which you put your left foot over the lead near to the dog's shoulder and take the strain on the

Above: The send-away during sheepdog trials. Here the dog is sent off on command towards the flock and is subsequently controlled by whistle, voice and gesture.

lead. You must practise this exercise before moving on to the next stage, but 'make haste slowly' – you must not let the dog get bored with any stage of the exercise. The dog must be given much praise to keep up its confidence.

To teach the 'down to the sit', hold the lead in the right hand, slide your right foot in front of the dog's paws, pushing them gently back at the same time using the left hand to pull the lead back and up behind the dog's head to give a lifting action. The command 'sit' must be given. This should be practised until the dog is working without help.

To teach the 'sit to stand', start by holding the lead in the right hand above the dog's head. Slide the left foot gently under the dog's middle, lifting the animal, and following this action by easing the lead backwards with the left hand.

The 'stand to sit' should be taught by holding the lead in the right hand, and using the left hand to bring the

Above: In advanced heelwork the leads are dispensed with – a natural progression from being on-lead. In competition, dogs are judged by their closeness to their handler.

lead behind the dog's head. Push the right foot up to the dog's front paws and give the command 'sit'. The dog should move back a pace in sitting.

Teach the 'down to stand' as follows. Hold the lead in the right hand and with the left hand move the lead up and back, moving the right foot against the dog's front paws as you do so, whilst the left foot slides into the dog's middle to urge it into the stand position. The command 'stand' must be given.

Practice all these moves patiently until you are satisfied each is being performed happily by the dog before attempting to move away from the dog's side. Do not rush this series of moves.

Once the dog is working well on-lead, the exercise can be performed off-lead. Step in front of the dog and repeat the commands, then slowly increase the distance between yourself and the dog until you are six, and then 10, paces away.

Heelwork: Turning Right and Left

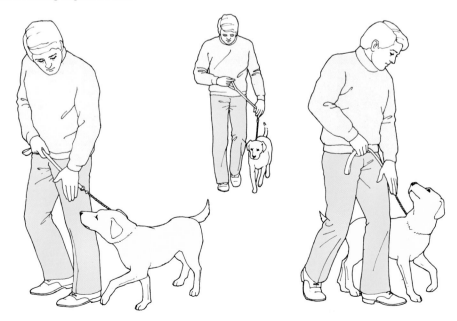

Turning right and left is instilled on-lead while basic heelwork is being taught. The objective is that *the dog must remain close — almost in contact with the left leg — during the turning exercises. This is done* *by constant use of the lead and check chain and continuous encouragement using the word 'close'.*

Advanced heelwork

This exercise involves off the lead heelwork at a fast and a slow pace, and may include left about turns and figures-of-eight. During the exercise the dog is required to respond to the commands of 'sit', 'down' or 'stand', in any order, whilst the handler continues to move forward.

As this is only performed in higher competitions, beginners are advised to wait until they are winning their way through the classes before attempting this exercise. If taught too early there is a danger of the dog anticipating the commands and slowing down in the heelwork.

The exercise is taught by taking one command at a time, the handler giving the command and stopping with the dog to see that the correct position is taken up. The handler walks round the dog, then stops again in order to get the dog to proceed. Each position should be practised until the dog is confident. Eventually, it will not be necessary for the handler to stop and circle round the dog. And soon, all the positions can be practised together. Timing of command is critical for this exercise — commands must be given at the exact moment you want the dog to stop.

AGGRESSION IN DOGS

Before advice can be given on controlling aggression in dogs it is first important to understand a dog's behavioural pattern. The dog, in the wild, is essentially a pack animal. The leader of that pack is the dog that, through brute strength, has proved its supremacy over its fellows. Even in the domestic situation those who keep a number of dogs soon get to recognize the pecking order; there is the boss dog, the second boss dog and so on. Such a system is nature's way of ensuring that the fittest of the species are bred from.

There are also unwritten rules within the pack. An adult dog is very unlikely to attack a puppy or an old weak dog, and will rarely attack a bitch. Two bitches, on the other hand, may be serious contenders.

The boss dog is treated with respect by the rest of the pack, even to the extent that members of the pack will keep their distance while the boss stands over a food dish, almost daring them to come forward. Similarly, it is not uncommon to witness a boss dog stand and intimidate a nervous dog, lower in the pecking order, by sheer presence alone, causing the latter to give up its position on a bed or cushion that the boss dog covets, and literally go and stand in a corner.

Having established, therefore, that there is in the dog a desire for dominance, it is essential that this instinct is not allowed to predominate when you bring home a companion dog. In other words, the dog must not be allowed to take over the dominant role, whereby the owner lives in nervous apprehension of the animal, and visitors are greeted with barred teeth. Such a situation is serious enough in the case of smaller breeds but can be positively dangerous in the case of larger, stronger breeds.

The human pack leader

Aggression in the pet dog should be eliminated from puppyhood, before a serious problem develops. While the sight of a puppy guarding its toy or bone may hold a certain charm, this same behaviour in the adult dog could prove dangerous. Imagine, for instance, a young child trying to take away a large juicy bone from an aggressive German Shepherd Dog!

Animals have a facility for detecting nervousness in humans. Because dogs are accustomed to obeying the dictates of a leader, human nervousness instils in them a sense of insecurity which, in turn, can lead to unacceptable behaviour. Therefore, once you have established the role of pack leader the relationship will be a more enjoyable one for you both.

Conversely, it is not advisable to be over protective of a dog. For instance, it is unnecessary to pick up your pet or cross to the other side of the street whenever you glimpse another animal in order to avoid a confrontation. By doing this you are merely convincing your dog that the other animal is an enemy. This will cause the pet to adopt a protective attitude towards you, with the result

Above: Dogs in the country must be trained to respect other animals. Initially, they must be kept leashed and commanded 'no-leave'.

Below: With two or more dogs, one will always assume dominance — a natural trait that stems from the dog's history as a pack animal.

that it will make a noisy and vigorous attempt to get to, and make short work of, any supposed aggressor.

Controlling aggression

How then should you curb the beginnings of aggression and cope with the occasional fight?

As in humans, there is variance in the canine intelligence quotient and in the dog's nervous reaction. Therefore, while with one dog the firmly voiced 'no', or the banging of a rolled up newspaper on the table, may be sufficient to make it instantly stop what it is doing (for instance, barking excessively or holding on to a bone and snarling), it may be necessary to put another dog firmly in its place — in other words, to put it in a position that is subservient to you by proving that you are the leader. You can do this by firmly shaking the animal by the scruff of the neck, looking at it unflinchingly while you do so.

Dog fights can also prove a problem. When a dog fight cannot be averted by a quick jerk of the lead, it may be necessary to throw a coat over the opponents, putting the animals temporarily off guard, so

Above: A dog being corrected for jumping up is made to sit and is given a verbal chastisement.

that you may quickly grab your animal from the rear. Cold water, if it is available, can also have the effect of dampening the combattants' fervour.

— The need for self expression —
While the excessive barker is a menace that must be controlled, the instinct to give a warning is a natural and useful one; it is the dog's way of attracting your attention for a number of reasons. There is a difference, however, between a re-minding bark at mealtimes or a warning when an intruder comes into the home and incessant yap-ping or barking for no reason at all.

Under extreme circumstances it is possible to have a dog's vocal chords removed, but this is definitely not recommended; a dog, like our-selves, has need to express itself. It is far better that a dog is taught from the onset when it should and should not bark, in other words, it must be taught to 'speak' on command and to 'be quiet' when commanded. In order to teach the latter, it is important that the dog first under-stand the former. This should not be difficult. Next time your dog barks,

you should praise it and give plenty of encouragement: 'Are you speak-ing, Jess?', 'Speak, Jess, Speak!' After a moment, raise your index finger, and give the command 'no' or 'be quiet' in a firm voice, making sure that the silence is achieved. Then, after a reasonable period, you can ask the dog to speak again until it will automatically 'speak' or 'be quiet' on command.

Punishment
It was mentioned earlier that the dog which, on returning belatedly ot its owner following a run, is rewarded with a severe reprimand or even a slap, will in future be less likely to respond to recall. This happens because the dog does not understand the real reason why it is receiving punishment. It can only assume the displeasure is associated with its own return. Similarly, if a puppy has chewed up one of your slippers in your absence, it will not understand its admonishment upon your return when it happily rushes forward to greet you. A dog must only be reprimanded at the *moment* of wrongdoing. It understands dis-

pleasure from the tone of your voice, and similarly praise and encouragement. When it does wrong, it must be left in no doubt of your feelings. Praise instantly when it stops off digging, chewing or whatever it was that caused your annoyance. It is in the dog's nature to want to please, not to offend. You must, therefore, never hit a dog. If a good telling off is required, a severe shake accompanied by the words 'no, bad boy' should be sufficient.

Remember also that dogs, like people, have a varying range of sensitivity and that just as one child may take a spanking in its stride and another become emotionally upset, there are those dogs which will go to any lengths to achieve their objec-tive, regardless of chastisement, and others which will flinch at the mere sight of an uplifted hand.

Bad habits
There are a number of other bad habits which are likely to evoke displeasure and which should be dealt with in varying ways. One is the habit, particularly in the young bitch, of relieving herself whenever she greets you. This does not warrant

punishment and on no account should any be given. Urination is the result of excitement. It is also a normal act of submission. In some bitches it is hard to eradicate, the best course being simply to ignore the bitch until she has got over her initial excitement.

Another annoying habit is that of young dogs who attempt to mount you, or your visitor's, leg in sex play. This act of sex play is normal adolescent behaviour which only needs simple correction. When it occurs, you should lift up your knee, say 'no' forcefully, and push the dog away. Providing you show your displeasure from the start the prob-lem should quickly cease.

Similarly, dogs that jump up at you or your visitors in greeting can cause great annoyance. This, too, should be corrected at an early stage by raising your knee whenever the dog attempts to jump up, stopping it in its tracks, and repri-manding it with the word 'no'.

OBEDIENCE TRIALS

Obedience trials are designed to test the ability of a dog and its handler to work together as a team, and it is this element of working together that makes the sport so enjoyable. Trials are organized by many kennel clubs throughout the world and though the rules governing them may vary from country to country, many of the exercises are basically the same — heel on-lead and off-lead, recall, retrieve, sit and down.

The Australian system follows closely in line with the UK system, whereas the American Kennel Club has a more extensive range of exercises which involves some agility, including the broad jump and high jump. The Club also includes tracking tests as part of the obedience trials system.

The United Kennel Club, the second oldest and largest all-breed dog registry in North America, also organizes obedience trials, along with conformation shows and working dog events such as hunting retriever tests and tracking events.

The Club is committed towards maintaining the working qualities of the various breeds and tries to encourage the 'total dog' concept — the idea that a dog must not only look good but also work or hunt well.

Obedience in the United Kingdom

The UK Kennel Club established an interest in obedience after witnessing the success with which dogs were trained during the First World War. Soon the Club had organized a series of trials in which dogs performed a range of exercises and were awarded points according to their merits. The rules now applying to obedience trials are given in full on pages 193-196, but the basic structure of the system is as follows.

In order to compete a dog must be a minimum of six months of age and must be registered with the Kennel Club. Spayed bitches and castrated dogs are permitted to compete but bitches in season are not. Handlers may only use a slip chain or smooth collar in the ring and are permitted to use a dog's name with a command or signal,

Above: In advanced obedience, the owner gradually slips the lead from the collar as an initial step in off-lead training for heelwork.

Top right: With leads still attached, the dogs perform the sit-stay exercise. One owner has returned to correct an erring pupil.

Right: A down-stay can last some minutes, with only minimal movement permitted. Handlers may be present (as here) or out of sight.

without incurring any penalty.

There are six grades of obedience tests, each grade representing a certain standard of training and cooperation between dog and handler. The stages are as follows: Pre-Beginners; Beginners; Novice; Class A; Class B; and Class C. Each stage involves precision control during the performance of the exercises and though the exercises are similar for all stages they do become increasingly demanding from one stage to the next, with the number of points attributed to each

exercise increasing accordingly.

The highest standard, Class C, is achieved by comparatively few. Each year, at some 40 Championship Obedience Shows throughout the United Kingdom, obedience certificates are awarded to the winning dogs and bitches in Class C trials, and any dog winning three such certificates earns the title Obedience Champion.

In most cases, the exercises commence and finish with the dog sitting at the handler's side, with the exception of the stay and distance control tests, and the recall for Beginners, Novice and Class A grades in which the dog may be left in either the sit or down position according to the handler's choice.

In the Novice Class there are seven exercises—a temperament test, heel on lead, heel free, recall, retrieve, sit and down. The temperament test requires the dog to be on-lead in the stand position with the handler standing by. The judge then approaches the dog quietly from the front and runs his hand gently down the dog's back. Any undue resentment, cringing, growling or snapping on the part of the dog is penalized. In the recall the dog must stay where it is until called and then respond promptly to the handler's command. The heel free exercise is to prove that the dog will obey the command 'heel' even when it is free of the lead.

In the Novice Class the 'sit' is executed for one minute and the 'down' for two minutes with the handler in sight. In Class A, on the other hand, the 'sit' is for one minute and the 'down' for five minutes with the handler *out* of sight. In Classes B and C the period of time for which the dog must obey the commands 'sit' and 'down' with the handler out of sight is increased to two and ten minutes respectively. These two exercises are intended to measure the amount of attention given by a dog to a command even when the handler is out of sight.

The various exercises in Classes A, B, and C, and their relative maximum scores, are shown in the table below.

Right: A dog obeys the command 'sit-stay' during an obedience trial, amidst the many distractions that such events involve.

Far right: The dog then exhibits a near-perfect sitting posture by its handler. This is, of course, the start and end point of all exercises.

Right: Many obedience shows are held on grass, out of doors. This gives rise to additional problems of distractions, especially with scent discrimination and distant control, which is the exercise this collie is undergoing. In competitive work, rehearsals and practise in fields are therefore of great importance.

UK OBEDIENCE EXERCISES

Class A

1	Heel on lead	15 points
2	Temperament test	10 points
3	Heel free	10 points
4	Recall from sit or down position	15 points
5	Retrieve	20 points
6	Sit	10 points
7	Down	30 points
8	Scent discrimination	30 points
	Maximum total score	150 points

Class B

1	Heel free	30 points
2	Send away, drop and recall	40 points
3	Retrieve	30 points
4	Stand one minute	10 points
5	Sit	20 points
6	Down	40 points
7	Scent discrimination	30 points
	Maximum total score	200 points

Class C

1	Heel work	60 points
2	Send away, drop and recall	40 points
3	Retrieve	30 points
4	Distant control	50 points
5	Sit	20 points
6	Down	50 points
7	Scent discrimination	50 points
	Maximum total score	300 points

Obedience in the United States

The American Kennel Club established obedience trials in the 1930s. The rules applying to these trials are laid out in full on pages 197-203 but the following is a brief explanation of the system.

In order to compete, a dog must be pure-bred, a minimum of six months of age and registered with the American Kennel Club. Unregistered dogs are eligible when an ILP (indefinite listing privilege) number has been issued by the American Kennel Club and may be entered indefinitely provided the ILP number is shown on each entry form. An ILP is issued upon adequate proof provided to indicate that the dog is pure-bred.

Spayed bitches, castrated dogs, monorchid or cryporchid males, and dogs that have faults which would disqualify them under standards for their breeds, may compete in obedience trials if otherwise eligible under these regulations. Blind or deaf dogs are prohibited from entry.

The obedience trials are divided into classes or grades of competition. Beginners compete in the Novice Classes. When a dog has won passing scores (170 or more) at three shows, under three different judges, it has earned the title of Companion Dog, and is entitled to carry the initials CD after its name. The next grade is the Open Classes. After a dog has won passing scores at three shows in these classes, it gains the title Companion Dog Excellent, or CDX.

Utility Class competitions follow. Three passing scores earn the title Utility Dog, or UD. Dogs which have won the UD title are then eligible for entry into the Obedience Trial Championship and having passed all the necessary requirements a dog will be awarded the title

Obedience Trial Champion, and will be entitled to use the prefix OTCh before its name.

Tracking tests, also run under the auspices of the American Kennel Club, do not take place at dog shows because they have to be run out of doors and are not, as a rule, considered a spectator sport. In this sport a dog may be awarded a T for tracking; or higher still, the title Utility Dog Tracking, UDT, if it also holds the title Utility Dog.

A perfect score in each obedience class is 200 points, a passing score being 170. However, no dog can qualify for a 'leg' towards its title unless it has scored more than 50% of the points allowed for each exercise of the competition.

There are six exercises in Novice competitions. If a dog makes a perfect score in five of these but scores zero in the sixth it could have a total score of 170 or more, but will still not qualify for a 'leg' towards its Companion Dog title.

Novice and Open Classes are divided into A and B, the difference between A and B classes being roughly the same as that between an amateur and a professional test. In other words, in Novice A and Open A the dog has to be handled by the owner or another member of the family. Novice B and Open B exercises are identical except that professional handlers and trainers can exhibit the dogs.

It is necessary for a judge to give a score of zero to any dog that fails to perform a principal part of an exercise upon the first command, and the judge must severely penalize the dog should it fail to complete any exercise. He will take

Below: Tracking in the United States is taught by long-leash methods. This does not unduly restrict the dog but gives the handler complete control.

Above: Advanced heelwork in America involves weaving, an exercise only seen in the United Kingdom as part of agility.

Right: A Shetland Sheepdog is tested on its advanced heelwork in Open Class obedience. It is performing the figure-of-eight off-leash.

off points should the dog appear sluggish, fail to pay attention to its handler, or be downright sloppy in its attitude towards the job in hand. Should a dog relieve itself in the ring it cannot make a qualifying score. The judge is also required to give credit in scoring for a dog's willingness and enjoyment while performing an exercise.

In the Novice Classes A and B the six exercises are as follows: heel on leash; stand for examination on leash; heel off leash; recall; long sit (1 minute's duration); and long down (3 minutes' duration).

The heel on leash is designed to prove that the dog has been taught to walk quietly at the side of its owner, not getting tangled up, and sitting when the handler stops.

In the stand for examination, the judge will touch the dog's head, body and hindquarters. If the dog sits during or before the examination, shows shyness or resentment, or growls and tries to bite, it will be disqualified and get zero marks. Slight movement of the feet, or moving after the examination, will bring lesser penalties.

The heel-free lesson proves that the dog will obey when free of the leash. In the recall the dog stays where left until called and responds promptly to the handler's command, 'come'. During the long sit and long down the handler remains in the ring, away from the dog, one minute for the sit, three minutes for the down exercise.

The Open Classes are for dogs that have passed all of the Novice requirements. No dog can enter these classes unless the American Kennel Club has awarded the dog the official Champion Dog (CD) title.

Dogs can be handled in the Open B Class by anyone. A feature of this class is that dogs that have won their Companion Dog Excellent (CDX) and Utility Dog (UD) titles may continue to compete in Open B. The exercises in Open Classes are similar to those performed in the Novice Class events.

Only dogs that hold the title CDX are qualified to enter the Utility Class. The exercises performed in Open and Utility Classes, with scores for a perfect performance, are shown on the right.

US OBEDIENCE EXERCISES

Open Class

1	Heel free	40 points
2	Drop on recall	30 points
3	Retrieve on flat	20 points
4	Retrieve over high jump	30 points
5	Broad jump	20 points
6	Long sit	30 points
7	Long down	30 points
	Maximum total score	200 points

Utility Class

1	Signal exercise	40 points
2	Scent discrimination:	
	leather article	30 points
	metal article	30 points
3	Directed retrieve of glove	30 points
4	Directed jumping	40 points
5	Group examination	30 points
	Maximum total score	200 points

Above left and right: In the retrieve over a jump, dogs must clear a hurdle both on their way out and on their return with the dumb-bell.

Right: The dog can lose many points if it drops the dumb-bell while jumping over the hurdle.

The signal exercise in the Utility Class requires the dog to obey only hand signals, rather than vocal commands. The directed retrieve is designed to test the dog's response to its handler's hand signal directing it to one of three gloves placed widely apart in the ring. The judge specifies which glove to retrieve. In the directed jump the dog is sent away from the handler, stops and sits on command, and jumps as directed. In the group examination the dogs are left standing near each other. The judge will examine each dog individually, as in a regular show ring, while the owners are some distance away. The dog must not show any fear or resentment of this. It must not move out of position until its handler is back in place.

7
Agility Tests and Working Trials

Competing in agility tests calls for fitness in the handler as well as the dog, for the former is required to run alongside the dog, against the clock, while the animal negotiates a prescribed course of obstacles. The choice of dog for this sport is all-important: sheepdogs predominate and the German Shepherd excels.

Working trials comprise a series of exercises designed to test a dog's breed characteristics, such as its ability to track, search, jump and retrieve. As in the case of obedience trials and agility tests, the ability of the dog and handler to work together as a team is an important aspect of the sport.

Tracking is performed both in working trials and in specialized events, and is also dealt with in this chapter. It is often associated with Bloodhounds, who are first taught the rudiments of the art as pups when they learn to play hide-and-seek with their owners.

Right: In agility, both the dog and the handler need to be very fit.

Below: The Bloodhound is a breed whose name is synonymous with tracking.

It is only in recent years that agility has been introduced as a competitive sport in the United Kingdom, since when it has also become increasingly popular in other parts of the world. Many of the obstacles used in agility today have been used in the past by the police, the Royal Air Force and certain dog training clubs for demonstrations. Indeed, the Royal Air Force Police Dogs Demonstration Flight appeared before the public to perform agility exercises as long ago as 1948, and subsequently took a tour of the United States.

However, it was not until 1978 that agility tests were first introduced at the Crufts Dog Show, using a method of faulting the dogs and putting them against the clock. With a few refinements, the Kennel Club legalized the sport in 1980 by drawing up a set of rules. The approved obstacles have been carefully designed to maximize spectator appeal and to minimize the possibility of injury or damage to the animal. Indeed, since 1980, there have been no recorded instances of damage, which is a credit to the rules drawn up by the Kennel Club.

The schedule of tests approved by the British Kennel Club are shown on page 192, though the rules are subject to some variation in other countries of the world. The schedule includes a list of the various obstacles which a dog must get over, under or through during the course of the competition.

Agility tests are considered to be a 'fun' type competition designed for spectator appeal. Anyone who is keen to participate in the sport should join the Agility Club, a club in the United Kingdom that has members world-wide. The Club can give help and advice on how and where to train, and also produces an informative, bi-monthly magazine.

Agility training

First and foremost, good control of a dog is essential before it can be taught agility. The animal must also be good at the 'down', 'send away', 'recall' and 'distant control' exercises. Teaching the dog to negotiate the obstacles is not past difficult; it is teaching it to do so accurately and consistently that is the hard part. And the hardest part of all in agility tests, usually overlooked, is controlling the dog at speed between each obstacle. This is where the classes may be won or lost.

One way to teach a dog to do something, such as jump an obstacle, is for the trainer and animal to do it together for the first few times until, with repetition, encouragement—and patience—the exercise is performed spontaneously.

If a dog is required to jump over a small fence, therefore, the owner, with the dog on the lead, should jump over it also. If a dog is required to jump through a hoop it should first be walked on the lead through the hoop which must be held at ground level. Gradually the hoop can be raised so that the dog has to jump to go through it. If the dog is expected to work its way through a tunnel there must be lots of encouragement from the handler and some incentive such as a titbit after the exercise has been performed correctly.

Below: Here a dog is seen leaving the rigid tunnel during an agility test. Confidence is essential if the dog is to keep up the momentum.

Below: The Crufts agility course, which varies slightly from year to year, is designed to demonstrate the dogs' ability and speed.

Right: This agility exercise consists of a tyre, suspended with its centre 3ft (1m) from the ground, through which the dog must jump.

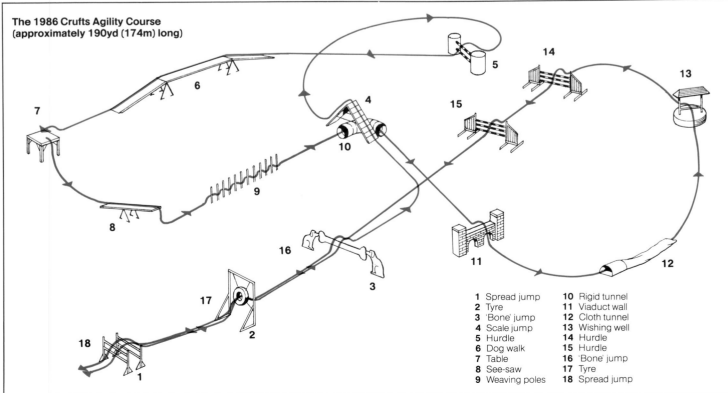

The 1986 Crufts Agility Course
(approximately 190yd (174m) long)

1 Spread jump	**10** Rigid tunnel
2 Tyre	**11** Viaduct wall
3 'Bone' jump	**12** Cloth tunnel
4 Scale jump	**13** Wishing well
5 Hurdle	**14** Hurdle
6 Dog walk	**15** Hurdle
7 Table	**16** 'Bone' jump
8 See-saw	**17** Tyre
9 Weaving poles	**18** Spread jump

Teaching the dog to negotiate the canvas tunnel

This agility exercise is best taught with the help of a friend. At first the dog will be suspicious of the tunnel, but with plenty of encouragement to give the animal confidence it can soon be coaxed from one end to the other.

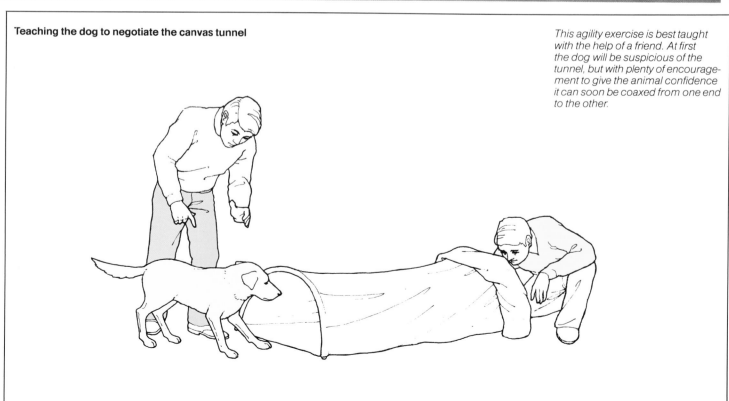

The procedure hardly varies in training dogs for a troupe in a circus where you can teach a dog to skip by first teaching it to jump through a hoop that is placed close to the ground. Gradually the dog will pick up the tempo and will eventually be able to jump over the rope.

It is important to remember during training that the dog's nature is such that it wants to please its handler. Because of this it is essential that every lesson ends on a successful note, even when a dog is experiencing difficulty with an exercise. If the dog cannot quite make a jump, the jump should be lowered until the dog has been successful, so that the animal can then be praised.

You can begin training by placing some obstacle at the backdoor and encouraging your dog to jump over it, letting the animal know what a 'good boy' it is when the obstacle has been negotiated. But make sure that it does *jump* over it, and not just walk round it.

Next you can make a little fence and jump it, with the dog on the lead, using the command 'up' as you both go over. It may be exhausting for you but is worth practising several times until the dog is enjoying the exercise and jumping readily. The dog should not be encouraged to jump the fence on the way back as this will teach it bad habits that would get it disqualified if performed during a competition.

You should next approach the jump with the dog as if you are also going to jump on the command 'up', but allow the dog to jump alone. The height of the fence can gradually be increased and the exercise practised until the dog is able to carry it out off the lead. Eventually, all you should need to do to get the dog to perform the jump is stretch out your right hand and give the command 'up'.

Teaching the dog to jump onto the table

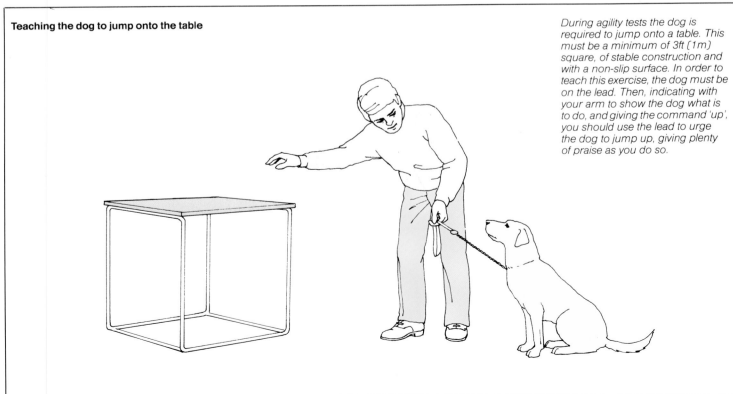

During agility tests the dog is required to jump onto a table. This must be a minimum of 3ft (1m) square, of stable construction and with a non-slip surface. In order to teach this exercise, the dog must be on the lead. Then, indicating with your arm to show the dog what is to do, and giving the command 'up', you should use the lead to urge the dog to jump up, giving plenty of praise as you do so.

Once the dog is jumping with ease it is time to think in terms of the long jump, the purpose of which is to ensure that your dog can get over a stream or some other sprawling obstacle in its path. Once again you can take the jump with the dog or, if you prefer, ask a friend to hold the dog while you make your way to the other side of the obstacle. The friend should release the dog when you call it, and you should give the appropriate 'up' (or 'over') command as the dog reaches the gap.

Left: A German Shepherd completing an agility high jump. The handler must be in control so that he can direct the dog to the next obstacle.

Below: During an agility exercise, the handler stands on the descent side of the A-frame and signals to the dog to continue down the ramp.

Some dogs have a greater jumping ability than others and it is interesting to note that while sheepdogs tend to predominate in agility tests, gaze hounds such as the Saluki, the Greyhound and the graceful Whippet appear the most agile of canines, capable of clearing a 7ft (2m) fence from a sitting start.

The highest obstacle to be scaled by a dog was a wall just over 11ft 5in (3.5m) high which was climbed by a German Shepherd Dog in 1980. Dogs should not, however, be encouraged to overcome such tall obstacles because the frequent impact of landing on the hard ground from a verticle height of 6ft (1·8m) or more can damage their shoulders.

The longest jump on record was achieved by a Greyhound in 1949, when one cleared a 5-barred gate and landed 30ft (9m) from where it took off.

WORKING TRIALS

Working trials are a popular sport in the United Kingdom where they date back to the 1920s when only German Shepherd Dogs took part. Today, any breed may take part, though German Shepherd Dogs, Collies, Labrador Retrievers, Dobermanns and Rottweilers are the most popular and successful breeds. Though working trials are also conducted in the United States, there is far less emphasis on them than on conformation showing and obedience trials.

Working trials are designed to make practical use of certain breed characteristics, such as scenting, retrieving, jumping and so forth, and the right sort of dog is essential in order to achieve success in this sport. Enrolment in a specialized training club where you can be

Teaching the dog to negotiate the A-frame

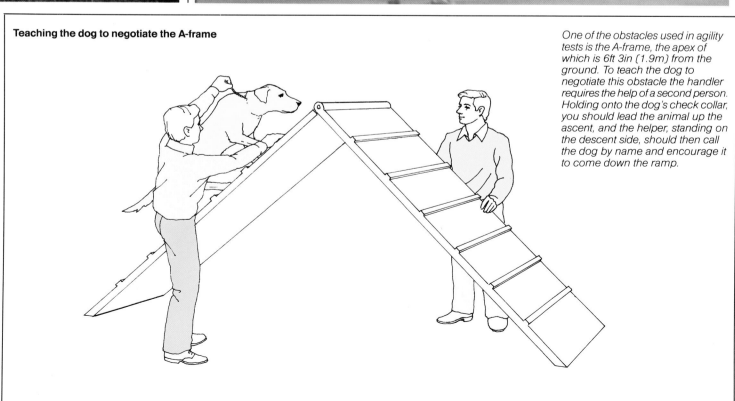

One of the obstacles used in agility tests is the A-frame, the apex of which is 6ft 3in (1.9m) from the ground. To teach the dog to negotiate this obstacle the handler requires the help of a second person. Holding onto the dog's check collar, you should lead the animal up the ascent, and the helper, standing on the descent side, should then call the dog by name and encourage it to come down the ramp.

given experienced instruction is also essential. The club will have the know-how to help you train your dog safely and will have the access to the sort of ground needed for searching and tracking.

The following is a summary of the various exercises that take place during working trials according to Kennel Club Rules in Britain.

Heelwork Performed both on and off the lead, this is to test the dog's ability to remain in the correct position. The dog stands on the handler's left hand side with its shoulder level with the handler's knee, and in this position must undergo a series of turns and halts, with commands and signals being kept to a minimum.

Sit- and down-stay Sit-stays of two minutes duration and down-stays of 10 minutes duration are performed, either in groups or singly. The handler must go to the place indicated by the judge until told to return. Meanwhile, the dog must remain in the sit or down position until released by the handler.

Recall to handler The dog is recalled from the sit or down position. The handler is instructed by the judge to stand at a given distance from the dog, and on the command of heel the dog must return to the handler at a brisk pace and sit in front of him.

Retrieve a dumb-bell The handler throws a dumb-bell as instructed by the judge. On command, the dog must move to retrieve the object, and on further command must return to present it to the handler, sitting in front of him to do so.

Send away and directional command The dog must confidently go away from the handler to a required distance, up to 50yd (46m) according to the test, and may be required to obey re-directional commands given by the handler at the behest of the judge.

Steadiness to gun-fire The dog may be on or off the lead while the gun is discharged, and excited barking, signs of fear or aggressive behaviour will be penalized.

Speak on command The dog is ordered to speak and cease speaking on command, and may be in the sit or down position according to the handler's discretion.

Agility scale jump The dog is required to scramble over the scale jump, the height of which is determined by the height of the dog at the shoulder — the height being 3ft (almost 1m) for dogs not exceeding 10in (25cm) at the shoulder, 4ft (1·2m) for dogs not exceeding 15in (38cm), and 6ft (1·8m) for dogs exceeding 15in at the shoulder. The dog and handler must approach the scale at a walking pace and halt at a determined distance. The dog is then ordered to scale the jump and on reaching the other side must stay in the down, sit or stand position as previously elected by the handler. The dog should then remain steady until recalled by the handler.

Agility clear and long jumps Except for smaller breeds, under 15in (38cm) in height, the clear jump usually consists of a 3ft (1m) high hurdle which the dog must clear from a standing start. The long jump is usually 9ft (2·7m) long for larger breeds, also taken from a standing

Right: During heelwork, dog and handler are directed by the steward to proceed forwards, the dog staying close to the handler's left leg.

Teaching the dog the long jump

To teach the long jump, the handler must accompany the dog alongside the jump, using the lead to control and encourage the animal over the length of the obstacle.

Above: The dog sits directly in front of the handler to present the dumb-bell during the retrieve.

Left: Obedience trials in America include exercises similar to those found in UK working trials, only here dogs must learn to retrieve over a jump as well as on the flat.

start. The handler may approach these jumps with the dog or may stand by the jumps and command the dog to jump. Once the dog has cleared a jump it should remain steady on the other side until joined by the handler.

Searching The dog is required to search an area 15yd (14m) square or 25yd (23m) square according to the test being taken. Three or four articles are positioned in the area and the dog must locate two of them to qualify. A time limit of four or five minutes is given to this exercise.

Tracking On the day prior to the trial, the steward lays the track, which may be a single line or include turns. The dog must follow the track and find the well-scented articles which have been left there.

TRACKING

In the minds of most people tracking is synonymous with the Bloodhound. It conjures up an immediate image of a pack of large beasts pursuing a desperate criminal over the moors. In fact, the Blood-hound, whose sense of smell is reckoned to be three million times more powerful than that of a human, is by no means the only dog possessed of scenting ability as witnessed, for instance, by the drug and explosive sniffer dogs who are trained to sniff out the presence of drugs such as cannabis, heroin or cocaine and various forms of explosives.

These dogs have the ability to recognize individual scents, and it is through channelling their natural instincts that they are taught to seek out the specific scent that the handler requires.

Dogs commonly used for this type of work include German Shepherds, Labradors, spaniels, pointers or any other bird dog breeds. In the United Kingdom, even an Irish Water Spaniel has been signed on for such duties.

German Shepherds are often used to seek out the elusive black box when an aircraft has met with disaster, and where wreckage has

Above and right: A German Shepherd Dog and handler practise tracking in preparation for a trialling event. The dog is on a long tracking lead and, despite the rough ground, is readily following the scent laid

two hours previously. During the actual trials the team will be followed by the judge, but here dog and handler are accompanied by an advisor who is commenting on how well both are performing.

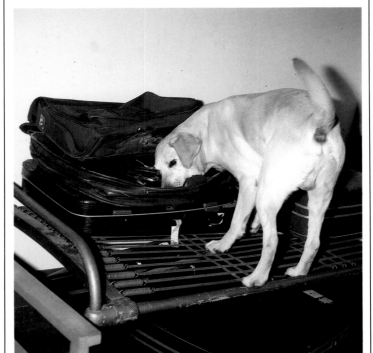

been scattered over a large area; in the United States they are also being taught to act as 'air scenters' in conjunction with helicopter and boat search teams.

The greatest tracking feat on record, in terms of a distance covered, was that performed by a Dobermann which, in 1925 in South Africa, followed a thief over 100 miles (160km) by scent alone.

The greatest drug sniffing dog recorded was a Golden Retriever named Intrepid, which could detect 16 different drugs and 11 different types of explosives. The animal was first handed over to the Dade County Sheriff's Department in Miami, Florida, in 1973 when it was four years old, and it discovered more than a ton of hashish worth two million dollars on its first assignment.

Left: A dog's acute sense of smell and its ability to distinguish between different scents is put to excellent use in the detection of drugs and explosives.

Scent trials

During tracking, or scent, trials the judge, dependent on his riding ability and the type of country being crossed, will be either mounted or on foot. Each hunt has a different line of approximately the same distance, a line being the scent where someone has walked and which the hound follows. The senior line is 3 miles (5km) long and two hours cold, which means that followers must set off two hours after the person laying the line has gone.

Time is a factor, though not the most important one. For a hound to become a scent trials champion in the United Kingdom, it has to win the senior stake twice under different judges, the criteria being that it must do the line without any assistance from the judge and must identify the runner at the end of the line.

Right: A young, inexperienced German Shepherd, wearing a tracking harness and on a very short lead, has quickly picked up the recently laid scent on the short grass.

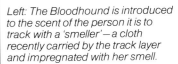

Left: The Bloodhound is introduced to the scent of the person it is to track with a 'smeller' — a cloth recently carried by the track layer and impregnated with her smell.

Training the young bloodhound

As with training for other sports, training Bloodhounds for tracking should be a game, though in this case it is a game of hide and seek.

The owner should hide while somebody unknown to the dog holds the animal. The owner then calls the dog so that it comes in search of him or her. Once the dog has got the idea of hunting its owner, the owner takes over holding it and accustoms it to hunting other members of the family. As soon as the dog has got used to hunting people it does know, it is put on to hunting people it does not know. This is achieved by leaving a 'smeller' behind — a piece of clothing, or perhaps a handkerchief which has been worn near to the skin so that it has become impregnated with the person's scent. This is held in the owner's hand and then left at the beginning of the line. The dog's nose is put down on the smeller so that the animal knows the smell of the person it is looking for.

Once the hound understands that it has to hunt a particular individual, the lines can be made colder and colder and should take in bends and go over obstacles. There are also other lessons to be learned, such as freedom from change, which means that the hound must not change on to someone else's scent, and freedom from riot, which means that it must not, in the course of its tracking, chase sheep and cattle.

The dog's instinct to track is there and it is up to the handler to bring it out. Different hounds are blessed with different abilities but few hounds are unable to track.

Equipment

Keen hounds should be worked in harness; it enables their speed to be controlled until they have settled on the line. However, the lead can be unclipped if desired enabling the hound to hunt free. The harness should be put on just before what is known as 'laying on' — the placing of the scented article at the beginning of the line. This way the hound will

associate the action with 'work'.

The harness for a growing puppy can be made from webbing, stitched in a figure of eight, with a buckled opening on the girth and a D-ring stitched to the cross-over point behind the shoulders. Once the dog is fully grown its harness can be made of leather or nylon webbing. The latter has the advantage of being resistant to mud. However, care should be taken that such a harness fits correctly.

The tracking leash should be approximately 10yd (9m) long, held high out of the hound's way so that the animal does not become entangled or trip over it. But it should not be attached to the hound's collar when working; if the dog's head is pulled up it will distract the animal from its work. The hound should be led up to the 'smeller' on the collar and leash and then the harness should be put on.

Bloodhound hunting

Another exciting form of sport is hunting with packs of Bloodhounds. One advantage is that it does not

Above and right: Trails are laid over as many different types of ground as possible in order to test the dog's scenting ability. Here the dog is seen confidently tracking across a stream and through thick woodland undergrowth.

upset the anti-blood sport lobby. Also, in the United Kingdom in particular, where railway lines, motorways, wire fences and other obstacles make certain areas of the countryside increasingly difficult for foxhunting, hunting with Bloodhounds has an added advantage in that the lines can be laid through terrain which is easily crossed and where farmers have given prior consent for their land to be used.

One reason why the sport is not perhaps more popular is that Bloodhounds are not really pack hounds and as such do not go in packs very well. They are, instead, hunting individuals who prefer to work alone, detecting cold difficult scents.

Above and right: The track layer lays the scent across rough ground and after a couple of hours, when the trail is two hours cold, the hound follows along the same route.

8

Sheepdogs and Gundogs

The televising of international sheepdog trials has introduced a new, widespread audience to the sport of trialling, resulting in the progeny of winning dogs selling for vast sums of money and being shipped all over the world. But, though training plays an important part in the development of a first-class sheepdog, the ability of these dogs to work sheep is instinctive; even a pup, for instance, the Border Collie will try to herd anything that moves and will crouch whenever it encounters sheep in a field.

Gundogs, too, have many devotees, which is hardly suprising when you consider how admirably this group combines the role of sporting dog and gentle family pet. Before training to the gun, these dogs must learn to distinguish various whistles and arm signals, and then, as they gain confidence, they must become accustomed to gun-fire.

Right: The Border Collie will herd sheep instinctively.

Below: A gundog is taught to retrieve using first a dummy and later a dead bird.

Sheepdogs were originally used to drive sheep and cattle to the markets and it was the role of the shepherd dog to herd, to guard and protect. Today, some breeds of sheepdog are no longer used for working sheep. The Old English (Bobtail) Sheepdog, for instance, once known as a cattle dog and guard, is now kept almost entirely as a family pet.

When talking about the working sheepdog, people usually think of the Border Collie, a dog bred for intelligence, speed and stamina. It takes its name from the English-Scottish border region where it originated. To avoid confusion when buying this breed, it is important to state its full name as several other breeds are also called collies, for example, the Rough Collie of American 'Lassie' fame, the Smooth Collie, similar to the Rough except for its coat, and the Bearded Collie which is really more suited to cattle driving than working sheep.

Sheepdog Trials

The North American Sheep Dog Society in Illinois has its growing band of trialling devotees. But the home of sheepdog trialling is the United Kingdom, where trials have been held almost annually since 1906 under the auspices of the International Sheep Dog Society (ISDS).

Each year in the United Kingdom there are four National Sheepdog Championships for Border Collies. These take place in England, Scotland, Ireland and Wales and culminate in the International Championships which are held in England, Scotland and Wales in successive years.

To qualify for entry in a National Trial a dog has to be entered in the society's stud book before June 1 of the year of the trial. The 15 highest pointed dogs in the English, Scottish, and Welsh National and the eight highest pointed dogs in the Irish National automatically make up the team for the International.

The International Trials take place over a three day period in conditions which resemble, as closely as possible, those which the shepherd and his dog encounter during their work in the hills.

The qualifying trials are run on a 'National' course. Five sheep are liberated some 400yd (366m) from the shepherd and his dog. The latter is directed to bring the sheep and goes off on a wide 'outrun'. The purpose of the dog running 'wide' (on the outside of the course) is, in theory, to shift sheep inside his run towards the middle ground so that when he 'lifts' (moves) the main flock any stragglers can be quickly

Right: In the qualifying trials the dog is sent out on a wide run to gather the five sheep and bring them through the gates to the shepherd. Following this, it must drive the sheep through two further gates and proceed to the shedding ring. Here, the dog sheds two of the unmarked sheep before penning the flock. Finally, it returns the flock to the shedding ring and singles out one marked sheep.

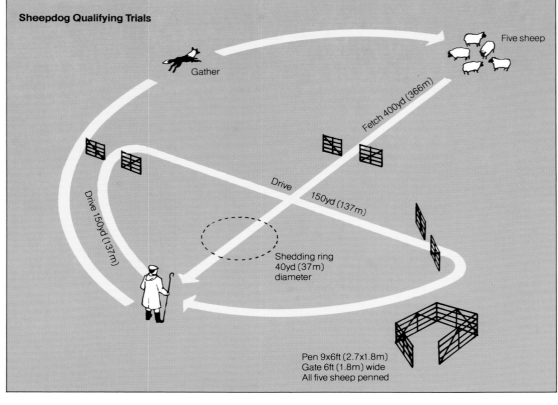

Sheepdog Qualifying Trials

Gather

Five sheep

Fetch 400yd (366m)

Drive 150yd (137m)

Drive 150yd (137m)

Shedding ring 40yd (37m) diameter

Pen 9x6ft (2.7x1.8m)
Gate 6ft (1.8m) wide
All five sheep penned

and easily collected. If the dog were to be sent directly, it would drive stragglers away from the flock.

Having completed the outrun, the dog arrives quietly behind the flock and waits momentarily for the sheep to settle down. It then approaches and 'lifts' its charges towards the shepherd, bringing them steadily in the most direct line to its master.

Once the sheep have reached the shepherd the gathering is completed. The shepherd next commands the dog to move the sheep behind him and then 'drive' them forward through a 'gate' which consists of a pair of hurdles positioned 150yd

(137m) away and 7yd (6·4m) apart. The dog must then turn the sheep across the field and drive them through a similar obstacle, again positioned 150yd away. The sheep are turned once more and returned to the shepherd where, within a 40yd (37m) circle called the shedding ring, the man and dog combine to 'shed' (separate) two sheep from the five. Two of the sheep are marked with red collars, and three are unmarked, and it is any two of the unmarked sheep which have to be shed and controlled by the dog.

Once this has been accomplished and the sheep are reunited, the

shepherd proceeds to a 9x6ft (2·7x1·8m) pen, one side of which is hinged and acts as a gate. Keeping the gate open with a 6-ft (1·8-m) rope, he then directs the dog to work the sheep into the pen.

The shepherd has to remain at the end of the rope to make sure that the dog does the major part of the work. Once 'penned' and consequently mixed up, the sheep are brought back to the ring where the dog has to 'single' (separate) one sheep from the rest. This time it has to be one of the two sheep marked with collars. The whole job has to be completed in 15 minutes.

Left: Having completed its outrun, the sheepdog crouches in position behind the flock, ready to lift it and drive it towards the shepherd.

Above: A sheepdog prepares to shed two of the unmarked sheep. In a working situation this manoeuvre may be used to isolate lame sheep.

Below: During penning, master and dog work closely together, the former holding the gate open while the dog directs the sheep into the pen.

Above: The 20 sheep have been gathered and are now ready to be driven through the gates. The dog must move steadily and confidently.

Below: During championship trials the dog must gather two lots of 10 sheep, going out first on one side to bring one group through the gates to a fixed post, and then out on the other side to unite the second group of sheep with the first. The dog then performs the triangular drive and proceeds to the shedding ring where it sheds off the 15 unmarked sheep. The dog finishes by penning the remaining five sheep.

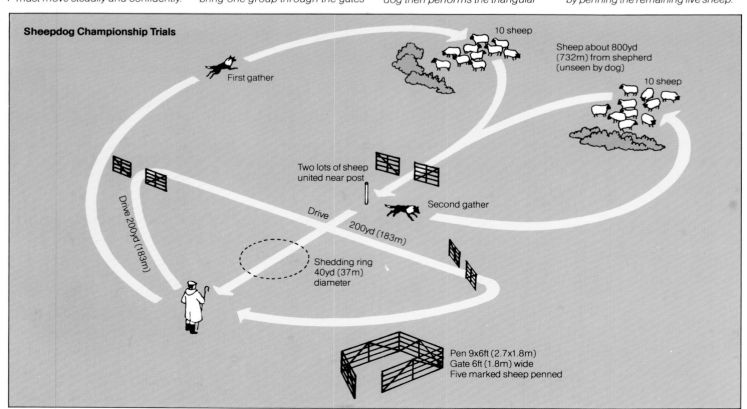

Sheepdog Championship Trials

First gather

10 sheep

Sheep about 800yd (732m) from shepherd (unseen by dog)

10 sheep

Two lots of sheep united near post

Second gather

Drive 200yd (183m)

Drive

200yd (183m)

Shedding ring 40yd (37m) diameter

Pen 9x6ft (2.7x1.8m)
Gate 6ft (1.8m) wide
Five marked sheep penned

On the third day of the trials the 15 highest scoring dogs compete in the championship event. The course has been increased to 800yd (732m), and the number of sheep increased to two lots of 10. The dog must go out on the right or left side as instructed and gather the first lot, bring it through the gate formed by the hurdles, and return on the other side to gather the second lot. It must then unite the two lots and bring them to the shepherd. Dog and shepherd continue, as in the earlier event, up to the shedding ring where 15 unmarked sheep have to be shed. The five marked sheep are then penned. The 'single' is not performed and the time limit is 30 minutes.

Marks are awarded in each section of the work—outrun and lift, fetch, drive, shedding, penning and singling—the manner in which the dog does its work and obeys the commands being of great importance. For instance, a dog which

moves sheep steadily and quietly without too many commands, but is unfortunate in missing the gate might gain more marks than the dog which gets the gate but rushes the sheep hither and thither and requires a lot of commands. It is the manner in which the work is done which really counts.

In addition to the single dog classes there is a class for doubles, two dogs working together being called a 'brace'. The work for this class follows the same course as used in the singles event, except that the dogs work on 10 sheep and are required to pen two lots of five on opposite sides of the field. The pens have openings only 5ft (1·5m) wide and no gate. The dog which pens first has to remain in charge of that pen, the shepherd and the second dog penning the remaining five in the other pen.

Sheepdog trials are essentially of a practical nature, the ISDS taking pains to discourage any

freak obstacles and circus tricks, their sole concern being the practical working capabilities of the Border Collie and its master.

Training sheepdogs

On average the working life of a Border Collie may be 11 or 12 years. Older dogs do not do the same amount of work as those who are still in their prime, but they have the skills of a lifetime behind them and are frequently used to help train the youngsters. The young dogs do the distance work in rounding up the sheep, and the old dog is then sent to bring them in. It will handle close up and do the shedding, which the younger dogs may not do so well.

The Border Collie's ability to work sheep is instinctive, for even as early as three months of age the dog will try to herd anything that moves, be it a sheep, a football or a person, and will crouch when seeing sheep in a field. Some may start working sheep as early as seven or eight months of age but it is sensible to let them come to the work when they are ready and not to rush them. All dogs are, after all, individuals and some mature earlier than others.

It would be impossible within the scope of this book to teach someone how to train a sheepdog but the advice given by the ISDS to anyone wishing to do so is 'not to overdo it'. Initially, you should work pups for very short periods of time, putting them round the work just to get the feel of them, and teaching them to go out on one side and then out on the other, to bring the sheep towards you (which is the natural thing for the dog to do) and to flank. Voice commands can be used until the dogs have got the hang of things at which point you can switch to whistle commands.

Only a few will make it to the top, but nearly all of them will make good working farm dogs.

Below: The brace trial is worked on similar lines to the singles trial, except there are two dogs and 10 sheep. With one dog on either side,

the brace must gather the sheep and then drive them through the two sets of gates. Finally, each dog must pen five sheep.

Above: Once the sheep are safely in the pen the shepherd shuts the gate and the dog drops down, still guarding its flock.

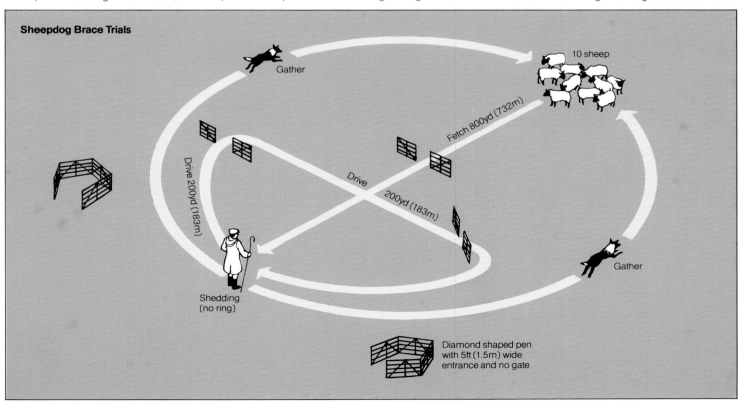

Sheepdog Brace Trials

Gather

10 sheep

Fetch 800yd (732m)

Drive 200yd (183m)

Drive

200yd (183m)

Shedding
(no ring)

Gather

Diamond shaped pen with 5ft (1.5m) wide entrance and no gate

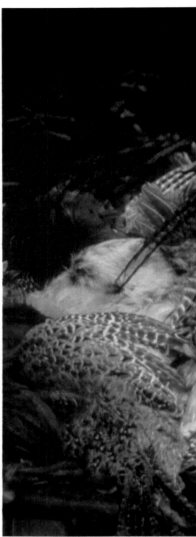

Left: The Yellow Labrador is a retriever which, having a short coat, is ideally suited to retrieving shot game from both land and water.

GUNDOGS

Gundogs, or bird dogs, are bred and subsequently trained to perform various tasks during the hunting of game. For example, the setter is bred to 'sett', that is, stand rigid on scenting game to indicate its presence and general direction, the pointer to 'point' — by its rigid stance indicate the presence and to point towards the position of game — the retriever to 'retrieve' shot game from land and water, and the spaniel to 'flush out' — drive birds from cover — and retrieve. Though each breed is renowned for a specific task, a good gundog will be taught to perform most of them.

The first bird dogs in England that were used for pointing were spaniels. And there exists evidence from as early as the 13th century that

spaniels were being taught to sett. The spaniel today is a good all purpose gundog, in its element hunting out rabbits and flushing out game, then remaining motionless until a shot has been fired. Early spaniels, however, were the forerunner of the setter.

The true pointing dogs were originally used to assist hawks and for netting game. In fact, it is thought that the tendency of present day setters to crouch when pointing is the result of having nets dragged over them during this latter form of hunting.

Pointers are said by some to have been of Spanish origin, brought to England around 1713 by soldiers returning from the war following the Peace of Utrecht. Some controversy exists, however, as to whether the Pointer did originate in Spain or was,

in fact, produced in England by crossing the Bloodhound, Foxhound and Greyhound. An authority on the breed, William Arkwright of Sutton Scarsdale, England, maintains that the Pointer originated in the East, found its way to Italy and then Spain — where it developed its classic head — and finally to Britain and South America.

The name English Setter is synonymous with that of Edward Laverack (1815-1877), a man who spent almost a lifetime breeding setters and who wrote in his famous work, *The Setter*, 'This breed is but a spaniel improved'.

The setting spaniel had been used as far back as the 16th century for setting partridges and quails. By interbreeding Laverack produced a strain that achieved not only the standard of excellence for which the

dogs were renowned in the 19th century, but also the standard on which the present English Setter was based.

Laverack's strain was to pass on to R.L. Purcell Llewellyn who ran and imported setters extensively to the United States and Europe. His strain is separately registered in the United States alone. The names of Llewelyn and Laverack are still in use in Europe today, signifying a dog's direct descendancy from Laverack's original stock.

The retrievers — the Flat Coat, Labrador, Golden and others — the Chesapeake Bay, which is a retriever of wild duck unsurpassed, and the fine Gordon and Irish (red) Setters are all bird dogs whose true purpose is not merely to locate game birds, but to find and raise them in such a manner that none of the shot birds is left behind.

Training Gundogs

In common with the pet dog that is learning obedience the gundog must respond to its name and learn the 'sit', 'down', 'down-stay' and 'recall' commands. Additionally, it must learn to distinguish whistles and arm signals (see table opposite).

Above: A Field Spaniel sits wearily amongst the day's bag. This breed is a good multipurpose gundog, efficient at both flushing out and retrieving.

Below: The English Setter has become very popular recently—apart from making an excellent gundog, its good nature makes it much sought after as a family pet.

SIGNALS FOR GUNDOGS

Arm Signals

Forward	Right arm by side, left arm forward
Right	Left arm by side, right arm extended
Left	Left arm by side, right arm across it
To ho (stop still)	Right arm by side, left arm held up above left shoulder
To ho (with gun)	Gun held in crook of right arm, left arm held above shoulder
Drop	Right arm up above shoulder, left arm by side
Drop (with gun)	Gun held upright in right arm, left arm by side

Words of command

No	Dead dead	To ho	On	Drop	Heel

Whistles

Drop	Short blast on whistle
Name and Come in	Repeated peeps
Look back and turn	Short blast, pause, short blast
Comeback	Continuous warbling note
On	Tweet tweet and hand signal

Left: The handler starts to train a young gundog using a dummy. This is first shown to the dog and then thrown a fair distance away.

Above: The dog must remain in the sit position until commanded to retrieve the dummy, then off it goes in hot pursuit.

In a manner not dissimilar to obedience training the dog should be taught attached to a long check cord so that it remains within calling distance. If, following a signal and the verbal command 'down', the instruction is not immediately obeyed, a quick tug is given on the line. Once the command has been obeyed the dog should be praised. With repetition the dog will, in response to the whistle and arm signal, immediately adopt the 'down' position.

The lesson should be repeated with a wider distance between dog and handler until, even when running free, the dog will immediately drop in response to a whistle or verbal command from its handler.

A gundog should not be introduced to guns until the end of its basic training for fear that the sound of a shot or of shouting will cow it. Getting the dog accustomed to the sound of gun-fire should be left until the dog has gained confidence. Later it must be taught to be 'steady' to gun-fire.

First of all, a shot should be fired with the dog perhaps in the 'down' position at a far end of the field. Once the dog's interest has been roused a shot may be fired a little nearer, with the dog still in the 'down' position, the handler taking pains to praise the dog on each occasion. Having trained the dog in this manner the handler will then progress by pretending to shoot an imaginary bird.

Quartering
By the time a gundog pup has reached 6 months of age it should be showing proof of its ability to scent, that is, to use its nose to recognize both people and objects. It is at this stage that a manoeuvre known as 'quartering' may be taught. Quartering is designed to enable the dog to drive the game up towards the guns.

As in all types of early training, sessions should be kept to 10 or 15 minutes' duration. Bear in mind that during the time taken for a man to advance 5-6yd (about 5-6m), a fast dog will move 40-50yd (about 40-50m) laterally. Thus, for every 200yd (about 200m) walked by the trainer his puppy may have run almost one mile (1·6km) and prolonged training at such a pace will soon rob a dog of its merry and zestful style.

A fine check cord should be used for lessons. This should be approximately 25yd (23m) long, attached to a slip lead. Handlers are advised to wear leather gloves. These prevent friction burns in the event of the check line passing quickly through the handler's fingers. Training sessions should take place in short grass, in stubble or in heather, not less than 6-8in (15-20cm) in height. If the height is less the dog will be inclined to put its nose to the ground, whereas if it is more the dog can merely jump over it.

The handler should face the oncoming breeze and, with the dog

Above: Having successfully located the dummy, the dog rushes back to present it to its handler, sitting in front of him to do so.

Below: A slightly more advanced retrieving exercise involves the dummy being hidden in woodland by an unseen party.

Above: As with all other forms of training, the dog must be praised when it has retrieved successfully. You should let it know you are pleased with it.

on a reasonably short lead, lead it on diagonally across the face of the wind. After proceeding a few paces he should give a double peep on the whistle and guide the dog into the wind, bringing it diagonally across its original path to an equal distance on the other side. Two further peeps and the trainer once again turns the dog into the wind and brings it diagonally back across the path. The whole process is repeated until the dog has learned that a double blast on the whistle is to be followed by a fairly sharp turn about, always facing into the wind.

The pattern is then repeated, but with the dog now being given more freedom on the check cord and being encouraged to trot. As the dog crosses before the hander, the handler must flick the check line across the dog's back to the windward side and then step forward so that, following the whistle signal, the dog may be guided into the wind and turned back across the mid-line.

Once the confidence of the animal has increased and, likewise, the pace, the handler will need but to flick the check cord quickly across the dog's back, and move forward several paces to get in front of the dog's beat, in order to get the dog to turn. Having blown the turn signal, the handler will need to move promptly in the direction of the dog so that the slip lead tightens only gradually about the neck, gently but firmly slowing the dog down and turning it into the wind.

Above: The dog, having been sent into the woodland area to find the planted game, may take a few seconds to pick up the scent.

This exercise should then be practised with a slightly longer check cord until the dog will successfully maintain its quartering pattern over an area which is consistent with a spaniel beat, approximately 20-30yd (18-27m) to right and left. Thereafter the pace should be increased and the beat widened until the limits of the line are used. Once this has been achieved the cord should be released and allowed to trail free. At this stage some handlers prefer to use a dog harness in place of a check cord to avoid unwarranted tugs on the dog's neck.

When a dog runs so close to birds that they are raised and scattered it is said to be flushing. However, if such a flush occurs when the dog is hunting upwind it is assumed that the animal has failed to detect the game or that it has flushed the birds on purpose; both these reasons are sufficient to eliminate a dog from a field trial.

When the dog runs downwind it is taken that it will not scent the game so easily, therefore a flush downwind does not constitute an eliminating fault. However, before a decision can be made about flushing of birds in field trials the judge has to consider the wind conditions.

Some young, inexperienced bird dogs may flush by drawing slowly into the birds after detecting their scent some distance away, but with practise they will learn the correct distance at which to stand and point game and, in training, it is best that they be permitted to judge the distance themselves.

Retrieving

You should not ask your dog to retrieve a dead bird until you have perfected its training with a dummy, both on land and in water. And some words of warning, never leave a check chain or collar on a dog when it is swimming; the dog might get a leg caught in a loose collar and drown.

Once you feel that your dog is ready to advance to retrieving the genuine article, start throwing a pigeon or a pheasant into long grass in the same way that you had the dummy. In its eagerness to retrieve the beginner dog may grab the offering rather clumsily, perhaps by a wing, so it is best in the early stages to tie the wings of the bird to its body or secure them with a rubber band.

The exercise should be repeated until the retriever has learned to roll the bird over and pick it up correctly. Otherwise it may have to literally stop and start in its retrieve as it tries to reposition the bird in its mouth, or tries to get a wing out of its eyes.

Do not allow your retriever to go after hare or rabbit until it is obedient to commands. Otherwise in its excitement it may run uncontrollably after the prey, oblivious to commands. A long, single blast on a whistle is used to command the dog to sit and await fresh instructions.

Field Trials

In the United Kingdom field trials take place in the field under shooting conditions for live wild game, fur and feather. The trial, working conditions and terrain are

Above: Once the dog is ready to retrieve the genuine article, a dead bird should be planted unseen by the dog in the undergrowth. Although possibly a little clumsy at first, the dog will soon learn how best to carry the game.

those appropriate to the game, the season of the year and the breed of gundog. Birds are free and the conditions are those that would be likely to be encountered on a normal day's shoot.

The field trials are divided into three main sections: pointers and setters, with a sub section for the German Short-haired Pointer and other similar all purpose breeds which have trials of their own; retrievers; and spaniels. All of these sections have separate functions to perform and have separate trials run under the requisite Kennel Club Rules and procedure.

In America, hunters, guns and spectators are usually mounted because the dogs hunt in taller cover than in the United Kingdom.

The American Kennel Club licenses four separate categories of field trials all of which are designed to test a dog's ability to carry out the job for which it was bred. Rules are different for each of the groups which are as follows: hounds in packs or pairs chase rabbits and hares; pointing breeds stop, point and permit the hunter to flush out game birds; retrievers fetch shot game from water and land; and spaniels flush game and retrieve.

Right and below: The dog returns directly to the handler and presents the bird, holding it in its mouth rather than dropping it.

9

Showing Your Dog

To spectators at any large dog show the art of exhibiting may seem easy; they may even wonder why the judge selected a particular animal when, in their opinion, another holds more appeal. But every breed has a standard of perfection laid down by the national kennel club, and it is the exhibit which conforms most exactly to that requirement that is selected as winner by the judge.

There is, as you will discover, far more to exhibiting than walking a dog in the ring. The exhibitor must prepare the dog beforehand and know how to present it to its very best advantage. Serious campaigning therefore involves a great deal of time spent on grooming, handling and travel, with exhibitors taking great pains to become established in their own breed, and often devoting several years to taking a good example to the top.

Right: A Samoyed receives some last minute preparation before entering the ring.
Below: A Coonhound takes up its show stance to display its good points.

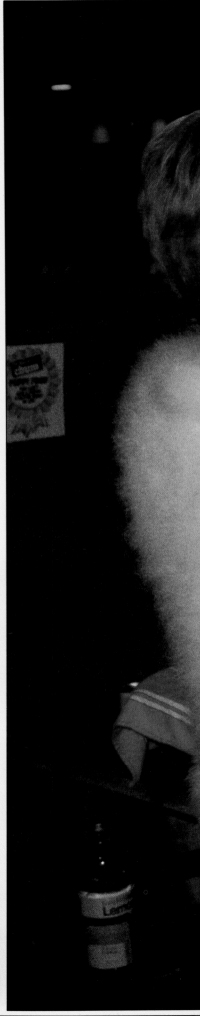

The proud owners of healthy, obedient dogs may well decide to try their luck at showing. If so, they will soon find themselves competing with all sorts of other dog owners and breeders. Some, like themselves, may be entering the ring for the first time. Others will be old hands, knowing all the tricks of presentation and how to catch the judge's eye. Shows also differ, from small local competitions for every variety — pedigree and non-pedigree alike — to large specialist shows with many pure-breed classes.

Why show your dog?
Shows are the shop window of the dog world. They are a means for individual breeders to show their wares and get the opportunity to see, through competition, how the standards for various breeds are being interpreted by the judges. By selecting dogs which correspond most closely to the breed standard drawn up by specialist breed clubs

(and approved by the national kennel club), breeds are kept true to their own conformation, style of movement, type and colour of coat, eye shape and colour, and temperament. Any owners' interest in their dog can soon extend to an interest in the breed, and then into a desire to challenge their own dog's standard of perfection against all comers. Showing dogs can become a compelling hobby or, for some, a lifetime's work.

Time and effort
There is no magic formula for producing the impeccably trained show dog or obedience dog. To be successful demands days, weeks, even years, of concentration so that the owner and dog become a successful winning team. Indeed, you will soon discover that the owner must learn as much as (if not more than) the dog to excel in the show ring or in obedience competitions.

How much time should you expect to devote to a promising show dog? In the case of a large breed, which takes a long time to mature, think in terms of two to three years of heavy campaigning to bring the dog up to title standard. In a smaller breed, you can reckon on two years. But be warned, it is not unusual for the novice exhibitor to 'waste' their dog through inexperience. Professional handlers are sometimes sought as a solution to this problem, particularly in the United States. While many dogs are handled by their owners in America, many others are put into the care of the professional. A really promising dog to be heavily campaigned will stay with its handler, living with him or her while travelling to shows across the entire country.

For the amateur, there is little more rewarding than taking a good dog to the top. But should business, disability, age, or some other reason prevent you from giving a really

Above: A proud owner displays the rosette awarded to her young Belgian Shepherd Dog for being chosen Best Puppy in Show. This is one of the most coveted awards in breed showing, the winner being chosen by the judge often from among many hundreds of entries.

promising dog its chance, then the answer must be not simply to ask a friend or neighbour to take the dog to a show for you, but to invest in the services of a professional.

Incidentally, there is little truth in the rumour that the show dog that is kept as a pet will never win through because it is likely to lean too affectionately towards its owner. Dogs that are cloying are those which are insecure in themselves. Many an uncrowned champion walking the streets today has that unmistakable air of arrogance, style and quality immediately apparent to the connoisseur.

How to begin

As a novice exhibitor you should start by visiting important dog shows well before you begin to campaign. By all means show your pup at small local shows to gain experience, but attend the bigger shows with the aim of increasing your own knowledge.

Watch seasoned exhibitors at important dog shows. In Britain, for instance, you can observe the people who are awarded CCs (Challenge Certificates), the highest award given at a Championship Show, for the Best Dog and Best Bitch in each breed. Watch these same people handling in Puppy and Minor Puppy classes and try to emulate them. Take note of the exhibitor entering the ring with a dog whose coat gleams to such an extent that it stands out boldly against its competitors.

Never be afraid to go up to experienced exhibitors—in quiet moments—and exchange a few words with them. Tell them that you admire the way in which they present their dog, and ask if you may watch while they groom it on the grooming table. Everybody enjoys a little flattery, and if an approach is made tactfully—obviously you must not waylay someone preparing to go into the ring—you can learn a great deal from successful breeders and exhibitors, not only about your own breed but also about many others. You will find that everyone will have his or her own ideas and tips on presentation.

Take the trouble to find out who the professional handlers are, and have a look at them too. Get to the show early, so that you can watch the exhibits being prepared. Then, when you feel you are ready, enter your young dog or bitch for its first Championship Show.

Breed clubs

The keen exhibitor will inevitably wish to become a member of a breed club; that is, a club which caters specifically for one given breed. The club liaises on behalf of that breed with the national kennel club under whose rules and breed standard (standard of perfection) the breed is exhibited.

Breed clubs are of immense help to the new member, who will benefit not only from attending the shows and getting to know other people, but from learning by word of mouth, as well as from the literature that is usually readily available, the correct way to prepare and present the variety in the show ring.

Acquiring a reputation

It is important in the early days of your show career to enter as many variety classes (those not confined to one breed) at Open Shows as possible. (A dog must not be entered for a variety class if it has not also been entered in a class for its breed where one has been provided. There is, however, no rule that prohibits it from entering a variety class as well as a breed class.) It is in variety classes that you will come up against Best in Show judges, and entering such classes enables the exhibitor to become seen and

Above: These two exhibitors are ideally dressed for showing off their dogs. Their clothes are casual but neat, in plain colours that do not detract attention from the beautiful English Setters.

known. If you attend only your own breed club and breed shows, you will know only your own breed and its judges. But by showing in variety classes, and indeed going to shows and wandering around on the days when your own breed is not being exhibited, you will gradually become acquainted with the judges and be able to nod and say 'Good morning' to those you have come under, so generally establishing yourself in the dog world.

What to wear

It is advisable to dress in a way that will complement your dog. Do not wear black if you are exhibiting a black dog, for example, and do not wear such brightly coloured clothes that the judge is tempted to look at you rather than your dog. Nor, on the other hand, should your clothes be too dreary; you should aim at adopting a happy medium. This you can achieve by undertaking some pre-show research. If the judge is a

young person, you can dress in a more relaxed style, whereas, if the judge is one of the 'old school', you would be well advised to wear something more formal such as a smart skirt or a suit and tie.

Dog shows are often held in country venues and may require a long journey, so it is good advice to travel in sweater and jeans, taking some smarter clothes with you, wrapped in polythene and carefully stowed in the boot of your car. Bad weather, too, can play havoc with 'best dress'. If, on a blustery day, you achieve qualification for Best of Breed with your dog, you will want to be able to change and look the part for the final judging.

Useful equipment

Watching fellow exhibitors at your first few shows, you are bound to wonder why you did not have the common sense to bring certain useful items. The following list of equipment should help you, but doubtless you will wish to add to it as time goes on.

Benching curtains
Cushion
Blanket and pegs
Fishing net (for protective action if necessary)
Grooming table and rubber mat (where applicable)
Water spray (where applicable)
Chalk block and/or powder
Tissues
Scissors
Damp sponge
First aid kit
Show lead
Advertising material
Pencil and paper
Velvet glove or polishing cloth
Brush and comb

PREPARING THE PUPPY

A litter of pups which has not been touched by human hands during the first few weeks of life may never integrate fully into a domestic environment. It is easy to understand, therefore, that the pup which has not been prepared for public attention, or been 'socialized' prior to a show career, may become so ring-shy that its chances of success are diminished.

The judge may be confronted by a promising pup which, at first glance, seems a deserving winner, but no matter how good an example of its breed, the judge cannot pick out an exhibit which is cowering in front of him, refusing to look up and shaking uncontrollably. Exhibiting such a specimen is particularly frustrating for the owner, who probably knows that the pup will gambol about happily as soon as it is taken from the show ring.

Temperament is partly governed by heredity. Nonetheless, the pup which prior to a show career — and after its inoculations — is taken on its lead to the local shops, introduced to the neighbours (and their dogs) and is sensibly handled by others, has more chance of developing into a confident animal than the pup which has seen nobody outside its human 'family'.

Travelling

During its show career the pup is likely to make innumerable journeys by road. If you do not want the mere sight of a vehicle to evoke panic, accustom it to taking trips for pleasure. All too often, the first trips a pup makes are to the veterinarian's surgery, where it receives routine inoculations. Why not ensure that your pup's first journeys are made for enjoyment? A ride in the vehicle will not then always be associated with having a needle jab. Of course, you must take care that the pup is not put on the ground before it has had its inoculations. Be sure, too, to cover the seats of the vehicle well in case the pup is sick. To avoid this happening, it is advisable not to feed the pup before the journey.

Benching

Your show dog must learn to be benched (placed in a three-sided kennel that forms part of a long bench) for considerable periods of time. At shows, the benching area is usually in a tent close to the exhibition area. You should never leave your dog bench unattended, so if you wish to walk round the show ground you should first ask a fellow exhibitor to keep an eye on your dog.

Benching can also be practised by leaving the dog in your car for short periods while, for instance, you visit a shop to buy a newspaper. Remember always to leave a window open to allow for fresh air, but not to leave it so wide that the pup can escape. Your dog will come to accept these short absences and learn to guard the car — and, eventually, the show bench.

At this early stage it is a good idea to encourage a stranger to poke a finger through the car window, just to test the pup's reaction. If the dog has

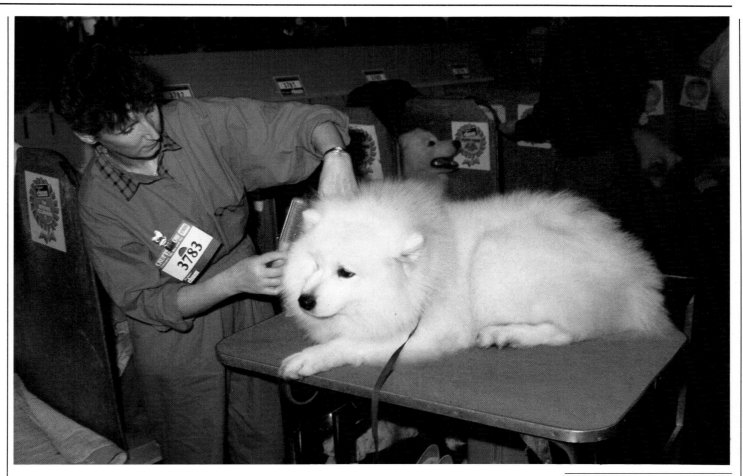

Above: Space is provided at shows for the grooming of breeds such as this Samoyed which requires painstaking attention.

Left: This Briard's owner has placed a soft rug in the bench to make sure the dog is comfortable while it awaits its turn to be shown.

Below: All show dogs must stand for examination by the judge. Here, a young Dobermann is being taught to stand in the required pose to show off its points.

a tendency to over-protect, it is a warning that a careless show visitor could at a later stage receive a nasty bite. Where a dog is over-protective, make a point of either putting a table in front of your bench at shows, putting some fisherman's net and pegs over your bench to protect it, or simply leaving a warning notice pinned to the bench, asking visitors not to touch. Biting incidents at shows are more often than not the fault of the spectator allowing a child to poke fingers in the face of a natural guard dog, or, even worse,

the spectators doing it themselves. The last thing you want, however, is for your dog to snap and have its show career promptly terminated.

At a show you will need a rug or cushion for the pup to sit on in its bench, and possibly benching curtains to fix around the three sides of the bench with pegs. Exhibitors of the smaller varieties take particular pride in setting off their bench areas to advantage. If you take a grooming table to a show, you will also need a blanket and rubber mat for the dog to stand on.

LEARNING RINGCRAFT

A pup may not be entered in a conformation show until it is six months old. But its chances of success will be much enhanced if the handler has prepared it for its show début beforehand. The show dog has to stand still for comparatively long periods in a required pose. It should look as if it is enjoying the proceedings (as indeed it should), move easily and correctly in the ring, behave well towards other dogs and take in its stride a physical examination by the judge.

You should start teaching your pup ringcraft early on by training it to stand for inspection. Smaller breeds are examined standing on the judge's table; larger breeds are examined at ground level. Start by standing your dog with its head erect and getting it accustomed to having its body and teeth examined, prior to being rewarded with a titbit. Then ask a friend to pretend to be the judge and to handle the pup, so that it accepts handling by a stranger as a matter of course.

A judge will approach the dog from the front and examine the head, eyes, ears and muzzle. Possibly he may ask you to show him the dog's teeth, or he may look at them himself. It is up to you to pose the dog, or 'stack' it, on the table although the judge may assist a beginner.

Movement

After each dog has been examined by the judge in the show ring, the handler is asked to walk or 'gait' the dog so that the judge may study its action, after which handler and dog should return to their original place

Above: All breeds, large or small, are required to move for the judge. Here, the judge is assessing the movement of a small Pomeranian.

in the line. Small breeds are walked in the ring; larger breeds are gaited, requiring more activity on the part of the handler, so that the judge may adequately assess the animal's movement.

Buy your dog a show lead (not to be confused with its everyday lead and collar) which loops over the head and is secured by a clasp. You should hold the lead in your left hand and always lead the dog on your left hand side. This allows the judge an unrestricted view of the dog from the centre of the ring. For most breeds, praise and the occasional titbit should be used to encourage the dog to show itself as naturally as possible.

Lead training is another activity best practised first at home or in the garden. For those without a garden, a quiet park or side street may be the best substitute. Practise walking, with the dog to your left, keeping its attention on you. Lead the pup in circles, triangles and straight lines. Pups learn most quickly if their early training is done by one person. Once they are walking well, other members of the family can take their turn. Gradually introduce the dog to areas where there is more activity

and noise, but keep its attention focused on you.

Large dogs have their own individual gait, and they should be allowed to slip gradually into this steady movement, a cross between a walk and a trot. The sequence of the gait is right hind foot forward, right front foot forward, followed by left hind foot then left front foot forward. Remember that good handlers pace themselves with the dog's movement rather than the other way round; they are also unobtrusive. The judge may be aware of the handler but it is the dog that is being presented.

In the show ring, your dog should always come to a stop unaided on all four feet. This is something you can practise. Move off together, holding a longish lead in your left hand. Come slowly to a halt, putting your right hand out in front of the dog to balance it until, eventually, the dog will stand instantly on all four legs without aid.

This exercise, in common with others, should obviously form part of a pleasurable outing. You should praise and talk to the dog throughout, so that it stands proudly with its head up. Having practised in this way you should then have little difficulty in posing the dog so that the judge can see the full quality of the animal and how well formed it is.

If you have access to a video camera, it is a good idea to ask

someone to accompany you to your first few shows to film the class. This will show you the way you move with your dog, and the action of your rivals. Compare your movement with that of the winners and you may see where you go wrong. You can then repeat the procedure in about six months and look for an improvement. If you have eradicated earlier mistakes, now is the time to watch people who are more successful than you and to discover the ways in which their showing of a dog is better than yours.

If you watch seasoned exhibitors in the ring, you may notice that they have a little piece of chopped liver, or some other delicacy, in their free hand. The titbit is used not only as a reward, but for attracting the dog's attention. The dog that learns how to walk and stand correctly, on a reward basis, will quickly learn to look on showing as a pleasant experience.

Stance

A dog is on show not merely from the time it appears in the line-up, but also beforehand. Many judges are making an assessment as you enter the show ring. Therefore, a sensible handler, having already run up and down to establish the correct gait, should sweep confidently into the ring to find a position in line.

The 'stacking' or standing position which a dog must take upon lining

up in the show ring varies according to the breed concerned, but the basic principle remains the same: the position must show the dog to its best advantage. Studying your chosen breed in the ring, and consulting with the breed club, should leave you in no doubt as to what is required.

Obviously the requirements in a Novice class are not as stringent as those where seasoned exhibitors are battling for honours. But certainly in a senior class it is important never to let your dog relax or lose its show stance. The judge may, while waiting for another dog to be stacked, turn around and note that your exhibit is always standing there in position. Keep your dog relaxed by talking to it. If it appears to be getting tired, move to the show side of the animal and groom it. In this way you will have your back between your dog and the judge, who will be looking at other dogs. If he looks up, your dog will not be in direct line of vision.

Giving a dog confidence

You should not fall into the bad habit of chatting to your neighbours in the ring, or becoming otherwise distracted to the detriment of showing your dog. Visit almost any dog show and you will see how bad it looks when exhibitors are so busy chatting to their friends, both inside and outside the ring, that they appear to have no interest in their own dog.

Left: An Afghan Hound is being gaited in the ring while the other exhibitors remain in line, ready to catch the judge's eye.

It is a good thing to keep in close contact with your dog while showing, and in countries where it is permissible you can do so by leaving your hand resting gently on some part of the animal's body. By running your hand down the dog's back or keeping your hand touching its head or ears, you can let your dog know that you are with it, and this in turn will increase its confidence. (Some countries, however, such as the United States, do not allow such physical contact while the dog is on show.)

Of course, you cannot adopt this practice with tiny breeds such as Chihuahuas because you cannot stand and touch the dog at the same time. But you can nonetheless keep instilling confidence with plenty of praise and encouragement.

Grooming

The breed of dog you choose will have much bearing on the actual time taken in show preparation, but all prospective show dogs must be accustomed to the necessary grooming sessions.

Smooth-coated breeds, such as the diminutive Smooth-coated Chihuahua, the Staffordshire Bull Terrier and the Dobermann need comparatively little pre-show grooming. Others require more time, such as the Airedale, which has to be hand stripped (clipping would spoil its coat for show purposes) the Bichon Frise which must be meticulously scissored, and the Yorkshire Terrier, which must spend much time with its hair done up in ribbons if its coat is to be maintained in show condition. Poodles, which are exhibited in the lion clip, and the Old English Sheepdog are but two other types of dog which require lengthy show preparation.

Ringcraft classes

Most aspiring exhibitors attend ringcraft or handling classes to learn how best to exhibit their dogs. Such classes are often run under the auspices of a canine society, and it is worth enquiring at your local reference library, pet store or kennels for the name, address and telephone number of the club secretary.

Attending ringcraft classes enables both dog and handler to practise. In addition it helps the handler to learn show procedure while the dog gains confidence and learns to mix with its kind. But bear in mind the different methods employed in exhibiting breeds. The class may not be beneficial to you, for instance, if the teacher is a gundog expert and it is your sole aim to exhibit a Toy Poodle.

Left: An instructor at a ringcraft class helps the handlers to set up their dogs. Much depends on the dogs' behaviour in the show ring, and time spent on practising ring procedure at training class is well rewarded.

DOG GROUPS IN THE BRITISH SHOW SYSTEM

Toys
Affenpinschers
Australian Silky Terriers
Bichons Frises
Cavalier King Charles Spaniels
Chihuahuas: Long-coated and Smooth-coated
Chinese Crested Dogs: Hairless and Powderpuff
English Toy Terriers: Black and Tan
Griffons Bruxellois
Italian Greyhounds
Japanese Chins
King Charles Spaniels
Lowchens
Maltese
Miniature Pinschers
Papillons
Pekingese
Pomeranians
Pugs
Yorkshire Terriers

Hounds
Afghan Hounds
Basenjis
Basset Hounds
Bassets Fauves de Bretagne
Beagles
Bloodhounds
Borzois
Dachsbracke
Dachshunds: Long-haired, Miniature Long-haired, Smooth-haired, Miniature Smooth-haired, Wire-haired and Miniature Wire-haired
Deerhounds
Elkhounds
Finnish Spitz
Foxhounds
Greyhounds
Hamiltonstovares
Ibizan Hounds
Irish Wolfhounds
Otterhounds
Petits Bassets Griffons Vendeen
Pharaoh Hounds
Portuguese Warren Hounds
Rhodesian Ridgebacks
Salukis
Sloughis
Swiss Laufhunds
Whippets

Terriers
Airedale Terriers
Australian Terriers
Bedlington Terriers
Border Terriers
Bull Terriers
Bull Terriers: Miniature
Cairn Terriers
Dandie Dinmont Terriers
Fox Terriers: Smooth and Wire
Glen of Imaal Terriers
Irish Terriers
Kerry Blue Terriers
Lakeland Terriers
Manchester Terriers
Norfolk Terriers
Norwich Terriers
Scottish Terriers
Sealyham Terriers
Skye Terriers
Soft-coated Wheaten Terriers
Staffordshire Bull Terriers
Welsh Terriers
West Highland White Terriers

Working breeds
Alaskan Malamutes
Anatolian Shepherd Dogs
Australian Cattle Dogs
Australian Kelpies
Bearded Collies
Beaucerons
Belgian Shepherd Dogs: Groenendaels, Laekenois, Malinois and Tervuerens
Bernese Mountain Dogs
Border Collies
Bouviers des Flandres
Boxers
Briards
Bullmastiffs
Collies: Rough and Smooth
Dobermanns
Eskimo Dogs
Estrela Mountain Dogs
German Shepherd Dogs
Giant Schnauzers
Great Danes
Hovawarts
Hungarian Kuvasz
Hungarian Pulis
Komondors
Lancashire Heelers
Maremma Sheepdogs
Mastiffs
Neapolitan Mastiffs
Newfoundlands
Norwegian Buhunds
Old English Sheepdogs
Pinschers
Polish Sheepdogs
Portuguese Water Dogs
Pyrenean Mountain Dogs
Rottweilers
St Bernards
Samoyeds
Shetland Sheepdogs
Siberian Huskies
Swedish Vallhunds
Tibetan Mastiffs
Welsh Corgis: Cardigan and Pembroke

Gundogs
Brittany Spaniels
Drentse Partridge Dogs
English Setters
German Long-haired Pointers
German Short-haired Pointers
German Wire-haired Pointers
Gordon Setters
Hungarian Vizslas
Hungarian Wire-haired Vizslas
Irish Setters
Irish Setters: Red and White
Italian Spinones
Large Munsterlanders
Pointers
Pointing Wire-haired Griffons
Retrievers: Chesapeake Bay, Curly-coated, Flat-coated, Golden and Labrador
Small Munsterlanders
Spaniels: American Cocker, American Water, Clumber, Cocker, English Springer, Field, Irish Water, Sussex and Welsh Springer
Weimaraners

Utility breeds
Boston Terriers
Bulldogs
Canaan Dogs
Chow Chows
Dalmatians
French Bulldogs
German Spitz: Klein and Mittel
Iceland Dogs
Japanese Akitas
Japanese Spitz
Keeshonds
Leonbergers
Lhasa Apsos
Mexican Hairless
Miniature Schnauzers
Poodles: Standard, Miniature and Toy
Schipperkes
Schnauzers
Shar-Peis
Shih Tzus
Tibetan Spaniels
Tibetan Terriers

DOG GROUPS IN THE AMERICAN SHOW SYSTEM

Toys
Affenpinschers
Brussels Griffons
Chihuahuas: Long Coat and Smooth Coat
English Toy Spaniels: Blenheim and Prince Charles, King Charles and Ruby
Italian Greyhounds
Japanese Chin
Maltese
Manchester Terriers: Toy
Miniature Pinschers
Papillons
Pekingese
Pomeranians
Poodles: Toy
Pugs
Shih Tzu
Silky Terriers
Yorkshire Terriers

Hounds
Afghan Hounds
Basenjis
Basset Hounds
Beagles
Black and Tan Coonhounds
Bloodhounds
Borzois
Dachshunds: Long-haired, Smooth-haired and Wire-haired
Foxhounds: American and English
Greyhounds
Harriers
Ibizan Hounds
Irish Wolfhounds
Norwegian Elkhounds
Otter Hounds
Pharaoh Hounds
Rhodesian Ridgebacks
Salukis
Scottish Deerhounds
Whippets

Terriers
Airedale Terriers
American Staffordshire Terriers
Australian Terriers
Bedlington Terriers
Border Terriers
Bull Terriers: Coloured and White
Cairn Terriers
Dandie Dinmont Terriers
Fox Terriers: Smooth and Wire
Irish Terriers
Kerry Blue Terriers
Lakeland Terriers
Manchester Terriers: Standard
Miniature Schnauzers
Norfolk Terriers
Norwich Terriers
Scottish Terriers
Sealyham Terriers
Skye Terriers
Soft-coated Wheaten Terriers
Staffordshire Bull Terriers
Welsh Terriers
West Highland White Terriers

Working breeds
Akitas
Alaskan Malamutes
Bernese Mountain Dogs
Boxers
Bullmastiffs
Dobermann Pinschers
Giant Schnauzers
Great Danes
Great Pyrenees
Komondorok
Kuvaszok
Mastiffs
Newfoundlands
Portuguese Water Dogs
Rottweilers
St Bernards
Samoyeds
Siberian Huskies
Standard Schnauzers

Herding breeds
Australian Cattle Dogs
Bearded Collies
Belgian Malinois
Belgian Sheepdogs
Belgian Tervuren
Bouviers des Flandres
Briards
Collies: Rough and Smooth
German Shepherd Dogs
Old English Sheepdogs
Pulik
Shetland Sheepdogs
Welsh Corgis: Cardigan and Pembroke

Sporting breeds
Brittanys
German Short-haired Pointers
German Wire-haired Pointers
Pointers
Retrievers: Chesapeake Bay, Curly-coated, Flat-coated, Golden and Labrador
Setters: English, Gordon and Irish
Spaniels: American Water, Clumber, Cocker, English Cocker, English Springer, Field, Irish Water, Sussex and Welsh Springer
Vizslas
Weimaraners
Wire-haired Pointing Griffons

Non-sporting breeds
Bichons Frises
Boston Terriers
Bulldogs
Chow Chows
Dalmatians
French Bulldogs
Keeshonden
Lhasa Apsos
Poodles: Miniature and Standard
Schipperkes
Tibetan Spaniels
Tibetan Terriers

SHOW GUIDE

Part of the preparation for showing your dog involves studying the various types of show open to entry. Shows are run under the auspices of the national kennel club of individual countries, and therefore eligibility and entry rules may vary, as does the character of the shows themselves. Find out as much as you can about the particular requirements for each type of show, so that you can be sure of your dog's eligibility for the class you intend to enter.

Shows may either be specific to one breed (or variety of breed) — called a specialty show — or they may be for all breeds. In an all-breed show, once the Best of Breed has been selected for each breed, winners may then go on to compete against each other in the group judging. Here, dogs are grouped according to the roles for which they were originally bred. The continental system has 10 groups, the United Kingdom six, and the United States

seven. How the breeds are divided amongst the various groups in the latter two countries is shown in the table opposite. Group winners then compete against each other for the coveted Best in Show title.

The UK show system

In the United Kingdom there are seven different types of dog show. These are as follows.

Exemption Show This is a relaxed affair, often held in conjunction with a fête or horse show and run in aid of charity. Such shows present an excellent opportunity for new-comers to get a feel of the atmosphere. In addition to the pure-bred classes allowed, there are usually a number of novelty or fun classes for cross-breeds and mongrels. Entries are accepted on the field.

Primary Show This is a small show run by an individual breed club or society and only open

to club members. Dogs which have won a first prize or hold a Challenge Certificate are ineligible.

Sanction and Limited Shows These are generally restricted to members of the promoting club or society, and prove an excellent training ground for ambitious new exhibitors. Some entrants may also feel that they have a better chance of making a name for themselves, because Challenge Certificate (CC) winners are ineligible.

Open Show This is a fairly big affair, often held in conjunction with an agricultural or county show. The dogs may be benched or otherwise. There are no Challenge Certificates on offer.

Championship Show Such events are of prime importance in the canine calendar, for it is at these shows that the coveted Challenge Certificates (CCs) are on offer. Some such shows are held over two

Above: A typical scene at an Exemption Show. These shows are relaxed affairs and provide good experience for novice exhibitors and their dogs.

or three days, so that perhaps toy dogs and hounds are exhibited on one day, working breeds and utility dogs on another, and so on. A limited number of Championship Shows are held in any given year. In the United Kingdom, one has to attain a first-class certificate in given classes at a Championship Show to qualify for the famous Crufts Championship Dog Show, so competition is intense.

The match A match, held under Kennel Club Rules in the United Kingdom, is a competition on knock-out lines between pairs of dogs of the same breed or invited breeds. Its chief purpose is to educate and stimulate the interest of dog club members.

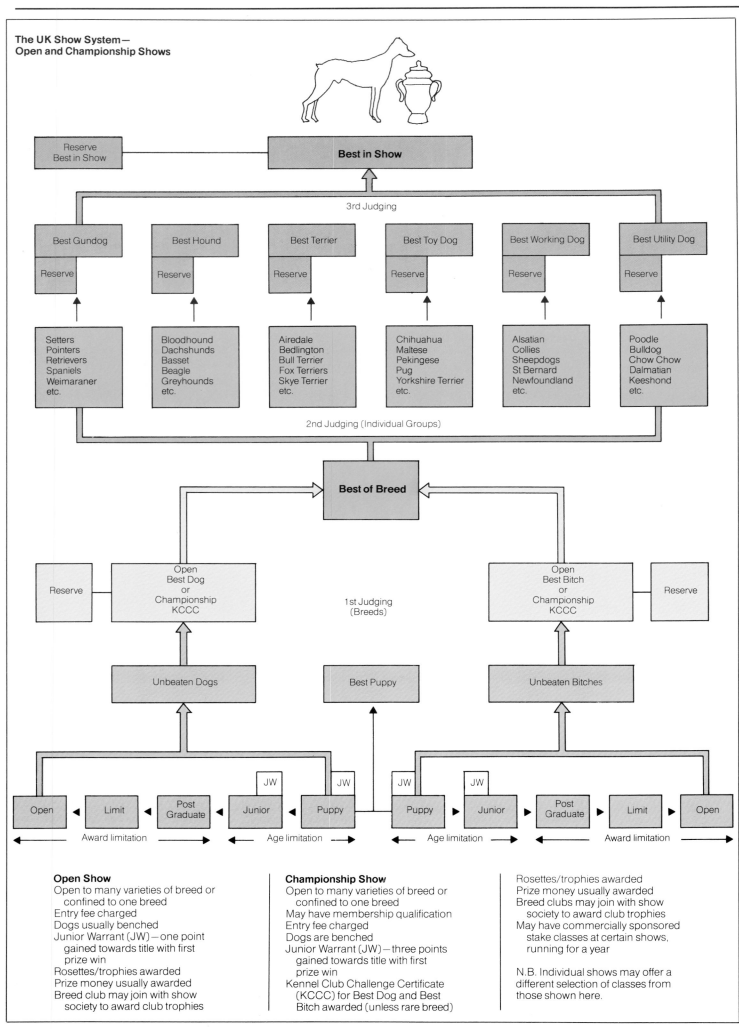

**The UK Show System—
Open and Championship Shows**

Reserve Best in Show — **Best in Show**

3rd Judging

Best Gundog	Best Hound	Best Terrier	Best Toy Dog	Best Working Dog	Best Utility Dog
Reserve	Reserve	Reserve	Reserve	Reserve	Reserve

| Setters Pointers Retrievers Spaniels Weimaraner etc. | Bloodhound Dachshunds Basset Beagle Greyhounds etc. | Airedale Bedlington Bull Terrier Fox Terriers Skye Terrier etc. | Chihuahua Maltese Pekingese Pug Yorkshire Terrier etc. | Alsatian Collies Sheepdogs St Bernard Newfoundland etc. | Poodle Bulldog Chow Chow Dalmatian Keeshond etc. |

2nd Judging (Individual Groups)

Best of Breed

| Reserve | Open Best Dog or Championship KCCC | 1st Judging (Breeds) | Open Best Bitch or Championship KCCC | Reserve |

| Unbeaten Dogs | Best Puppy | Unbeaten Bitches |

| Open | Limit | Post Graduate | Junior [JW] | Puppy [JW] | Puppy [JW] | Junior [JW] | Post Graduate | Limit | Open |

Award limitation — Age limitation — Age limitation — Award limitation

Open Show
Open to many varieties of breed or confined to one breed
Entry fee charged
Dogs usually benched
Junior Warrant (JW) — one point gained towards title with first prize win
Rosettes/trophies awarded
Prize money usually awarded
Breed club may join with show society to award club trophies

Championship Show
Open to many varieties of breed or confined to one breed
May have membership qualification
Entry fee charged
Dogs are benched
Junior Warrant (JW) — three points gained towards title with first prize win
Kennel Club Challenge Certificate (KCCC) for Best Dog and Best Bitch awarded (unless rare breed)

Rosettes/trophies awarded
Prize money usually awarded
Breed clubs may join with show society to award club trophies
May have commercially sponsored stake classes at certain shows, running for a year

N.B. Individual shows may offer a different selection of classes from those shown here.

A useful definition of typical classes held at Open and Championship Shows is given here. Note that the use of the term 'Special' applies to any class not specifically defined by the Kennel Club.
Minor Puppy For dogs of six and not exceeding nine calendar months of age.
Puppy For dogs of six and not exceeding 12 calendar months of age.
Junior For dogs of six and not exceeding 18 calendar months of age.
Maiden For dogs which have not won a Challenge Certificate at an Open or Championship Show (Puppy, Special Puppy, Minor Puppy and Special Minor Puppy classes excepted).
Novice For dogs that have not won a Challenge Certificate, or three or more first prizes at Open and Championship Shows (Puppy, Special Puppy, Minor Puppy and Special Minor Puppy classes excepted).
Tyro For dogs that have not won a Challenge Certificate, or five or more first prizes at Open and Championship Shows (Puppy, Special Puppy, Minor Puppy and Special Minor Puppy classes excepted).
Undergraduate For dogs that have not won a Challenge Certificate or three or more first prizes at Championship Shows, (Puppy, Special Puppy, Minor Puppy, and Special Minor Puppy classes excepted).
Graduate For dogs that have not won a Challenge Certificate or four or more first prizes at Championship Shows in Graduate, Minor Limit, Mid Limit, Limit and Open classes.
Post Graduate For dogs that have not won a Challenge Certificate or five or more first prizes at Championship Shows in Post Graduate, Minor Limit, Mid Limit, Limit and Open classes.
Minor Limit For dogs that have not won two Challenge Certificates or three or more first prizes in all at Championship Shows in Minor Limit, Mid Limit and Open classes confined to the breed at shows where Challenge Certificates were offered for the breed.
Mid Limit For dogs that have not won three Challenge Certificates or five or more first prizes in all at Championship Shows in Mid Limit, Limit and Open classes confined to the breed at shows where Challenge Certificates were offered for the breed.
Limit For dogs that have not won three Challenge Certificates under three different judges or seven or more first prizes in all at Champion-

Above: A retriever competes for the Best of Gundogs award. Group judging takes place at Open and Championship Shows, with individual breed winners competing.

ship Shows in Limit and Open classes confined to the breed at shows where Challenge Certificates were offered for the breed.
Open For all dogs of the breed for which the class is provided and eligible for entry at the show.

In addition to these, there are Veteran classes for dogs over five years of age, Brace and Team classes for pairs and teams of dogs respectively, and Sweepstake classes, open to Veteran, Brace, Team, Stud Dog, Brood Bitch and Breeders classes, in which some of the fees may be awarded as prize money.

REGULATIONS GOVERNING THE ENTRY OF DOGS FOR CRUFTS SHOW 1986

1 Entry in Breed Classes at Crufts Show 1986 where Challenge Certificates are offered except German Wire-Haired Pointers and Siberian Huskies.

A dog is eligible for entry in breed classes where Challenge Certificates are offered if it has qualified in any of the following ways under the Rules and Regulations of the Kennel Club.

(a) If it is a Champion, Show Champion, Field Trial Champion, Working Trial Champion or Obedience Champion.

(b) If it has been awarded a Challenge Certificate at a Show held between January 1st 1985 and December 16th 1985.

(c) If it has been awarded a Reserve Challenge Certificate at a Show held between January 1st 1985 and December 16th 1985.

(d) If it has won any of the following prizes in a breed class (as defined in Kennel Club Regulations for the Definitions of Classes at Championship Shows) at a Championship Show where Challenge Certificates were offered for the breed, between January 1st 1985 and December 16th 1985.
First in Minor Puppy Class
First in Puppy Class
First in Junior Class
First in Post Graduate Class
First in Limit Class
First in Open Class

(e) If it has won a first prize in the following classes at Crufts Show 1985:
Special Puppy Class
Special Junior Class
Post Graduate Class
Limit Class
Open Class

(f) If it has been awarded a 5-point or higher Green Star at a Show held between December 18th 1984 and December 16th 1985 under Irish Kennel Club Rules and Regulations.

(g) If a Beagle, it has won a first prize at a Hound Show between January 1st 1985 and December 16th 1985 held under the Rules of the Masters of Harriers and Beagles Association.

2 Entry in Classes at Crufts Show 1986 for German Wire-Haired Pointers, Siberian Huskies and Any Other Variety Not Separately Classified.

A dog is eligible for entry in classes for German Wire-Haired Pointers, Siberian Huskies and Any Other Variety Not Separately Classified if it has qualified in any of the following ways under the Rules and Regulations of the Kennel Club.

(a) If it has been declared Best of Sex or Reserve Best of Sex of breed or gained any of the following prizes in Breed or Variety classes (as defined in the Kennel Club Regulations for the Definitions of Classes at Championship Shows) at a Championship Show held between January 1st 1985 and December 16th 1985.
First in Minor Puppy Class
First in Puppy Class
First in Junior Class
First in Post Graduate Class
First in Limit Class
First in Open Class
(subject to notes below)

(b) If it has won a first prize in a class for Any Other Variety Not Separately Classified at Crufts Show 1985.

(c) If it has been awarded a 5-point or higher Green Star at a Show held between December 18th 1984 and December 16th 1985, under Irish Kennel Club Rules and Regulations.

3 Entry in Field Trial Classes at Crufts Show 1986.

A dog is eligible for entry in Field Trial Classes if it has at any time won a prize, an Award of Honour, a Diploma of Merit or a Certificate of Merit in actual competition at a Field Trial held under Kennel Club or Irish Kennel Club Field Trial Rules and Regulations.

4 Obedience Championships at Crufts Show 1986.

A dog is eligible for entry if it has won a Kennel Club Obedience Certificate at a Show held between January 1st 1985 and December 16th 1985.

Notes

1 A breed class is a class confined to one breed.

2 Qualifying awards as above in Minor Puppy, Puppy, Junior, Post Graduate, Limit and Open Classes qualify a dog for entry at Crufts Show 1986 only if the class in which the award was gained was not made 'Special' in any way, ie by age, colour, height, weight, to members of a Society, to breeders, etc. An exception is made only in the case of prize winners in Special Puppy and Special Junior at Crufts Show 1985. Wins in Brace, Team and Sweepstake Classes do not qualify nor do wins in any classes other than those stated above.

3 In any class scheduled at Crufts Show 1986 for which an age limit appears in the definition, the age will be calculated to December 1985, and not to the date of the show.

4 No entries will be accepted as 'Not for Competition'.

5 Wins in breed classes at 1985 Championship Shows where Challenge Certificates are not offered will not qualify for entry in breed classes where Challenge Certificates are on offer at Crufts Show 1986 except for German Wire-Haired Pointers and Siberian Huskies.

6 Dogs which gained Challenge Certificates prior to 1985 but have not qualified as above during the year will not be eligible for entry.

7 Eligibility of Champions is restricted to those whose title was gained under Kennel Club Rules and Regulations.

8 Show awards which count towards the title of Champion under the Rules of any governing body other than the Kennel Club, will not count as qualification for Crufts 1986 except the award of a 5-point Green Star at a Show held between December 18th 1984 and December 16th 1985 under Irish Kennel Club Rules and Regulations.

Above: A moment of great joy and excitement at the 1986 Crufts Show, the major showing event of the year. This Airedale, having been chosen Best in Breed and Best in Terrier Group, then won the supreme award of Best in Show.

Right: A Newfoundland and its owner relax together at a small outdoors show, having successfully picked up an award.

UK winners and awards

In the United Kingdom a Challenge Certificate (CC) is awarded to the Best Dog and Best Bitch in each breed, and any dog or bitch that has won three Challenge Certificates at three Championship Shows and under three different judges attains Championship status.

A Reserve Challenge Certificate is also awarded to the Reserve Best Dog and Best Bitch, and in the event of the Challenge Certificate winner being disqualified the Reserve Best of Sex (Dog or Bitch) is awarded the Challenge Certificate.

The Junior Warrant is an award the definition of which seems to baffle many newcomers, and indeed it is something that very few manage to attain. To gain such a warrant a dog

has to attain 25 points before it reaches 18 months of age in breed classes at Open and Championship Shows (not necessarily where Challenge Certificates are on offer). At an Open Show one point is awarded to the winner of each breed class; at a Championship Show, three points. Bearing in mind that a dog cannot be exhibited until it is six months of age it must obviously be exceptional to achieve this recognition.

Entry procedure

Entries for shows, other than Exemption Shows, are made by post on the appropriate application form, available from the show secretary. Entries must be submitted, together with fees, by a given

closing date. The regulations governing the entry of dogs into the world's most famous dog show, the Crufts Show in London, are given in the table above.

To complete an entry form correctly, you need to consult your dog's certificate of pedigree: you will be required to enter your dog's (or bitch's) date of birth, its registered name, the name of the breeder, and the registered names of its sire and dam. You may also need to fill in the Kennel Club registered numbers.

There is a growing practice for entries not to be acknowledged unless a stamped addressed envelope or stamped postcard is enclosed. However, in the case of Championship Shows you will be sent a ring card bearing your entry

number prior to the show. Otherwise, on arrival at the show you must check your number in the catalogue; it will correspond with the number on your bench (or in the United States, carried on your arm band) in the tent where your breed is being housed.

When you enter the show ring in the United Kingdom the steward will check your number against his or her list, and give you the relevant ring card if you have not received one. This should then be attached to your lapel with a ring clip; a safety pin will suffice if you do not have one, but the clip would appear more professional. In the United States, an arm band bearing your number will be given to you prior to entering the ring. It is worn on the left arm.

**The American Show System—
Specialty and All-breed Shows**

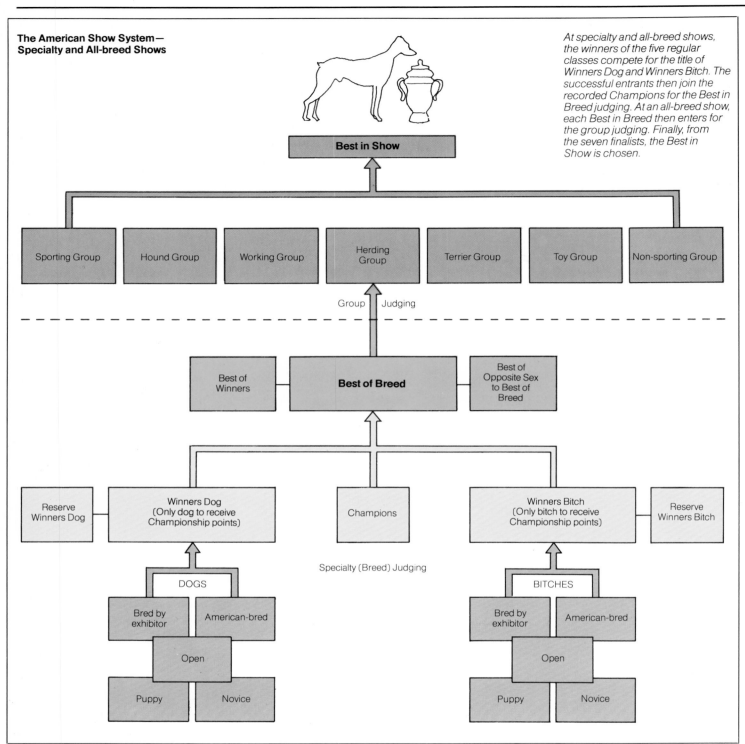

At specialty and all-breed shows, the winners of the five regular classes compete for the title of Winners Dog and Winners Bitch. The successful entrants then join the recorded Champions for the Best in Breed judging. At an all-breed show, each Best in Breed then enters for the group judging. Finally, from the seven finalists, the Best in Show is chosen.

Best in Show

| Sporting Group | Hound Group | Working Group | Herding Group | Terrier Group | Toy Group | Non-sporting Group |

Group │ Judging

Best of Winners | **Best of Breed** | Best of Opposite Sex to Best of Breed

Reserve Winners Dog | Winners Dog (Only dog to receive Championship points) | Champions | Winners Bitch (Only bitch to receive Championship points) | Reserve Winners Bitch

Specialty (Breed) Judging

DOGS

Bred by exhibitor | American-bred

Open

Puppy | Novice

BITCHES

Bred by exhibitor | American-bred

Open

Puppy | Novice

US all-breed shows

The American group system of judging is somewhat different from the British in that there are only five regular classes for each breed or variety of breed: Puppy; Novice (for dogs which have never won a prize except in a Puppy class); Bred by exhibitor (excluding Champions); American-bred (restricted to dogs born in the United States, and as a result of a US mating), and Open (for all dogs including Champions). Only these five classes count towards the required number of points to become a Champion.

After the judge has judged these

Right: An Afghan Hound displays its beautiful flowing movement as it is gaited for the judge at a top American all-breed show.

Above: A judge examines closely the head of a Bullmastiff at an all-breed show. The dog is expected to stand quietly during the inspection.

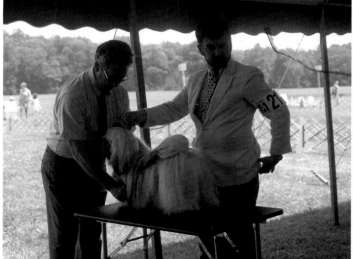

Left: A Lhasa Apso is examined on the judge's table. The breed's abundant coat makes it more difficult for the judge to detect faults.

five classes the winners are brought back to compete against each other in the Winners class. The best dog, called the Winners Dog, and the best bitch—the Winners Bitch—both receive Championship points.

The judge must then choose which dog he considers Best of Breed. The Best of Breed class has in it all the recorded Champions competing in the show, both male and female, plus the Winners Dog and Winners Bitch. The judge goes over all the animals and selects one he considers to be the best— the Best of Breed. From the Winners Dog and Winners Bitch he selects

the Best of Winners. If either the Winners Dog or Winners Bitch is selected Best of Breed, it automatically becomes Best of Winners. The judge then finishes the breed judging by selecting a Best of Opposite Sex to Best of Breed.

This same process of elimination takes place in every breed. Then each Best of Breed winner competes in its group, and finally, from the winners of the seven groups, the Best of Show is selected.

To attain Championship status, a dog or bitch must gain a total of 15 points under at least three different judges. The system commences in

Above: The seven group winners line up for the judge's appraisal at an all-breed American dog show. From among these seven dogs will be chosen the Best in Show.

Above: The selection for Best in Show having been made and the award presented, the winning dog, a handsome Bloodhound, stands on display with its owner.

the Winners class, where a given number of points are awarded to Winners Dog and Winners Bitch. The number of points are allocated according to the number of dogs entered and present, *not* those that have been entered for the class but do not appear. The most points that may be awarded at one show is five, known as a Major. After that a really good dog may gain a Championship in three straight shows.

── American specialty shows ──
At a specialty show the same classes are offered as for an all-breed show but there is no group judging. Both the Open classes and the Puppy classes may be divided by colour at specialty and all-breed shows.

Left: The hound group finalists line up before the judge, each one a breed winner in the show. The winner will then compete for the Best in Show title.

Clubs may also wish to offer additional classes not available at all-breed shows. The 12–18 month classes for both dogs and bitches provide a competition for dogs that are not mature but are not really puppies either. This class is usually offered instead of the Novice class. Dogs between the ages of 12 and 18 months of age that are not Champions may enter. Veteran Bitch and Veteran Dog classes may also be held. The age of the veteran may be determined by the specialty club. The winner of the Veteran Bitch and Veteran Dog class may go on to compete for Best of Breed or Best of Variety. Dogs in this class may or may not be Champions and the winners do not compete in Winners Dog or Winners Bitch class.

Non-regular classes are sometimes offered at shows. There are Stud Dog and Brood Bitch classes. The Stud Dogs and Brood Bitches are shown with their offspring, who must be entered in the regular classes as well. The parents may or

may not be. Only the offspring are judged on conformation merits. Other non-regular classes may be Brace or Team classes.

── US sanctioned matches ──
In the United States, a sanctioned match is an informal meeting at which pure-bred dogs may compete but not for Championship points. It can be held by a club or association, whether or not a member of the American Kennel Club, by obtaining sanction from the Club.

These matches provide an ideal opportunity for dog clubs, judges, stewards and exhibitors and their dogs to gain the experience needed for licenced events.

── US varieties within the breeds ──
In breeds which have varieties within the breed, the varieties are shown separately. The classes offered are the same as for those breeds without varieties. The Best of Variety designation is given, rather than Best of Breed; and Best Opposite Sex to Best of Variety, rather than Best of Opposite Sex to Best of Breed. At all-breed shows each variety is represented in its group. Therefore, in the Best in Show competition there would be a

Rough Collie and a Smooth Collie in the herding group, representing the best from both varieties. But it is not uncommon to see a Standard Poodle from the non-sporting Group and a Toy Poodle from the toy group both competing for Best in Show. The recognized breeds with varieties are as follows:

Cocker Spaniels Solid Colour Black, including Black and Tan; any solid colour other than black; Parti-colour.

Beagles Not exceeding 13in (33cm); over 13in (33cm) but not exceeding 15in (38cm) in height.

Dachshunds Long-haired; Smooth-haired; Wire-haired.

Bull Terriers Coloured; White

Manchester Terriers Standard, over 12 pounds (5kg) and not exceeding 22 pounds (10kg); Toy, not exceeding 12 pounds (5kg).

Poodles Miniature, over 10in (25cm) and not exceeding 15in (38cm); Standard, over 15in (38cm); Toy, not exceeding 10in (25cm).

Collies Rough Coat; Smooth Coat

Chihuahuas Long Coat; Smooth Coat

English Toy Spaniels Blenheim and Prince Charles; King Charles and Ruby.

The Continental system

It is rather difficult to generalize about the rules governing dog shows in Europe, because they vary slightly from one country to another. But they are all very similar in most respects, because, instead of each country having its own rules, all are governed by the regulations laid down by the FCI (Fédération Cynologique Internationale). Each country has its own national equivalent of the Kennel Club, but for shows each must stick to the rules laid down by the FCI.

Speaking generally, shows are either of championship status or are much smaller shows—usually held by the breed clubs—more in the nature of fun shows or matches.

At a Championship Show, the judge has to write a critique on every exhibit, and also give it a grade: excellent, very good, good or sufficient. Any dog that tries to bite is disqualified. Generally, the critique has to be written on the spot, and it is then handed to the exhibitor by the judge. In the Netherlands there is slightly less pressure on the judge, because the local rules lay down that such critiques must be sent to the Dutch Kennel Club within 14 days of the show. This kind of judging obviously takes a long time, so it is as well that the classes in European shows are neither as numerous nor as well filled as they are in the United Kingdom and the United States. Usually there are only Youth, Open and Championship classes, although additional classes are permitted. Occasionally there are Brace or Team classes. But it is very rare to find a European show that has any of the featured Variety classes that are staged in Britain and America. Whether this is a good thing or not depends upon your point of view; but it certainly takes away some of the appeal of the show to the general public.

Only a dog that has received the grading Excellent may be taken into account for the award of Best of Sex. Many countries do not permit the award of an Excellent grade to a dog in the Youth class, but some do allow this. The Youth class is governed by age limits, and this is usually from 9-24 months.

It is rare for a European show to have an award for Best of Breed, though this occasionally happens. Without the award of Best of Breed, there cannot be any Group or Best in Show judging, which is a great pity, as there is then no great final climax to the show, and the onlookers tend to melt away disconsolately at the end of the day.

After all the dogs have been graded, some may be awarded the CACIB (Certificat d'Aptitude au Championat International de Beauté) or the CAC (Certificat d'Aptitude au Championat). The CACIB is awarded only at an International Championship Show. A certificate may be awarded to the winner of the grading Excellent, but not necessarily so, because a judge may not consider such a dog, even though Excellent, to be of such outstanding merit as to warrant the award of a certificate. Because a dog in the Youth class may not

Above: At a European show, dogs do not generally compete against each other for Best of Breed, but are judged individually and graded, the best ones receiving certificates.

receive the grading Excellent, it may well happen that, in one of the few countries that allow an award for Best of Breed, the judge may put the Youth class winner above the winner of a certificate.

To obtain the title of Champion, a dog must obtain three certificates, either CACIB or CAC, under two different judges; and the first and last certificates must be won with an interval of 12 months between them. They can be won in any country that is affiliated to the FCI, and since movement of dogs is not restricted between most continental European countries by regulations regarding rabies, there is a fairly large area from which an exhibitor can choose a show.

Most British and American shows are thought to be fairly 'cut-throat' in their outlook, but European exhibitors seem to have a different attitude to their shows, and there is a feeling that they are even more 'out for blood'. There are fewer dogs competing, yet the owners appear to take a much more serious view of what happens to them: they confront one another with grave faces and troubled brows, and there is little chatter until all the judgements have been declared.

Shows in Europe are also rather more rigorous in their attitude to permitting removal of exhibits: you will never find a show that says participants may go home at 3.00 p.m., even when there is no real need to stay longer. Perhaps as there are far fewer shows than in Britain and the United States, the organizers want the dogs to remain so that they can be seen by the late-comers.

But wherever they take place, dog shows are always interesting and usually fun too, and it is from this point of view that a wise owner should regard them.

The Scandinavian system

The Scandinavian showing system is a mixture of the Continental and British systems. There are three main classes: Junior (for exhibits 8-15 months old), Open (for exhibits over 15 months old), and Champion classes (for exhibits that have already obtained the title of Swedish, Finnish, Danish, Norwegian or International Champion).

In the Junior and Open classes exhibits are graded on their own merits: they are not in competition against each other. The gradings are: 1st prize (a very good specimen of the breed), 2nd prize (a moderately good specimen), 3rd prize (an exhibit lacking in construction), and 4th prize (a very untypical exhibit).

All those that gain a 1st grading in Junior then compete against each other and are placed in order of 1st to 4th. The 1st prize winners in the Open class enter a Winners class

with Companion Dog (CD) awarded on a points system at trials.

Most breeds have specialist breed clubs, which use the UK Kennel Club breed standards.

The Australian states have individual kennel control organizations overseen by an advisory Australian Kennel Control Council. The availability of dog shows, field trials and obedience tests varies from state to state, and is determined by the number of pedigree dogs in the area.

The Royal Agricultural Societies of Australia all have dog show sections. The Melbourne Show, for example, runs over 11 days, with only a few breeds judged each day. These shows also cater for breed club obedience displays. Show stewards are professional people and have to pass stringent examinations before taking up their duties.

At these larger shows, the classes usually offered are: Baby puppy (pup may be shown from three months of age), Minor Puppy, Puppy, Junior, Intermediate, Novice, Graduate, Limit, State-bred, Australian-bred, and Open. These are self-explanatory or similar to the UK classification. The group classification is: toys, terriers, gundogs, hounds, working, and non-sporting.

Australian Champions have to gain 100 points from at least four different judges. The method by which a Champion gains its crown is complicated, but ensures that a superb specimen of a numerically small breed stands an almost equal chance with a superb specimen of a popular breed.

After all the breed classes have been judged, the first prize winners in each sex over six months old compete for the Challenge Certificate (CC). The winner gains five points plus one point for each competing exhibit of the same sex over six months old, to a maximum of 25 points. (A winning bitch would gain five points for the CC on its own merit, and if the total entry of bitches over six months old is 10 this would result in 15 points towards the Championship of that particular bitch.) The dog CC and bitch CC then compete for Best of Breed.

At multi-breed shows the Best of Breed then enters the group judging. The winner of each group receives five points plus one point for every exhibit in the group, to a maximum of 25 points. The six group winners then compete for Best in Show, from which the winner gains five points plus one point for every other exhibit entered in ordinary classes, to a maximum of 25 points. No exhibit may receive more than 25 points in one show.

Once 100 points have been gained, the record of the animal's wins is checked by its respective state control, the appropriate fee is paid, and an Australian Champion Certificate is issued.

and are also placed 1st to 4th.

Some breeds with a well-defined original function have to be highly placed at trials to test that function before they can enter Winners classes, for example, field trials for retrievers.

The International Championship Shows in Scandinavia approved by the FCI award the CACIB and the CACIT (Certificat d'Aptitude au Championat International de Travail). An International Champion has to gain four CACIBs from three different judges and in three different countries. Between the first and last CACIB there must be an interval of 12 months.

The Australian system

In spite of, or perhaps because of, a strong anti-dog movement in Australia, there is a tremendous enthusiasm among dog owners for basic training, and huge membership of training and breed clubs. Obedience training is on a par with everyday sit/stay/heel UK training,

Left: Salukis are given time to relax at an Australian show. In this country the types of shows and classes are similar to those held in the United Kingdom, though the Championship points system differs.

10

Dogs and the Law

The laws concerning dog ownership and conduct not only differ from one country or state to another, they may also differ from one district, street or park to the next. Therefore, before buying a dog, you should always find out what leash, licencing and other laws pertain in your area.

Quarantine laws also differ from one country to another; the United Kingdom for example, in order to remain rabies-free, requires dogs entering the country to undergo a six-month quarantine period. Many other countries require proof of inoculation against rabies.

There are also various licences required for the boarding, breeding and exporting of dogs, and laws regarding performing dogs, strays and animal transportation. Perhaps most importantly, there are laws to protect dogs against cruelty and mis-use.

Right: By law, stray dogs can be rounded up and impounded.

Below: Dog owners should find out if there are any restrictions on dogs in their local park.

The law in relation to dogs varies throughout the world, so it is sensible to check up to date requirements with the relevant embassy.

In Italy the cost of a licence to keep a dog varies from province to province so that the fee for keeping a dog in a large city such as Florence or Rome might be somewhat higher than that charged in a rural community.

In the People's Republic of China the tax on dogs rose so sharply in 1947 that few people could afford to retain them and now it is an offence to keep a dog at all, although rumours persist that several may still be maintained in remote areas. Fortunately many dogs were sent to the United States for refuge and happily dogs of Chinese origin should be with us for very many years to come.

Germany, a country famous for the splendid breeds it has produced, is becoming an exceedingly expensive place to keep a dog with sharp increases in the cost of both licences and dog food.

France seems more lenient towards its dog owners and there is a ruling that everyone automatically has the right to keep a cat and dog in their apartment.

Law and responsibilities in the United Kingdom

Boarding kennels The Animals Boarding Establishments Act (1963) requires that boarding kennels for dogs (and indeed cats) should be licensed by the respective district council (or borough council where appropriate). The requirement pertains if the kennels are being run as a 'business', irrespective of whether the boarding takes place at a private dwelling.

Generally speaking, if animals are boarded as a regular practice it is construed that a business is being run for 'profit'. You are unlikely to need a licence if you merely look after your friends' and neighbours'

dogs during holiday periods and they pay you for the requisite number of cans of pet food.

There is no maximum fee for a licence, which may be granted at a council's discretion, that council having satisfied itself as to the conditions in which the dogs will be kept, fed and exercised and protected from various eventualities.

There are certain exceptions from licence requirements, for instance, where the boarding is carried on as a sideline to a main business such as a veterinary practice.

Breeding The Breeding of Dogs Act (1973) evoked some criticism when first introduced. However, it has done much to eradicate the breeding of dogs under inadequate or unhygienic conditions. Breeding establishments have to be inspected and certain, not unreasonable, conditions complied with before the granting of a licence by the local authority.

A licence is required where more than two bitches are kept for the purpose of breeding and selling for profit. You do not need to apply for a licence if you keep a certain number of bitches as pets and do not intend to breed from them.

Cruelty The Protection of Animals Act (1911) is still in force having been strengthened over the years by various acts of parliament and statutory regulations.

Broadly speaking, the act covers such matters as abandonment or transportation of an animal in such a manner as to cause unnecessary suffering, using a dog for draught purposes (on the highway) — a questionable ruling because the practise of harnessing up Bernese Mountain dogs, and other breeds, in the United Kingdom is common-place at fêtes and charity events where the dogs are *not* taken on to the highway — unlawful experimentation or operations, and of course dog fighting (there have been a

number of convictions in recent times where fine breeds such as the Staffordshire Bull and English Bull Terriers have been put to this outdated and cruel use.

Diseases When the United Kingdom joined the Common Market considerable fear was expressed lest quarantine regulations should be relaxed and rabies, which has been moving steadily westward since the Second World War, be allowed to penetrate the island shores. Doubtless renewed plans for a channel tunnel will bring further fears of quarantine evasion.

Currently it is a serious offence to bring a dog into the United Kingdom without an import licence (see Importing dogs), and dogs entering the country must spend six months in quarantine kennels approved by the Ministry of Agriculture, Fisheries and Food. This has caused much controversy in the past and is likely to continue to do so. However, the fact remains that the United Kingdom remains rabies free, it has not as yet become necessary to introduce a law whereby all dogs must be vaccinated against the disease.

There are also legal responsibilities for any injury or damage incurred where, for instance, a dog is sold with a warranty claiming that the animal is disease free and this does not prove to be the case, or where a dog which the owner knows to be diseased is allowed to mingle with healthy animals.

Dog licences Until recently, the keeper of a dog over six months of age was required to licence it, the same charge being levied for any other dog (or dogs) in the possession of the keeper. Licences were not, however, required for guide dogs for

Right: Boarding kennels must be licensed by the local district council which will ensure that the premises are adequately run.

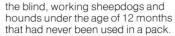

the blind, working sheepdogs and hounds under the age of 12 months that had never been used in a pack.

The cost of this licence had remained virtually unchanged since it was introduced in 1878, when it was set at 7s 6d. But recently, with the fee standing at the decimal equivalent of 37p, the system was costing more in administrative and other costs than was being collected. After much discussion in Parliament over whether to increase the fee substantially or to abolish it altogether, the latter course was finally agreed upon in 1986 and a licence is now no longer required.

Dogs in the home Despite the British having the reputation of being a nation of dog lovers, the signs are that with increasing urbanisation and flat dwelling the keeping of dogs will become difficult. Generally, the owner of a freehold

Left: Owners are, by law, held responsible for their dog's actions, and many now insure against claims for damages caused by their dog.

property has the right to keep such domestic pets as he wishes provided that they do not constitute a health hazard, for instance, a pig or goat, kept in unhygienic circumstances in a small back garden or yard would not be tolerated.

Nonetheless, it is a wise precaution, when thinking of moving house, to check whether your new neighbours like dogs. A complaint brought by a neighbour and backed up by others, could well lead to hefty defence costs.

Most standard leases contain a clause prohibiting the keeping of pets without the written consent of the landlord and, while in many cases, the obtaining of such consent is a mere formality, it is sensible to obtain it before purchasing a pet to prevent any possible future heartbreak. Many council home agreements preclude the keeping of dogs except where such homes have access to a garden, for instance a dog might only be allowed in a house or ground floor flat. Again, it is best to check out the position and get permission before buying your dog.

Identification The Control of Dogs Order (1930) requires that every dog, when in a public place, should wear a collar, with a disc attached clearly showing the name and address of the person to whom it belongs. A common practice is to show the dog's name on the disc also, so that if the animal is lost and frightened it will respond to the familiar sound of its name.

The tattooing of dogs with an identifying number or mark, allied with a central registry, is a common practice in the United States and is slowly increasing in popularity in the United Kingdom, though, as yet, there is no national registry in this country.

Importing dogs The chief legislations concerned with importing dogs into the United Kingdom are the Animal Health Act (1981) and the Rabies (Importation) of Dogs, Cats and other Mammals Order (1974).

Before importing a dog an import licence must be obtained from the Ministry of Agriculture, Fisheries and Food, (or, in Scotland, the

Secretary of State). There are two exceptions to this rule:
1) Where a dog has been a resident for six months or more in Northern Ireland, the Channel Islands or the Isle of Man.
2) Where the dog is landed, or put ashore, with the aim of re-exporting it within 48 hours from the same port or airport. However, arrangements must be made beforehand to avoid illegal entry.

An import licence requires a dog, upon arrival, to be detained for a six months period at a quarantine establishment approved by the Ministry of Agriculture, Fisheries and Food, or, for Scotland, the Secretary of State.

Exporting dogs Obviously where a dog is to exported the requirements of the country of import must be met. Enquiries should be addressed to the Ministry of Agriculture, Fisheries and Food and also to the Department of Trade and Industry, Export Licensing Branch, as a British export licence is also required. (See International travel requirements, page 189.)

Owner's responsibilities Prior to the Animals' Act (1971), the owner whose dog slipped out of the garden gate and caused an accident, could not be held responsible for its action. The 1971 Act changed all that and owners are now legally responsible for their pets' actions irrespective of whether the animals were deemed to be under their control at the time.

It stands to reason, therefore, that the owner of a dog which causes a traffic accident might face a serious claim for damages. That is why an increasing number of dog owners are seeking insurance protection either through specialist insurance companies or through welfare societies such as The National Dog Owners' Association, which offers cover as a membership benefit.

Some roads in the United Kingdom have been designated no dog areas—unless, that is, the animals are kept on the lead.

Country dwellers are well aware of the importance of preventing their dogs from worrying sheep or indeed from worrying any livestock, and farmers have the right to shoot on sight any dog which appears to be a threat to their livestock.

The fouling of footpaths by dogs causes more complaints from people than any other canine act, and in some areas, anyone whose dog is caught performing such an act may be liable to pay a fine, the amount varying according to the area. The main offenders are strays and dogs which are allowed by their owners to wander through the streets at will. Needless to say, there are also those owners who fail to train their dogs not to foul pavements even while the animal is under their control on the lead.

In the United Kingdom the motorist who has the misfortune to run over a dog is required by law to report the accident to the police within 24 hours of the incident. Strangely, this requirement does not apply to cats which do not have the same protection under the law.

Performing dogs In recent times, no doubt due to the success of certain dogs which appear on television and in advertising, various animal agencies have been formed which offer dogs for roles in film, stage and television productions.

Not generally known is that the training of dogs for public performance and entertainment requires a licence under the Performing Animals' Act (1925). However, registration and the obtaining of a licence (in the area where the trainer lives) would appear to be a fairly simple formality.

There are also laws protecting animals from being cruelly treated, for instance, being frightened or goaded into fury in the course of a filming sequence.

Sales of dogs The validity of advice to 'buy from a breeder' is borne out by the number of calls welfare societies regularly receive from people who have bought a pure bred dog from some other source, paying out substantial sums, only to discover thereafter that the certificate of pedigree received was virtually worthless.

A breeder cannot guarantee that the dog you buy is going to be a show winner, but many will be prepared to give you a receipt to confirm whether the dog has been sold to you for pet or show purposes.

If a dog is sold with a 'false' certificate of pedigree, and for the price that one would reasonably be expected to pay were that document genuine, this would constitute the criminal offence of obtaining money by false pretences, and the trading standards officer or your local authority should be consulted.

Stray dogs The Dogs' Act (1906) gave the police in the United Kingdom statutory responsibility for the capture, custody and disposal of stray dogs. Members of the public who lose a dog are invited to notify a local police station, where a detailed descripton of the animal is taken. Similarly, stray dogs found by members of the public should be taken to the police.

A stray dog may be kept by the police over-night, subsequent to which it is dispersed to various kennels pending claim, homing or, alas, eventual painless destruction. Everything possible is done to ensure that the latter course does not take place. For instance, in London, dogs found within the Metropolitan Police area are collected each morning from police stations in a distinctive red van and taken to the renowned Battersea Dogs' Home.

The law provides for dogs to be retained at Battersea for seven days, pending claim by their owners. Thereafter they may be retained for a period of time during which they are offered on sale to the public; thousands of Londoners choose their family pets from Battersea.

Transport and shops In London, and other parts of the United Kingdom, dogs may travel on buses providing the conductor agrees. If the bus is a double decker they are required to travel on the upper deck. Dogs can also travel on both underground and overground trains. There is no charge if they are transported in a container of specified dimensions, otherwise half price or child's fare is requested.

A dog may be taken into a railway carriage, but it is not allowed on a seat or in the refreshment car, or anywhere that food is being served. If another passenger objects to a dog's presence it must be transferred to the guard's van. Most large dogs usually do travel with the guard.

It is generally supposed that dogs are prohibited by law from being taken into shops. In fact this is not so. The position is that according to the Food Hygiene (General) Regulations of 1970 made under the Food and Drugs Act of 1955 (or in Scotland the Food Hygiene (Scotland) Regulations of 1959) food traders are obliged to take all such steps as may be reasonably necessary to protect the food from risk of contamination. This places the responsibility of whether or not to ban dogs on the shopkeeper, and there has been an increase over the past ten years in the number of establishments banning dogs.

Many people believe, quite mistakenly, that they cannot take a dog into a hotel. This is by no means the case. Many hotels, particularly those in country areas, welcome canine guests, but it is as well to check the position when making a booking rather than assuming that dogs are accepted. In hotels where dogs are welcomed it is usually permissible for the animal to share the owner's bedroom and sometimes to accompany them into public rooms, but never into a restaurant or anywhere that food is being served.

The American situation
Dog laws and legislations in the United States come under several categories. Humane laws, federal legislation, animal welfare acts, and laws, restrictions and regulations for states, counties, towns and cities are all part of a network to protect dogs from humans and vice versa. Before taking up residence in a new

Above: In New York City, owners are required by law to clear up after their dogs, for which purpose many people use a 'poop scoop'.

area it is therefore advisable to determine the laws pertaining. In some areas, for instance, the number of dogs that may be kept in a home is restricted. The local Humane Society should, in most cases, be able to answer any questions concerning dog laws in their specific area.

It is usual for dogs to be licensed from four months of age. In some areas six months is the minimum age and, in all cases, proof of rabies inoculation is required before a licence can be issued.

Leash laws exist in almost every city, county and state, the enforcement of which varies considerably. There are, however, particularly strict leash laws in New York City and owners there are responsible for cleaning up any mess deposited by their dogs—the 'poop and scoop law'. However, one of the strictest dog laws would appear to be that passed in the state of Ohio in 1965 whereby dogs must be on a leash, tied or fenced in, 24 hours a day, except when hunting.

The cost of a dog licence also varies from state to state and in some cases there is a reduced rate for spayed females or neutered males, castration being encouraged in an effort to reduce the huge number of stray and unwanted dogs.

In regard to inter-state travel, all states require a health certificate and only the states of New Jersey and New York do not require proof of rabies vaccination. Dogs taken to Hawaii must undergo 120 days quarantine at the owner's expense. Before a dog may travel by air, the owner or shipper must present a current health certificate and proof of rabies inoculation to the airline. Most, if not all, commercial airlines will not accept dogs travelling unaccompanied if air temperatures are above or below accepted levels. It is wise to check ahead for rules and regulations before travelling with, or shipping, a pet. Trains will not take dogs at any time, even in the baggage cars.

Australia
In Australia laws regarding the control, seizure and registration of dogs vary from state to state. However, there has, in recent times, been some relaxation in that German Shepherd Dogs can now be imported into any part of Australia and breeding is permitted.

Guide dogs for the blind can accompany their owners into any

building or public place.

There is an excellent canine registration system in New South Wales. Owners have to complete a form and, on payment of a fee, are issued with a registration collar disc engraved with the name of the area, the registration number and year of expiry.

It is only permitted for dogs to enter Australia from, or via, the United Kingdom, New Zealand and specified Pacific Islands.

INTERNATIONAL TRAVEL REQUIREMENTS

Austria Proof of inoculation against rabies and a valid health certificate required, inoculation to have been given 30 days before date of entry, but not over a year before.

Belgium Proof of inoculation against rabies required, such inoculation to have been given 30 days before date of entry.

Bulgaria Valid health certificate and written confirmation that the country of origin is free from infectious disease required.

Czechoslovakia Valid health certificate required along with written

confirmation that, as at two days before arrival, no outbreak of rabies has occurred in place of origin within 90 days period.

Denmark Proof of inoculation against rabies required, such inoculation to have been given at least four weeks before date of entry, but within the past 12 months.

Finland Proof of inoculation against rabies and distemper required; also health certificate and entry permit from The Ministry of Agriculture. There is a quarantine period of six months, two months of which may be spent at the owner's residence.

France Proof of inoculation against rabies required in the case of dogs over one year of age. Puppies between 3-12 months additionally need injections against distemper and contagious liver infection. Special arrangements have to be made in the case of puppies under three months of age.

Germany, East Proof of inoculation against rabies required, such inoculation to have been administered at least 30 days before date of entry; also approved health certificate, made out no more than five days before entry into the country.

Germany, West Proof of inoculation against rabies required, such inoculation to have been administered at least 30 days before date of entry.

Greece Proof of inoculation against rabies affording 12 months protection required.

Ireland See United Kingdom.

Italy Proof of inoculation against rabies required, such inoculation to have been given at least 20 days before date of entry; also approved health certificate.

Luxembourg Proof of inoculation against rabies required, such inoculation to have been given 30 days before date of entry.

Netherlands Proof of inoculation against rabies required, such inoculation having been given 30 days before date of entry.

Norway Entry permit must be obtained from the Ministry of Agriculture. Six-month quarantine period required, two months of which is spent at owner's residence.

Poland Proof of inoculation against rabies required; also health certificate (duplicated) which must have been made out at least four days prior to date of entry.

Portugal Proof of inoculation against rabies and valid health certificate required. Both to be approved by the Veterinary Health Office.

Rumania Proof of inoculation against rabies and valid health certificate required.

Spain Proof of inoculation against rabies and health certificate required. The rabies inoculation must have been administered at least 30 days prior to date of entry, but not in excess of 12 months before such a date. The name of the injection fluid and that of the manufacturer should appear on the vaccination certificate. Dogs arriving at the border without correct documentation are subject to 20 days quarantine. No vaccination requirements for puppies under eight weeks of age.

Sweden Entry permit must be obtained from the Ministry of Agriculture. Six months quarantine required, two months of which is spent at the owner's home.

United Kingdom Import and export only allowed where prior permission has been granted. Compulsory six-month quarantine period must be spent in quarantine kennels approved by the Ministry of Agriculture, Fisheries and Food.

United States All states require a valid health certificate and, with the exception of New Jersey and New York, proof of rabies inoculation. Hawaii requires dogs entering the state to undergo 120 days quarantine at the owner's expense.

Yugoslavia Proof of inoculation against rabies required, such inoculation to have been administered at least 15 days before date of entry. Health certificate also required.

Appendices

KENNEL CLUB REGULATIONS FOR AGILITY TESTS

(Reproduced by kind permission of The Kennel Club)

1 Registered Clubs, Societies, Dog Training Clubs, Kennel Club Licensed Shows and other organisations approved by the Kennel Club may hold Agility Tests. The Kennel Club reserves the right to refuse any application for a licence.

2 Applications for permission to hold Agility Tests must be made in the form of a letter to the Secretary of the Kennel Club at least six months before the date of the proposed event. A fee of £2.87 (inclusive of VAT) must be forwarded with the application together with a schedule for the event which must contain:—

(a) The date, place and time of event.
(b) A separate official entry form which must be an exact copy of wording of the specimen entry form issued by the Kennel Club.
(c) The amounts of entry fees and any prize money.
(d) The method by which the judge will mark the tests.
(e) The qualifications for entry in the tests scheduled.
(f) An announcement that the Tests are held Kennel Club Regulations for Agility Tests.
(g) An announcement that the organising committee reserve the right to refuse any entry.
(h) The names of the judges.

3 A dog must, at the time of the competition, be registered at the Kennel Club. The Committee of the organising Club may reserve the right to refuse entry.

4 Puppies under 12 calendar months of age and bitches in season are not eligible for competition in Agility Tests.

5 If a dog competes which has been exposed to the risk of any contagious or infectious disease during the period of six weeks prior to the Agility Tests and/or if any dog shall be proved to be suffering at Agility Tests from any contagious or infectious disease, the owner thereof shall be liable to be dealt with under Kennel Club Rule 17.

6 The organising Club shall keep a list of the names of all competing dogs with awards and the names and addresses of their owners for a period of twelve months from the date of the Agility Tests.

7 A judge at an Agility Test can not compete at that event on the same day.

8 Fraudulent or Discreditable Conduct at Agility Tests to be Reported:—

The Executive of the organising Club of an Agility Test must immediately report to the Secretary of the Kennel Club any case of alleged fraudulent or discreditable conduct, any default or omission at or in connection with the Agility Test which may come under its notice, and at the same time forward to the Secretary of the Kennel Club all documents and information in connection therewith, which may be in its possession or power. Where fraudulent or discreditable conduct is alleged at an Agility Test in Scotland, the Executive of the organising Club must make such report in the first instance to the Secretary of the Scottish Kennel Club.

Agility Tests are considered to be a "fun" type competition designed for spectator appeal. However, competitors are reminded that they are subject to other Kennel Club Rules & Regulations where applicable.

SCHEDULE OF TESTS

Agility Tests—Courses and Obstacles

The following obstacles meet with the approval of the Committee of the Kennel Club but organisers may submit others for approval if desired. No practice is to be allowed on the course.

1 Test Area The test area must measure not less than 40 yards x 30 yards and have a non-slip surface.

2 Course A minimum of ten and a maximum of 18 comprise a test course.

3 Obstacles

Hurdle: Height 2ft 6in maximum. Width: 4ft 0in minimum.

Dog Walk: Height: 4ft 0in minimum, 4ft 6in maximum. Walk plank width: 8in minimum, 12in maximum. Length: 12ft 0in minimum, 14ft 0in maximum. Ramps to have anti-slip slats at intervals to be firmly fixed to top plank.

Hoop: Aperture diameter: 1ft 3in minimum. Aperture centre from ground 3ft 0in in maximum.

Brush Fence: Dimensions as for hurdle.

Table: Surface: 3ft 0in square minimum. Height: 3ft 0in maximum. To be of stable construction with non-slip surface.

Collapsible Tunnel: Diameter: 2ft 0in minimum, 2ft 6in maximum. Length: 12ft 0in. Circular of non-rigid material construction with entrance of rigid construction and fixed or weighted to the gorund.

'A' ramp: Length: 3 yards minimum, 3½ yards maximum. Width: 3ft 0in. Height of apex from ground 6ft 3in. Two ramps hinged at apex. Surface of ramps slatted at intervals.

Weaving Poles: Number 6 minimum, 12 maximum. Distance apart 2ft 0in maximum.

Pipe Tunnel: Diameter: 2ft minimum. Length: 10ft 0in minimum.

See-Saw: Width: 8in minimum, 12in maximum. Length: 12ft 0in minimum, 14ft 0in maximum. Height of central bracket from ground, 2ft 3in maximum. A plank firmly mounted on central bracket.

Long-jump: Length: 5ft maximum. Width: 4ft minimum. Height: 1ft maximum.

Pause Box: Defined area 4ft x 4ft.

Marking

Standard Marking

5 faults for each failure to negotiate any obstacle correctly.
Failure to correctly complete the course—disqualified.

Other marking

Any form of marking other than 'Standard' must be stated in the schedule.

Below: Negotiating the weaving poles during an agility test.

KENNEL CLUB REGULATIONS FOR TESTS FOR OBEDIENCE CLASSES

(Reproduced by kind permission of The Kennel Club)

1 Kennel Club Show Regulations shall where applicable and as amended or varied from time to time apply to Obedience Classes as follows:—

Kennel Club Championship Show Regulations } to Championship Obedience Shows.

Kennel Club Licence Show Regulations } to Licence Obedience Shows.

Kennel Club Regulations for Sanction Shows } to Sanction Obedience Shows.

2 A Show Society may schedule any or all of the following classes at a show. No variation to any test within a class may be made. "Run-offs" will be judged, one at a time, by normal scheduled tests.

Classes may be placed in any order in the schedule but this order must be followed at the show except that a Society, by publication in the schedule, may reserve the right to vary the order of judging when the entry is known.

The maximum number of entries permitted in a Class for one Judge to judge with the exception of Class C where Obedience Certificates are on offer shall be sixty. If this number is exceeded the Class shall be divided by a draw into two equal halves, each to be judged separately. The prizes for each Class shall be the same as that offered for the original Class. No Judge shall judge more than sixty dogs in one day and if a Judge is appointed for two or more Classes the combined total entries of which exceed sixty, a Reserve Judge shall be called upon to officiate appropriately. Show Societies should ensure that when appointing Judges for Shows sufficient numbers are appointed for the expected entries. The Reserve Judge may enter dogs for competition at the Show and if not called upon to judge may compete.

Where a Class is divided into two halves exhibitors who have entered for that Class shall be notified accordingly of all changes or alterations and no timed stay exercises are to be held earlier than those advertised for the original class.

In Class C where Obedience Certificates are on offer one Judge only may be appointed for each sex. Judges must be present at all times dogs are under test including stay exercises.

3 *(a)* In all the classes the handler may use the dog's name with a command or signal without penalty. Except in the Stay Tests and Distant Control, all tests shall commence and finish with the dog sitting at the handler's side except in Beginners, Novice and Class A Recall Tests where the dog may be left in either the Sit or Down position at the handler's choice.

(b) Food shall not be given to a dog in the ring.

(c) In any test in which judge's articles are used, none of them should be injurious to the dog, and they must be capable of being picked up by any breed entered in that test.

(d) Spayed bitches and castrated dogs are permitted to compete in Obedience Classes.

(e) No bitch in season shall be allowed to compete in Obedience Classes.

(f) In all tests the points must be graduated.

(g) Handlers may use only a slip chain or smooth collar in the ring.

(h) Every handler must wear his ring number prominently displayed when in the ring.

(i) The Show Executive shall also appoint a Chief Steward whose name must be announced in the schedule and who must not work a dog at the Show. The Chief Steward shall be responsible for the control of any running order and for the smooth running of each class, and whose decision in such matters shall be final.

The Show Executive shall also ensure that Ring or "Caller" Stewards are appointed for each class scheduled who must not work a dog at the Show.

(j) A draw for the running order in Class C at Championship Shows must be made prior to the Show and exhibitors and judges must be notified of the running order before the day of the Show. The Kennel Club will ballot for the running order for Championship Class C and Show Secretaries must forward lists of entries by recorded delivery or registered post to the Kennel Club for a ballot within 7 days after the closing of entries. Where a complete draw for the running order of classes other than Championship Class C is not made, Show Managements must ensure that at least 10 competitors/dogs are available by means of a ballot for judging in the first hour following the scheduled time for the commencement of judging of that class and these competitors must be notified prior to the Show. All competitors must report to the Ring Scoreboard Steward and book in within one hour of the scheduled time for the commencement of judging for the class and those reporting late will be excluded from competition unless they have reported previously to the Chief Steward that they are actually working a dog entered in another Championship Class C or in the Stay Tests of another class. Where a complete running order is made, all competitors must be notified prior to the day of the Show and must book in on arrival at the Show. Published orders of running must be strictly adhered to.

Where timed stays will take place it must be announced in the schedule that they take priority over other tests, the times of such tests to be promulgated at the Show and published in the catalogue. In the case of Championship Class C stays must not be judged before 1 p.m.

Where Championship Class C competitors are required to compete in another Class at the Show the Chief Steward will agree with the judges of these other classes that the judging of such competitors be re-arranged in the running order. It will be the responsibility of competitors to advise the Chief Steward of the clash of judging.

In all Scent Tests, dogs should compete in the same order as for previous tests, but the judge may relax the running order where necessary. Scent tests must not be carried out during the main ring work but will take place as a separate test at the judges' discretion.

(k) Judging rings shall not in any circumstances contain less than 900 square feet of clear floor space and shall be not less than 20 feet in width except that for Championship Class C the ring must contain not less than 1,600 square feet.

(l) No person shall carry out punitive correction or harsh handling of a dog at any time whilst within the boundaries of the Show.

(m) Judges at Championship Shows

(1) For Class C at Championship Shows judges must have had at least five years judging experience and must have judged at thirty Open Obedience Shows at which they must have judged Class C not less than 15 times. Judging experience of other classes must include at least 2 each of the following at Open or Championship Shows, Beginners, Novice, Class A and Class B.

(2) For all other classes, other than Class C, the judge must have had at least three years judging experience at twenty Open Obedience Shows and have judged Beginners, Novice, Class A and Class B each on at least 2 occasions at Open Shows.

(n) Judges at Open Shows

(1) On first appointment must satisfy the Show Committee that they have at least two years experience judging at a lower level and have worked a dog in Licensed Obedience Shows and have also acted as a Caller Steward or Marker Steward working with the judge in the ring on at least six occasions at Licensed Shows.

(o) A Judge of Class C at an Open Show must record in the judging book the number of points awarded to each dog with 290 or more points. The Show Secretary will record these in the official marked catalogue.

(p) The judge may allow a dog to be withdrawn from competition only on application by the competitor to the judge.

4 Imperfections in heeling between tests will not be judged but any physical disciplining by the handler in the ring, or any uncontrolled behaviour of the dog, such as snapping, unjustified barking, fouling the ring, or running out of the ring, even between tests, must be penalised by deducting points from the total score and the judge may bar the dog from further competition in that class.

5 *(a)* In all the following Definitions of Classes, First Prize wins in Limited and Sanction Show Obedience Classes will not count for entry in Open and Championship Show Obedience Classes. No dog is eligible to compete in Obedience Classes at Limited and Sanction Shows which has won an Obedience Certificate or obtained any award that counts towards the title of Obedience Champion or the equivalent thereof under the rules of any governing body recognised by the Kennel Club. Obedience Champions are eligible only for Class C at Open and Championship Shows.

(b) A dog may be entered in any two classes at a Show for which it is eligible with the exception of Championship Class C for which only dogs appropriately qualified may be entered. (Note the qualification for Championship Class C and Obedience Warrant).

PRE-BEGINNERS

Pre-Beginners Classes may only be scheduled at Limited and Sanction Obedience Shows. If owner or handler or dog have won a first prize in any Class they may not compete in Pre-Beginners.

Handlers will not be penalised for encouragement or extra commands except in the Sit and Down tests. In these tests, at the discretion of the judge, handlers may face their dogs. Judges or Stewards must not use the words "last command" except in the Sit and Down tests.

1. Heel on Lead	15 points
2. Heel Free	20 points
3. Recall from sit or down position at handler's choice. Dog to be recalled by handler when stationary and facing the dog. Dog to return smartly to the handler, sit in front, go to heel—all on command of judge or steward or handler. Distance at discretion of judge. Test commences when handler leaves dog	10 points
4. Sit One Minute, handler in sight	10 points
5. Down Two Minutes, handler in sight	20 points
	Total 75 points

BEGINNERS

If owner or handler or dog have won a total of two or more first prizes in the Beginners Class, they may not compete in Beginners. Winners of one first prize in any other Obedience Class are ineligible to compete in this Class.

Handlers will not be penalised for encouragement or extra commands except in the Sit and Down tests. In these tests, at the discretion of the judge, handlers may face their dogs. Judges or stewards must not use the words "last command" except in the Sit and Down tests.

1. Heel on Lead	15 points
2. Heel Free	20 points
3. Recall from sit or down position at handler's choice. Dog to be recalled by handler when stationary and facing the dog. Dog to return smartly to handler, sit in front, go to heel—all on command of judge or steward to handler. Distance at discretion of judge. Test commences when handler leaves dog.	10 points
4. Retrieve any article. Handlers may use their own article	25 points
5. Sit One Minute, handler in sight	10 points
6. Down Two Minutes, handler in sight	20 points
	Total 100 points

NOVICE

For dogs that have not won two first prizes in Obedience Classes (Beginners Class excepted).

Handlers will not be penalised for encouragement or extra commands except in the Sit and Down tests. In these tests, at the discretion of the judge, handlers may face their dogs. Judges or stewards must not use the words "last command" except in the Sit and Down tests.

1. Temperament Test. To take place immediately before heel on lead. Dog to be on lead in the Stand position. Handler to stand by dog. Judge to approach quietly from the front and run his hand gently down the dog's back. Judge may talk quietly to dog to reassure it. Any undue resentment, cringing, growling or snapping to be penalised. This is not a stand for examination or stay test.	10 points
2. Heel on Lead	10 points
3. Heel Free	20 points
4. Recall from sit or down position at handler's choice. Dog to be recalled by handler when stationary and facing the dog. Dog to return smartly to handler, sit in front, go to heel—all on command of judge or steward to handler. Distance at discretion of judge. Test commences when handler leaves dog.	10 points
5. Retrieve a Dumb-bell. Handlers may use their own bells	20 points
6. Sit One Minute, handler in sight	10 points
7. Down Two Minutes, handler in sight	20 points
	Total 100 points

CLASS A

For dogs which have not won three first prizes in Classes A, B, and Open Class C in total.

Simultaneous command and signal will be permitted. Extra commands or signals must be penalised.

1. Heel on Lead	15 points
2. Temperament Test. Will take place before Heel Free. Dog to be in the stand position and off lead. Handler to stand beside dog. Conditions as for Novice Temperament Test, except that Test will commence with order "last command" and end with order "test finished". Extra commands will be penalised. This is not a stand for examination or stay test	10 points
3. Heel Free	20 points
4. Recall from Sit or Down, position at handler's choice. Dog to be recalled to heel by handler, on command of judge or steward, whilst handler is walking away from dog, both to continue forward until halted. The recall and halt points to be the same for each dog and handler. Test commences following handler's last command to dog	15 points
5. Retrieve a Dumb-bell. Handlers may use their own dumb-bells	20 points
6. Sit One Minute, handler out of sight	10 points
7. Down Five Minutes, handler out of sight	30 points
8. Scent Discrimination, handler's scent on handler's article. The total number of articles shall not exceed ten, all of which shall be clearly visible to the dog	30 points
	Total 150 points

CLASS B

For dogs which have not won three first prizes in Class B and Open Class C in total.

One command, by word or signal, except in Test 2. Extra commands or signals must be penalised.

1. Heel Free. The dog shall be required to walk at heel free and shall also be tested at fast and slow pace. Each change of pace shall commence from the "halt" position	30 points
2. Send Away, Drop and Recall. On command of judge or handler, dog to be sent away in direction indicated by judge. After the dog has been dropped, handler will call the dog to heel whilst walking where directed by judge and both will continue forward. No obstacle to be placed in path of dog. Simultaneous command and signal is permitted but as soon as the dog leaves the handler the arm must be dropped. (N.B. an extra command may be simultaneous command and signal, but an extra command must be penalised)	40 points
3. Retrieve any one article provided by the Judge but which must not be in any manner injurious to the dog (definitely excluding food or glass). The article to be picked up easily by any breed of dog in that Class and to be clearly visible to the dog. A separate similar article to be used for each dog. Test commences following Judge or Steward's words "last command" to handler	30 points
4. Stand One Minute, handler at least ten paces away from and facing away from the dog	10 points
5. Sit Two Minutes, handler out of sight	20 points
6. Down Ten Minutes, handler out of sight	40 points
7. Scent Discrimination. Handler's scent on article provided by judge. A separate similar article to be used for each dog and the total number of articles shall not exceed ten, all of which shall be clearly visible to the dog and shall be similar to the article given to the handler. Judges must use a separate similar scent decoy or decoys for each dog. No points will be awarded if the article is given to the dog	30 points
	Total 200 points

Right: The dog receives lavish praise from its handler at the end of a successfully performed obedience exercise.

CLASS C

At Championship Shows: For dogs which have been placed on at least one occasion not lower than third in each class of Novice Class, Class A and Class B and have won Open Class C with not less than 290 marks on one occasion and have gained at least 290 marks in Open Class C on three further occasions under different judges. Dogs which qualified for entry in Championship Class C prior to 1st May 1980 are also eligible.

At Limited and Sanction Shows: Open to all dogs except Obedience Certificate winners and dogs which have obtained any award that counts towards the title of Obedience Champion or the equivalent thereof under the rules of any governing body recognised by the Kennel Club.

One command, by word or signal, except in Test 2 where an extra command may be simultaneous command and signal. Extra commands or signals must be penalised.

1. Heel Work. The dog shall be required to walk at heel free, and also be tested at fast and slow pace. At some time during this test, at the discretion of the judge, the dog shall be required, whilst walking to heel at normal pace, to be left at the Stand, Sit and Down in any order (the order to be the same for each dog) as and when directed by the judge. The handler shall continue forward alone, without hesitation, and continue as directed by the judge until he reaches his dog when both shall continue forward together until halted. Heel work may include left about turns and figure-of-eight at normal and/or slow pace   60 points
2. Send Away, Drop and Recall as in Class B   40 points
3. Retrieve any one article provided by the Judge but which must not be in any manner injurious to the dog (definitely excluding food or glass). The article to be picked up easily by any breed of dog in that Class and to be clearly visible to the dog. A separate similar article to be used for each dog. Test commences following Judge or Steward's "last command" to handler   30 points
4. Distant Control. Dog to Sit, Stand and Down at a marked place not less than ten paces from handler, in any order on command from judge to handler. Six instructions to be given in the same order for each dog. Excessive movement, i.e. more than the length of the dog, in any direction by the dog, having regard to its size, will be penalised. The dog shall start the exercise with its front feet behind a designated point. No penalty for excessive movement in a forward direction shall be imposed until the back legs of the dog pass the designated point   50 points
5. Sit Two Minutes, handler out of sight   20 points
6. Down Ten Minutes, handler out of sight   50 points
7. Scent Discrimination. Judge's scent on piece of marked cloth. Neutral and decoy cloths to be provided by the Show Executive. The judge shall not place his cloth in the ring himself, but it shall be placed by a steward. A separate similar piece to be used for each dog and the total number of separate similar pieces of cloth from which the dog shall discriminate shall not exceed ten. If a dog fetches or fouls a wrong article this must be replaced by a fresh article. At open-air shows all scent cloths must be adequately weighted to prevent them being blown about. The method of taking scent shall be at the handler's discretion but shall not require the judge to place his hand on or lean towards the dog. A separate similar piece of cloth approximately 6in by 6in but not more than 10in by 10in shall be available to be used for giving each dog the scent. Judges should use a scent decoy or decoys   50 points

Total 300 points

---

6 The Kennel Club will offer an Obedience Certificate (Dog) and an Obedience Certificate (Bitch) for winners of 1st prizes in Class C Dog and Class C Bitch at a Championship Show, provided that the exhibits do not lose more than 10 points out of 300, and provided also that the classes are open to all breeds.

Judges must also award a Reserve Best of Sex provided that the exhibit has not lost more than 10 points out of 300.

---

7 The Kennel Club will offer at Crufts Dog Show each year the Kennel Club Obedience Championship—(Dog) and the Kennel Club Obedience Championship—(Bitch). A dog awarded one or more Obedience Certificates during the calendar year preceding Crufts Show shall be entitled to compete.

The Tests for the Championships shall be those required for Class C in these regulations. If the winning dog or bitch has lost more than 10 points out of 300, the Championship award shall be withheld.

---

8 As provided in Kennel Club Rule 4(c), the following dogs shall be entitled to be described as Obedience Champions and shall receive a Certificate to that effect from the Kennel Club:—
- (a) The winners of the Kennel Club Obedience Championships.
- (b) A dog awarded three Obedience Certificates under three different judges in accordance with these Regulations.

EXPLANATORY NOTES FOR OBEDIENCE TESTS

In all classes the dog should work in a happy natural manner and prime consideration should be given to judging the dog and handler as a team. The dog may be encouraged and praised except where specifically stated.

Instructions and commands to competitors may be made either by the judge or his steward by delegation.

In all tests the side of a handler will be regarded as the "working side", unless the handler suffers from a physical disability and has the judge's permission to work the dog on the right-hand side.

To signal the completion of each test the handler will be given the command "test finished".

It is permissible for handlers to practise their dogs before going into the ring provided there is no punitive correction and this is similar to an athlete limbering up before an event.

Time Table of Judging — To assist show executives the following guide time table is issued: —

Class C . . . . 6 dogs per hour
Class B . . . . 8 dogs per hour
Class A . . . . 12 dogs per hour
Novice . . . . 12 dogs per hour
Beginners . . . . 12 dogs per hour

The dog should be led into the ring for judging with a collar and lead attached (unless otherwise directed) and should be at the handler's side. Competitors in Championship Class C who have lost more marks than would enable them to qualify with 290 marks at the conclusion of the judging to volunteer to withdraw from the Class with the judge's approval. This decision to withdraw is entirely at the discretion of the competitor and judges must not compel such competitors to withdraw.

1 Heel on Lead

The dog should be sitting straight at the handler's side. On command the handler should walk briskly forward in a straight line with the dog at heel. The dog should be approximately level with and reasonably close to the handler's leg at all times when the handler is walking. The lead must be slack at all times. On the command "Left Turn" or "Right Turn" the handler should turn smartly at a right angle in the appropriate direction and the dog should keep its position at the handler's side. Unless otherwise directed, at the command "about turn" the handler should turn about smartly on the spot through an angle of 180° to the right and walk in the opposite direction, the dog maintaining its position at the handler's side. On the command "halt" the handler should halt immediately and the dog should sit straight at the handler's side. Throughout this test the handler may not touch the dog or make use of the lead without penalty.

2 Heel Free

This test should be carried out in a similar manner as for Heel on Lead except that the dog must be off the lead throughout the test.

3 Retrieve a Dumb-Bell/Article

At the start of this exercise the dog should be sitting at the handler's side. On command the handler must throw the dumb-bell/article in the direction indicated. The dog should remain at the Sit position until the handler is ordered to send it to retrieve the dumb-bell/article. The dog should move out promptly at a smart pace to collect the dumb-bell/article cleanly. It should return with the dumb-bell/article at a smart pace and sit straight in front of the handler. On command the handler should take the dumb-bell/article from the dog. On further command the dog should be sent to heel. In Classes A, B and C the test commences on the order "last command" to handler.

4 (a) Sit/Stay

The Judge or Steward will direct handlers to positions in the ring. The command "last command" will be given when all are ready and handlers should then instantly give their final command to the dogs. Any further commands or signals to the dogs after this "last command" will be penalised. Handlers will then be instructed to leave their dogs and walk to positions indicated until ordered to return to them. Dogs should remain at the Sit position throughout the test. This is a group test and all dogs must compete together — but where this is impracticable at indoor shows it may be split into two groups for judging but all judging of groups must follow without interval.

(b) Stand/Stay

This test should be carried out exactly as for the Sit/Stay, except that dogs will be left in the Stand position throughout the Test. This is a group test and all dogs must compete together — but where this is impracticable at indoor shows it may be split into two equal groups for judging but all judging of groups must follow without interval.

(c) Down/Stay

This test should be carried out exactly as for the Sit/Stay, except that dogs will be left in the Down position throughout the Test. This is a group test and all dogs must compete together — but where this is impracticable at indoor shows it may be split into two equal groups for judging but all judging of groups must follow without interval.

5 Scent Discrimination

A steward will place the scented article amongst up to a maximum of nine other articles.

In a scent test if a dog brings in a wrong article or physically fouls any article (i.e. mouths it) this article will be replaced.

The dog should at this time be facing away from the articles. On command the handler should bring the dog to a point indicated, give the dog scent and stand upright before sending the dog to find and retrieve the appropriate article. The dog should find the article and complete the test as for the Retrieve test. In all tests, scent articles are to be placed at least 2 feet apart. Limiting the time allowed for this test is at the Judge's discretion.

Class A — Handler's Scent on Handler's Article.

The Judge should reject any articles he considers to be unfit by nature of their size, shape or substance and which in his opinion could have the effect of converting this elementary Scent Test into a Sight Test. In this test at least one other article must be scented by someone other than the handler and the decoy article(s) must be similar for each dog.

Class B — Handler's Scent on Article provided by the Judge.

The article must not be given to the dog. All articles must be separate and similar.

Class C — Judge's Scent on piece of marked cloth. A decoy steward should not handle a cloth for a period longer than the Judge.

Below: A successful retrieve during a scent discrimination exercise.

REGULATIONS FOR THE AMERICAN KENNEL CLUB
LICENSED OBEDIENCE TRIALS

*(These regulations are copyrighted by The American Kennel Club, and are
reproduced by special permission)*

NOVICE

Novice A Class

Section 1. The Novice A class shall be for dogs not less than six months of age that have not won the title C.D. A dog that is owned or co-owned by a person who has previously handled or regularly trained a dog that has won a C.D. title may not be entered in the Novice A class, nor may a dog be handled in this class by such person.

Each dog in this class must have a different handler who shall be its owner or co-owner or a member of the immediate family of the owner or co-owner, provided that such member has not previously handled or regularly trained a C.D. dog. The same person must handle the same dog in all exercises. No person may handle more than one dog in the Novice A class.

Novice B Class

Section 2. The Novice B class shall be for dogs not less than six months of age that have not won the title C.D. Dogs in this class may be handled by the owner or any other person. A person may handle more than one dog in this class, but each dog must have a separate handler for the Long Sit and Long Down exercises when judged in the same group. No dog may be entered in both Novice A and Novice B classes at any one trial.

Novice Exercises and Scores

Section 3. The exercises and maximum scores in the Novice classes are:

1. Heel on Leash and Figure Eight.................... 40 points
2. Stand for Examination........................... 30 points
3. Heel Free...................................... 40 points
4. Recall... 30 points
5. Long Sit....................................... 30 points
6. Long Down..................................... 30 points
Maximum Total Score............................. 200 points

C.D. Title

Section 4. The American Kennel Club will issue a Companion Dog certificate for each registered dog, and will permit the use of the letters "C.D." after the name of each dog that has been certified by three different judges to have received Qualifying scores in Novice classes at three Licensed or Member Obedience Trials, provided the sum total of dogs that actually competed in the Regular Novice classes at each trial is not less than six.

Heel on Leash & Figure Eight

Section 5. The principal feature of this exercise is the ability of the dog and handler to work as a team.

Orders for the exercise are "Forward", "Halt", "Right turn", "Left turn", "About turn", "Slow", "Normal" and "Fast". "Fast" signifies that the handler must run, handler and dog moving forward at noticeably accelerated speed. In executing the About turn, the handler will always do a Right About turn.

The orders may be given in any sequence and may be repeated as necessary, but the judge shall attempt to standardize the heeling pattern for all dogs in any class.

The leash may be held in either hand or in both hands, providing the hands are in a natural position. However, any tightening or jerking of the leash or any act, signal or command which in the judge's opinion gives the dog assistance shall be penalized.

The handler shall enter the ring with his dog on a loose leash and stand with the dog sitting in the Heel position. The judge shall ask if the handler is ready before giving the order, "Forward". The handler may give a command or signal to Heel, and shall walk briskly and in a natural manner with his dog on a loose leash. The dog shall walk close to the left side of the handler without swinging wide, lagging, forging or crowding. Whether heeling or sitting, the dog must not interfere with the handler's freedom of motion at any time. At each order to Halt, the handler will stop and his dog shall sit straight and promptly in the Heel position without command or signal, and shall not move until the handler again moves forward on order from the judge. It is permissible after each Halt, before moving again, for the handler to give a command or signal to Heel. The judge shall say "Exercise finished" after this portion of the exercise.

Before starting the Figure Eight the judge shall ask if the handler is ready. Figure Eight signifies that on specific orders from the judge to Forward and Halt, the handler and dog, from a starting position about equidistant from the two stewards and facing the judge, shall walk briskly twice completely around and between the two stewards, who shall stand 8 feet apart. The Figure Eight in the Novice classes shall be done on leash. The handler may choose to go in either direction. There shall be no About turn or Fast or Slow in the Figure Eight, but the judge must order at least one Halt during and another Halt at the end of this portion of the exercise.

Heel on Leash & Figure Eight, Scoring

Section 6. If a dog is unmanagable, or if its handler constantly controls its performance by tugging on the leash or adapts pace to that of the dog, the dog must be scored zero.

Substantial deductions shall be made for additional commands or signals to Heel and for failure of dog or handler to change pace noticeably for Slow and Fast.

Substantial or minor deductions shall be made for such things as lagging, heeling wide, forging, crowding, poor sits, handler failing to walk at a brisk pace, occasional guidance with leash and other imperfections in heeling.

In scoring this exercise the judge shall accompany the handler at a discreet distance so that he can observe any signals or commands given by the handler to the dog. The judge must do so without interfering with either dog or handler.

Stand for Examination

Section 7. The principal features of this exercise are that the dog stand in position before and during the examination, and that the dog display neither shyness nor resentment.

Orders are "Stand your dog and leave when you are ready", "Back to your dog" and "Exercise finished". There will be no further command from the judge to the handler to leave the dog.

The handler shall take his dog on leash to a place indicated by the judge, where the handler shall remove the leash and give it to a steward who shall place it on the judge's table or other designated place.

On judge's order the handler will stand and/or pose his dog off leash by the method of his choice, taking any reasonable time if he chooses to pose the dog as in the show ring. When he is ready, the handler shall give his command and/or signal to the dog to Stay, walk forward about six feet in front of the dog, turn around and stand facing the dog.

The judge shall approach the dog from the front, and shall touch only the dog's head, body and hindquarters, using the fingers and palm of one hand only. He shall then order, "Back to your dog", whereupon the handler shall walk around behind his dog and return to the Heel position. The dog must remain standing until after the judge has said "Exercise finished"

Stand for Examination, Scoring

Section 8. The scoring of this exercise will not start until the handler has given the command and/or signal to Stay, except for such things as rough treatment of the dog by its handler or active resistance by the dog to its handler's attempts to make it stand. Either of these shall be penalized substantially.

A dog shall be scored zero if it displays shyness or resentment, growls or snaps at any time, sits before or during the examination, or moves away from the place where it was left either before or during the examination.

Minor or substantial deductions, depending on the circumstances, shall be made for a dog that moves its feet at any time or sits or moves away after the examination has been completed.

Heel Free, Performance and Scoring

Section 9. This exercise shall be executed in the same manner as Heel on Leash and Figure Eight except that the dog shall be off leash and that there shall be no Figure Eight. Orders and scoring shall also be the same.

Recall

Section 10. The principal features of this exercise are that the dog stay where left until called by its handler, and that the dog respond promptly to the handler's command or signal to "Come".

Orders are "Leave your dog", "Call your dog" and "Finish".

On order from the judge, the handler may give command and/or signal to the dog to Stay in the Sit position while the handler walks forward about 35 feet to the other end of the ring, where he shall turn and stand in a natural manner facing his dog. On judge's order or signal, the handler will give command or signal for the dog to Come. The dog must come straight in at a brisk trot or gallop and sit straight, centred immediately in front of the handler's feet, close enough that the handler could readily touch its head without moving either foot or having to stretch forward. The dog must not touch the handler or sit between his feet.

On judge's order the handler will give command or signal to Finish and the dog must go smartly to the Heel position and Sit. The manner in which the dog finishes shall be optional with the handler provided that it is prompt and that the dog Sit straight at Heel.

——— Recall, Scoring ———

Section 11. A dog must receive a score of zero for the following: not Staying without additional command or signal, failure to Come on the first command or signal, moving from the place where left before being called or signalled, not sitting close enough so that the handler could readily touch its head without stretching or moving either foot.

Substantial deductions shall be made for a slow response to the Come, varying with the extent of the slowness; for the dog's standing or lying down instead of waiting in the Sit position; for failure to Sit in Front; failure to Finish or Sit at Heel; or for extra command or signal to Sit or Finish.

Minor deductions shall be made for slow or poor Sits or Finishes, for touching the handler on coming in or while finishing, and for sitting between the handler's feet.

——— Group Exercises ———

Section 12. The principal feature of these exercises is that the dog remain in the Sitting or Down position, whichever is required by the particular exercise.

Orders are "Sit your dogs" or "Down your dogs", "Leave your dogs" and "Back to your dogs".

All the competing dogs in the class take these exercises together, except that if there are 12 or more dogs they shall, at the judge's option, be judged in groups of not less than 6 nor more than 12 dogs. When the same judge does both Novice A and Novice B, the two classes may be combined provided there are not more than 12 dogs competing in the combined classes. The judge shall divide his class into approximately equal sections. The Group exercises shall be judged after each section. The dogs that are in the ring shall be lined up in catalogue order along one of the four sides of the ring. Handler's armbands, weighted with leashes or other articles if necessary, shall be placed behind the dogs.

For the Long Sit the handlers shall, on order from the judge, command and/or signal their dogs to Sit if they are not already sitting. On further order from the judge to leave their dogs, the handlers shall give a command and/or signal to Stay and immediately leave their dogs. The handlers will go to the opposite side of the ring, turn and stand facing their respective dogs.

If a dog gets up and starts to roam or follows its handler, or if a dog moves so as to interfere with another dog, the judge shall promptly instruct the handler or one of the stewards to take the dog out of the ring or to keep it away from the other dogs.

After one minute from the time he has ordered the handlers to leave their dogs, the judge will give the order to return, whereupon the handlers must promptly go back to their dogs, each walking around and in back of his own dog to Heel position. The dogs must not move from the Sitting position until after the judge has said, "Exercise finished". The judge shall not give the order "Exercise finished" until the handlers have returned to the Heel position.

Before starting the Long Down the judge shall ask if the handlers are ready. The Long Down is done in the same manner as the Long Sit except that instead of sitting their dogs the handlers shall, on oder from the judge, down their dogs to a position facing the opposite side of the ring, without touching either the dogs or their collars, and except further that the judge will order the handlers to return after three minutes. The dogs must not move from the Down position until after the judge has said, "Exercise finished".

The dogs shall not be required to sit at the end of the Down exercise.

——— Group Exercises, Scoring ———

Section 13. During these exercises the judge shall stand in such position that all the dogs are in his line of vision, and where he can see all the handlers in the ring without having to turn around.

Scoring of the exercises will not start until after the judge has ordered the handlers to leave their dogs, except for such things as rough treatment of a dog by its handler or resistance by a dog to its handler's attempts to make it Sit or lie Down. These shall be penalized substantially; in extreme cases the dog may be excused.

A handler whose dog assumes a position in such a manner that it could interfere with an adjacent competing dog shall be required to reposition his dog and shall also be substantially penalized; in extreme cases the dog may be excused.

A score of zero is required for the following: the dog's moving at any time during either exercise a substantial distance away from the place where it was left, or going over to any other dog, or staying on the spot where it was left but not remaining in whichever position is required by the particular exercise until the handler has returned to the Heel position, or repeatedly barking or whining.

A substantial deduction shall be made for a dog that moves even a minor distance away from the place where it was left or that barks or whines only once or twice. Depending on the circumstance, a substantial or minor deduction shall be made for touching the dog or its collar in getting the dog into the Down position.

There shall be a minor deduction if a dog changes position after the handler has returned to the Heel position but before the judge has said, "Exercise finished". The judge shall not give the order "Exercise finished" until the handlers have returned to the Heel position.

The judge stands by while dog and handler perform the figure eight exercise off-leash during US obedience trials.

OPEN

Open A Class

Section 1. The Open A class shall be for dogs that have won the C.D. title but have not won the title C.D.X. Obedience judges or persons who have owned, trained or exhibited a dog that has earned an O.T.Ch. may not enter or handle dogs in this class. Each dog must be handled by its owner or by a member of his immediate family. Owners may enter more than one dog in this class but the same person who handled each dog in the first five exercises must handle the same dog in the Long Sit and Long Down exercises, except that if a person has handled more than one dog in the first five exercises he must have an additional handler, who must be the owner or a member of his immediate family, for each additional dog, when more than one dog that he has handled in the first five exercises is judged in the same group for the Long Sit and Long Down.

Open B Class

Section 2. The Open B Class will be for dogs that have won the title C.D. or C.D.X. A dog may continue to compete in this class after it has won the title U.D. Dogs in this class may be handled by the owner or any other person. Owners may enter more than one dog in this class but the same person who handled each dog in the first five exercises must handle each dog in the Long Sit and Long Down exercises, except that if a person has handled more than one dog in the first five exercises he must have an additional handler for each additional dog, when more than one dog that he has handled in the first five exercises is judged in the same group for the Long Sit and Long Down. No dog may be entered in both Open A and Open B classes at any one trial.

Open Exercises and Scores

Section 3. The exercises and maximum scores in the Open classes are:
1. Heel Free and Figure Eight . . . . 40 points
2. Drop on Recall . . . . 30 points
3. Retrieve on Flat . . . . 20 points
4. Retrieve over High Jump . . . . 30 points
5. Broad Jump . . . . 20 points
6. Long Sit . . . . 30 points
7. Long Down . . . . 30 points

Maximum Total Score . . . . 200 points

C.D.X. Title

Section 4. The American Kennel Club will issue a Companion Dog Excellent certificate for each registered dog, and will permit the use of the letters "C.D.X." after the name of each dog that has been certified by three different judges of Obedience Trials to have received Qualifying scores in Open Classes at three Licensed or Member Obedience Trials, provided the sum total of dogs that actually competed in the Regular Open classes at each trial is not less than six.

Heel Free and Figure Eight, Performance and Scoring

Section 5. This exercise shall be executed in the same manner as the Novice Heel on Leash and Figure Eight exercise, except that the dog is off leash. Orders and scoring are the same as in Heel on Leash and Figure Eight.

Drop on Recall

Section 6. The principal features of this exercise, in addition to those listed under the Novice Recall, are the dog's prompt response to the handler's command or signal to Drop, and the dog's remaining in the Down position until again called or signalled to Come. The dog will be judged on the promptness of its response to command or signal and not on its proximity to a designated point.

Orders for the exercise are "Leave your dog", "Call your dog", an order or signal to Drop the dog, another "Call your dog" and "Finish". The judge may designate in advance a point at which, as the dog is coming in, the handler shall give his command or signal to the dog to Drop. The judge's signal or designated point must be clear to the handler but not obvious or distracting to the dog.

On order from the judge, the handler may give command and/or signal for the dog to Stay in the Sit position while the handler walks forward about 35 feet to the other end of the ring, where he shall turn and stand in a natural manner facing his dog. On judge's order or signal, the handler shall give command or signal to Come and the dog must start straight in at a brisk trot or gallop. On the judge's order or signal, or at a point designated in advance by the judge, the handler shall give command or signal to Drop, and the dog must immediately drop completely to the Down position, where he must remain until, on judge's order or signal, the handler again gives command or signal to Come. The dog then completes the exercise as in the Novice Recall.

Drop on Recall, Scoring

Section 7. All applicable penalties listed under the Novice Recall shall apply. In addition, a score of zero is required for a dog that does not drop completely to the Down position on a single command or signal, and for a dog that drops but does not remain down until called or signalled.

Substantial deductions, varying with the extent, even to the point of zero, shall be made for delayed or slow response to the handler's command or signal to Drop, for delay or slowness to Down, and for slow response to either of the Recalls. All penalties as in the Novice Recall shall apply.

Retrieve on the Flat

Section 8. The principal feature of this exercise is that the dog retrieve promptly.

Orders are "Throw it", "Send your dog", "Take it" and "Finish".

The handler shall stand with his dog sitting in the Heel position in a place designated by the judge. On order, "Throw it", the handler shall give command and/or signal to Stay, which signal may not be given with the hand that is holding the dumbbell, and throw the dumbbell a distance of at least 20 feet. On order to send his dog, the handler shall give command or signal to retrieve. The retrieve shall be executed at a brisk trot or gallop, the dog going directly to the dumbbell and retrieving it without unnecessary mouthing or playing. The dog must sit straight to deliver, centred immediately in front of the handler's feet, close enough that the handler can readily take the dumbbell without moving either foot or having to stretch forward. The dog must not touch the handler nor sit between his feet. On order from the judge to take it, the handler shall give command or signal and take the dumbbell.

The Finish shall be executed as in the Novice Recall.

The dumbbell, which must be approved by the judge, shall be made of one or more solid pieces of one of the heavy hardwoods, which shall not be hollowed out. It may be unfinished, or coated with a clear finish, or painted white. It shall have no decorations or attachments but may bear an inconspicuous mark for identification. The size of the dumbbell shall be proportionate to the size of the dog. The judge shall require the dumbbell to be thrown again before the dog is sent if, in his opinion, it is thrown too short a distance, or too far to one side, or too close to the ringside.

Retrieve on the Flat, Scoring

Section 9. A dog that fails to go out on the first command or signal, or goes to retrieve before the command or signal is given, or fails to retrieve, or does not return with the dumbbell sufficiently close that the handler can easily take the dumbbell as described above, must be scored zero.

Substantial deductions, depending on the extent, shall be made for slowness in going out or returning or in picking up the dumbbell, for not going directly to the dumbbell, for mouthing or playing with or dropping the dumbbell, and for reluctance or refusal to release the dumbbell to the handler. All other applicable penalties listed under the Novice Recall shall apply.

Retrieve over High Jump

Section 10. The principal features of this exercise are that the dog go out over the jump, pick up the dumbbell and promptly return with it over the jump.

Orders are "Throw it", "Send your dog", "Take it" and "Finish".

This exercise shall be executed in the same manner as the Retrieve on the Flat, except that the dog must clear the High Jump both going and coming. The handler must stand at least 8 feet, or any reasonable distance beyond 8 feet, from the jump but must remain in the same spot throughout the exercise, and he must throw the dumbbell at least 8 feet beyond the jump.

The jump shall be as nearly as possible one and one-half times the height of the dog at the withers, as determined by the judge, with a minimum height of 8 inches and a maximum height of 36 inches. This applies to all breeds with the following exceptions:

The jump shall be once the height of the dog at the withers or 36 inches, whichever is less, for the following breeds—

Bloodhounds	Greater Swiss Mountain Dogs
Bullmastiffs	Mastiffs
Bernese Mountain Dogs	Newfoundlands
Great Danes	St. Bernards
Great Pyrenees	

The jump shall be once the height of the dog at the withers or 8 inches, whichever is greater, for the following breeds—

Spaniels (Clumber)	Norwich Terriers
Spaniels (Sussex)	Scottish Terriers
Basset Hounds	Sealyham Terriers
Dachshunds	Skye Terriers
Welsh Corgis (Cardigan)	West Highland White Terriers
Welsh Corgis (Pembroke)	Maltese
Australian Terriers	Pekingese
Cairn Terriers	Bulldogs
Dandie Dinmont Terriers	French Bulldogs
Norfolk Terriers	

The jumps may be preset by the stewards based on the handler's advice as to the dog's height. The judge must make certain that the jump is set at the required height for each dog. He shall verify in the ring with an ordinary folding rule or steel tape to the nearest one-half inch, the height of each dog at the withers. He shall not base his decision as to the height of the jump on the handler's advice.

The side posts of the High Jump shall be 4 feet high and the jump shall be 5 feet wide and shall be so constructed as to provide adjustment for each 2 inches from 8 inches to 36 inches. It is suggested that the jump have a bottom board 8 inches wide including the space from the bottom of the board to the ground or floor, together with three other 8 inch boards, one 4 inch board, and one 2 inch board. A 6 inch board may also be provided. The jump shall be painted a flat white. The width in inches, and nothing else, shall be painted on each side of each board in black 2 inch figures, the figure on the bottom board representing the distance from the ground or floor to the top of the board.

Retrieve over High Jump, Scoring
Section 11. Scoring of this exercise shall be as in Retrieve on the Flat. In addition, a dog that fails, either going or returning, to go over the jump, or that climbs or uses the jump for aid in going over, must be scored zero. Touching the jump in going over is added to the substantial and minor penalties listed under Retrieve on the Flat.

Broad Jump
Section 12. The principal features of this exercise are that the dog stay where left until directed to Jump and that the dog clear the jump on a single command or signal.

Orders are "Leave your dog", "Send your dog" and "Finish".

The handler will stand with his dog sitting in the Heel position in front of and at least 8 feet from the jump. On order from the judge to "Leave your dog", the handler will give his dog the command and/or signal to Stay and go to a position facing the right side of the jump, with his toes about 2 feet from the jump, and anywhere between the lowest edge of the first hurdle and the highest edge of the last hurdle.

On order from the judge the handler shall give the command or signal to Jump and the dog shall clear the entire distance of the Broad Jump without touching and, without further command or signal, immediately return to a sitting position in front of the handler as in the Novice Recall. The handler shall change his position by executing a right-angle turn while the dog is in mid-air, but shall remain in the same spot. The dog must sit and finish as in the Novice Recall.

The Broad Jump shall consist of four hurdles, built to telescope for convenience, made of boards about 8 inches wide, the largest measuring about 5 feet in length and 6 inches high at the highest point, all painted a flat white. When set up they shall be arranged in order of size and shall be evenly spaced so as to cover a distance equal to twice the height of the High Jump as set for the particular dog, with the low side of each hurdle and the lowest hurdle nearest the dog. The four hurdles shall be used for a jump of 52" to

72", three for a jump of 32" to 48", and two for a jump of 16" to 28". The highest hurdles shall be removed first. It is the judge's responsibility to see that the distance jumped is that required by these Regulations for the particular dog.

Broad Jump, Scoring
Section 13. A dog that fails to Stay until directed to Jump, or refuses the jump on the first command or signal, or walks over any part of the jump, or fails to clear the full distance, with its forelegs, must be scored zero. Minor or substantial deductions, depending on the specific circumstances in each case, shall be made for a dog that touches the jump in going over or that does not return directly to the handler. All other applicable penalties listed under the Novice Recall shall apply.

Open Group Exercises, Performance and Scoring
Section 14. During the Long Sit and the Long Down exercises the judge shall stand in such a position that all of the dogs are in his line of vision, and where he can see all the handlers in the ring, or leaving and returning to the ring, without having to turn around.

These exercises in the Open classes are performed in the same manner as in the Novice classes except that after leaving their dogs the handlers must cross to the opposite side of the ring, and then leave the ring in single file as directed by the judge and go to a place designated by the judge, completely out of sight of their dogs, where they must remain until called by the judge after the expiration of the time limit of three minutes in the Long Sit and five minutes in the Long Down, from the time the judge gave the order to "Leave your dogs". On order from the judge the handlers shall return to the ring in single file in reverse order, lining up facing their dogs at the opposite side of the ring, and return to their dogs on order from the judge.

Orders and scoring are the same as in the Novice Group exercises.

UTILITY

Section 1. The Utility class shall be for dogs that have won the title C.D.X. Dogs that have won the title U.D. may continue to compete in this class. Dogs in this class may be handled by the owner or any other person. Owners may enter more than one dog in this class, but each dog must have a separate handler for the Group Examination when judged in the same group.

Division of Utility Class
Section 2. A club may choose to divide the Utility class into Utility A and Utility B classes, provided such division is approved by The American Kennel Club and is announced in the premium list. When this is done the Utility A class shall be for dogs which have won the title C.D.X. and have not won the title U.D. Obedience judges or persons who have owned, trained, or exhibited a dog that has earned an O.T.Ch. may not enter or handle dogs in this class. Owners may enter more than one dog in this class but the same person who handled each dog in the first five exercises must handle the same dog in the Group Examination, except that if a person has handled more than one dog in the first five exercises he must have an additional handler, who must be the owner or a member of his immediate family, for each additional dog, when more than one dog he has handled in the first five exercises is judged in the same group for the Group Examination. All other dogs that are eligible for the Utility class but not eligible for the Utility A class may be entered only in the Utility B class to which the conditions listed in Chapter 5, Section 1 shall apply. No dog may be entered in both Utility A and Utility B classes at any one trial.

Utility Exercises and Scores
Section 3. The exercises, maximum scores and order of judging in the Utility classes are:

1. Signal Exercise	40 points
2. Scent Discrimination Article No. 1	30 points
3. Scent Discrimination Article No. 2	30 points
4. Directed Retrieve	30 points
5. Directed Jumping	40 points
6. Group Examination	30 points
Maximum Total Score	200 points

U.D. Title

Section 4. The American Kennel Club will issue a Utility Dog certificate for each registered dog, and will permit the use of the letters "U.D." after the name of each dog that has been certified by three different judges of Obedience Trials to have received Qualifying scores in Utility classes at three Licensed or Member Obedience Trials in each of which three or more dogs actually competed in the utility class or classes.

Signal Exercises

Section 5. The principal features of this exercise are the ability of dog and handler to work as a team while heeling, and the dog's correct responses to the signals to Stand, Stay, Drop, Sit and Come.

Orders are the same as in Heel on Leash and Figure Eight, with the additions of "Stand your dog", which shall be given only when dog and handler are walking at normal pace, and "Leave your dog". The judge must use signals for directing the handler to signal the dog to Drop, to Sit and to Come, in that sequence, and to Finish.

Heeling in the Signal Exercise shall be done in the same manner as in Heel Free, except that throughout the entire exercise the handler shall use signals only and must not speak to his dog at any time. On order from the judge, "Forward", the handler may signal his dog to walk at heel, and on specific order from the judge in each case, shall execute a "Left turn", "Right turn", "About turn", "Halt", "Slow", "Normal" and "Fast". These orders may be given in any sequence and may be repeated as necessary, but the judge shall attempt to standardize the heeling pattern for all dogs in the class.

On order from the judge, and while the dog is walking at heel, the handler shall signal his dog to Stand in the Heel position near one end of the ring. On further order, "Leave your dog", the handler shall signal his dog to Stay, go to the other end of the ring and turn to face his dog. On separate and specific signals from the judge, the handler shall give his signals to Drop, to Sit, to Come and to Finish as in the Novice Recall. During the heeling part of this exercise the handler may not give any signal except when a command or signal is permitted in the Heeling exercises.

Signal Exercise, Scoring

Section 6. A dog that fails, on a single signal from the handler, to Stand or remain standing where left, or to Drop, or to Sit and Stay, or to Come, or that receives a command or audible signal from the handler to do any of these parts of the exercise, shall be scored zero.

Minor or substantial deductions depending on the specific circumstances in each case, shall be made for a dog that walks forward on the Stand, Drop or Sit portions of the exercise.

A substantial deduction shall be made for any audible command during the Heeling or Finish portions of the exercise.

All the penalties listed under the Heel on Leash and Figure Eight, and the Novice Recall exercises shall apply.

Scent Discrimination

Section 7. The principal features of these exercises are the selection of the handler's article from among the other articles by scent alone, and the prompt delivery of the right article to the handler.

Orders are "Send your dog", "Take it" and "Finish".

In each of these two exercises the dog must select by scent alone and retrieve an article which has been handled by its handler. The articles shall be provided by the handler and shall consist of two sets, each comprised of five identical objects not more than six inches in length, which may be items of everyday use. One set shall be made entirely of rigid metal, and one of leather of such design that nothing but leather is visible except for the minimum amount of thread or metal necessary to hold the object together. The articles in each set must be legibly numbered, each with a different number and must be approved by the judge.

The handler shall present all 10 articles to the judge, who shall designate one from each set and make written note of the numbers of the two articles he has selected. These two handler's articles shall be placed on a table or chair within the ring until picked up by the handler, who shall hold in his hand only one article at a time. The judge or steward will handle each of the remaining 8 articles as he places them on the floor or ground at random and about six inches apart, with the closest article being about 20 feet from the handler and the dog. Before the dog is sent, the judge must make sure that the articles are clearly visible to the dog and handler, and that the articles are properly separated so that there will be no confusion of scent between the articles.

Handler and dog shall turn around after watching the judge or steward spread the articles, and shall remain facing away from those articles until the judge has taken the handler's scented article and given the order, "Send your dog".

The handler may use either article first, but must relinquish each one immediately when ordered by the judge. The judge shall make certain that the handler imparts his scent to each article only with his hands and that, between the time the handler picks up each article and the time he gives it to the judge, the article is held continuously in the handler's hands which must remain in plain sight.

On order from the judge, the handler will immediately place his article on the judge's book or work sheet. The judge, without touching the article with his hands, will place it among those on the ground or floor.

On order from the judge to "Send your dog", the handler may give the command to Heel before turning, and will execute a Right About turn, stopping to face the articles with the dog sitting in Heel position. The handler shall then give the command or signal to retrieve. Handlers may at their discretion on order from the judge to "Send your dog", execute with their dog a Right About turn to face the articles, simultaneously giving the command or signal to retrieve. In this instance the dog shall not assume a sitting position, but shall go directly to the articles. The handler may give his scent to the dog by gently touching the dog's nose with the palm of one open hand, but this may only be done while the dog and handler have their backs to the articles and the arm and hand must be returned to a natural position before handler and dog turn to face the articles.

The dog shall go at a brisk trot or gallop directly to the articles. It may take any reasonable time to select the right article, but only provided it works continuously. After picking up the right article the dog shall return at a brisk trot or gallop and complete the exercise as in the Retrieve on the Flat.

These procedures shall be followed for both articles. Should a dog retrieve a wrong article in the first exercise, that article shall be placed on the table or chair. The correct article must be removed, and the second exercise shall be conducted with one less article on the ground or floor.

Scent Discrimination, Scoring

Section 8. Deductions shall be the same as in the Novice Recall and the Retrieve on the Flat. In addition, a dog that fails to go out to the group of articles, or retrieves a wrong article, or fails to bring the right article to the handler, must be scored zero for the particular exercise.

Substantial deductions shall be made for a dog that picks up a wrong article, even though he puts it down again immediately, for any roughness by the handler in imparting his scent to the dog, and for any excessive motions by the handler in turning to face the articles.

Minor or substantial deductions, depending on the circumstances in each case, shall be made for a dog that is slow or inattentive, or that does not work continuously. There shall be no penalty for a dog that takes a reasonably long time examining the articles provided the dog works smartly and continuously.

Directed Retrieve

Section 9. The principal features of the exercise are that the dog stay until directed to retrieve, that it go directly to the designated glove, and that it retrieve promptly. The orders for the exercise are "One", "Two" or "Three", "Take it" and "Finish". In this exercise the handler will provide three predominantly white, cotton work gloves, which must be open and must be approved by the judge. The handler will stand with his back to the unobstructed end of the ring with his dog sitting in the Heel position midway between and in line with the two jumps. The judge or steward will then drop the three gloves across the end of the ring, while the handler and dog are facing the opposite direction, one glove in each corner and one in the centre, about 3 feet from the end of the ring and for the corner gloves, about 3 feet from the side of the ring. All three gloves will be clearly visible to the dog and handler, when the handler turns to face the glove designated by the judge. There shall be no table or chair at this end of the ring.

The gloves shall be designated "One", "Two" or "Three" reading from left to right when the handler turns and faces the gloves. The judge will give the order "One", or "Two" or "Three". The handler then must give the command to Heel and turn in place, right or left to face the designated glove. The handler will come to a halt with the dog sitting in the Heel position. The handler shall not touch the dog to get it into position nor may he reposition the dog. The handler will then give his dog the direction to the designated glove with a single motion of his left hand and arm along the right side of the dog, and will give the command to retrieve either simultaneously with or immediately following the giving of the direction. The dog shall then go directly to the glove at a brisk trot or gallop and retrieve it without unnecessary mouthing or playing with it, completing the exercise as in the Retrieve on the Flat.

The handler may bend his body and knees to the extent necessary in giving the direction to the dog, after which the handler will stand erect in a natural position with his arms at his sides.

The exercise shall consist of a single retrieve, but the judge shall designate different glove numbers for successive dogs; each glove shall be used approximately the same number of times.

Directed Retrieve, Scoring

Section 10. All applicable penalties listed under the Novice Recall and the Retrieve on the Flat shall apply. In addition, a score of zero is required for any commands or signals by the handler, after turning, to position the dog to face the designated glove, for not going directly to the designated glove, or for not retrieving the glove.

Depending on the extent, substantial or minor deductions shall be made for a handler who over-turns, or touches the dog or uses excessive motions while turning to face the glove.

Directed Jumping

Section 11. The principal features of this exercise are that the dog go away from the handler in the direction indicated, stop when commanded, jump as directed and return as in the Recall.

The orders are "Send your dog", the designation of which jump is to be taken, and "Finish".

The jumps shall be placed midway in the ring at right angles to the sides of the ring and 18 to 20 feet apart, the Bar Jump on one side, the High Jump on the other. The judge must make certain that the jumps are set at the required height for each dog by following the procedure described in Retrieve over the High Jump.

The handler, from a position on the centre line of the ring and about 20 feet from the line of the jumps, shall stand with his dog sitting in the Heel position and on order from the judge shall command and/or signal his dog to go forward at a brisk trot or gallop to a point about 20 feet beyond the jumps and in the approximate centre. When the dog has reached this point the handler shall give a command to Sit; the dog must stop and sit with his attention on the handler but need not sit squarely.

The judge will designate which jump is to be taken first by the dog and shall order either "High" or "Bar" when designating either the High or Bar Jump. The handler shall command and/or signal the dog to return to him over the designated jump. While the dog is in mid-air the handler may turn so as to be facing the dog as it returns. The dog shall sit in front of the handler and, on order from the judge, Finish as in the Novice Recall. The judge will say "Exercise Finished" after the dog has returned to the Heel position.

When the dog is again sitting in the Heel position the judge will ask, "Are you ready?" before giving the order to send the dog for the second part of the exercise. The same procedure shall be followed for the second jump.

It is optional with the judge which jump is taken first, but both jumps must be taken to complete the exercise and the judge must not designate the jump until the dog is at the far end of the ring. The dog shall clear the jumps without touching them.

The height of the jumps shall be the same as required in the Open classes. The High Jump shall be the same as that used in the Open classes, and the Bar Jump shall consist of a bar between 2 and 2½ inches square with the four edges rounded sufficiently to remove any sharpness. The bar shall be painted a flat black and white in alternate sections of about 3 inches each. bar shall be supported by two unconnected 4 foot upright posts about 5 feet apart. The bar shall be adjustable for each 2 inches of height from 8 inches to 36 inches, and the jump shall be so constructed and positioned that the bar can be knocked off without disturbing the uprights.

Directed Jumping, Scoring

Section 12. A dog must receive a score of zero for the following: anticipating the handler's command and/or signal to go out, not leaving the handler, not going out between the jumps, not stopping on command and remaining at least 10 feet beyond the jumps, anticipating the handler's command and/or signal to Jump, not jumping as directed, knocking the bar off the uprights, and climbing or using the top of the High Jump for aid in going over.

Substantial deductions shall be made for a dog that does not stop in the approximate centre of the ring about 20 feet beyond the jumps, for a dog that turns, stops or sits before the handler's command to Sit and for a dog that fails to sit.

Substantial or minor deductions, depending on the extent, shall be made for slowness in going out or for touching the jumps. All of the penalties listed under Novice Recall shall also apply.

Group Examination

Section 13. The principal features of this exercise are that the dog Stand and Stay, and show no shyness or resentment.

All the competing dogs take this exercise together; except if there are 12 or more, they shall be judged in groups of not less than 6 nor more than 12 dogs, at the judge's option. The judge shall divide his class into approximately equal sections. The Group exercise shall be judged after each section. The handlers and dogs in the ring shall line up in catalogue order, side by side, down the centre of the ring, with the dogs sitting in the Heel position. Each handler shall place his armband, weighted with leash or other article if necessary, behind his dog. The judge must instruct one or more stewards to watch the other dogs while he conducts the individual examination, and to call any faults to his attention.

On order from the judge, "Stand your dogs", all the handlers will stand or pose their dogs and on further order, "Leave your dogs", will give command and/or signal to Stay and walk forward to the side of the ring where they shall turn and stand facing their respective dogs. The judge will approach each dog in turn from the front and examine it, going over the dog with his hands as in dog show judging except that under no circumstances shall the examination include the dog's mouth or testicles.

When all dogs have been examined and after the handlers have been away from their dogs for at least three minutes, the judge will promptly order the handlers, "Back to your dogs" and the handlers will return, each walking around and in back of his own dog to the Heel position, after which the judge will say, "Exercise Finished". Each dog must remain standing at its position in the line from the time its handler leaves it until the end of the exercise, and must show no shyness or resentment. The dogs are not required to Sit at the end of this exercise.

Group Examination, Scoring

Section 14. There should be no attempt to judge the dogs or handlers on the manner in which the dogs are made to stand. The scoring will not start until after the judge has given the order to leave the dogs, except for such general things as rough treatment of a dog by its handler, or active resistance by a dog to its handler's attempts to make it stand. Immediately after examining each dog the judge must make a written record of any necessary deductions, subject to further deductions for subsequent faults.

A dog must be scored zero for the following: displaying shyness or resentment, moving a minor distance from the place where it was left, going over to any other dog, sitting or lying down before the handler has returned to the Heel position, growling or snapping at any time during the exercise, repeatedly barking or whining.

Substantial or minor deductions, depending on the circumstance, must be made for a dog that moves its feet repeatedly while remaining in place, or sits or lies down after the handler has returned to the Heel position.

OBEDIENCE TRIAL CHAMPIONSHIP

Dogs that May Compete

Section 1. Championship points will be recorded only for those dogs which have earned the Utility Dog title. Any dog that has been awarded the title of Obedience Trial Champion may continue to compete, and if such dog earns a First or Second place ribbon, that dog shall also earn the points.

Championship Points

Section 2. Championship points will be recorded for those dogs which have earned a First or Second place ribbon competing in the Open B or Utility Class (or Utility B, if divided), according to the schedule of points established by the Board of Directors of The American Kennel Club. In counting the number of eligible dogs in competition, a dog that is disqualified, or is dismissed, excused or expelled from the ring by the judge shall not be included.

Requirements for the Obedience Trial Champion are as follows:
1. Shall have won 100 points; and
2. shall have won a First place in Utility (or Utility B, if divided) provided there are at least three dogs in competition; and

3. shall have won a First place in Open B provided there are at least six dogs in competition; and

4. shall have won a third First place under the conditions of 2 or 3 above; and

5. shall have won these three First places under three different judges.

O.T. Ch. Title Certificate
Section 3. The American Kennel Club will issue an Obedience Trial Championship certificate for each registered dog and will permit the use of the letters O.T.Ch. preceding the name of each dog, that meets these requirements.

Triple Champion
Section 4. Any dog which has been awarded the titles of Champion of Record, Obedience Trial Champion and Field Champion may be designated as a "Triple Champion", but no certificate will be awarded for a Triple Champion.

Ineligibility and Cancellation
Section 5. If an ineligible dog has been entered in any Licensed or Member Obedience Trial or Dog Show, or if the name of the owner given on the entry form is not that of the person or persons who actually owned the dog at the time entries closed, or if shown in a class for which it has not been entered, or if its entry form is deemed invalid or unacceptable by The American Kennel Club, all resulting awards shall be cancelled. In computing the championship points, such ineligible dogs, whether or not they have received awards, shall be counted as having competed.

Move Ups
Section 6. If an award in any of the Regular classes is cancelled, the next highest scoring dog shall be moved up and the award to the dog moved up shall be counted the same as if it had been the original award. If there is no dog of record to move up, the award shall be void.

Return of Awards
Section 7. If the win of a dog shall be cancelled by The American Kennel Club, the owner of the dog shall return all ribbons and prizes to the show-giving club within ten days of receipt of the notice of cancellation from The American Kennel Club.

Point Schedule
Section 8.

OPEN B CLASS

Number competing	Points for first place	Points for second place
6-10	2	0
11-15	4	1
16-20	6	2
21-25	10	3
26-30	14	4
31-35	18	5
36-40	22	7
41-45	26	9
46-50	30	11
51-56	34	13

UTILITY CLASS

Number competing	Points for first place	Points for second place
3- 5	2	0
6- 9	4	1
10-14	6	2
15-19	10	3
20-24	14	4
25-29	18	5
30-34	22	7
35-39	26	9
40-44	30	11
45-48	34	13

Below: A dog is being trained to perform the retrieve over high jump exercise in preparation for an obedience event.

MAJOR KENNEL CLUBS OF THE WORLD

Australia
Australian National Kennel Council, Royal Show Grounds, Ascot Vale, Victoria (Incorporating: The Canine Association of Western Australia; North Australian Canine Association; The Canine Control Council (Queensland); Canberra Kennel Association; The Kennel Control Council; Kennel Control Council of Tasmania; The RAS Kennel Club; South Australian Canine Association.)

Barbados
Barbados Kennel Club, Wraysbury, Bucks, St Thomas, Barbados, W.1.

Belgium
Societe Royale Saint-Hubert, Avenue de l'Armee 25, B-1040, Brussels

Bermuda
The Bermuda Kennel Club Inc, PO Box 1455, Hamilton 5

Brazil
Brazil Kennel Club, Caixa Postal, 1468, Rio de Janeiro

Canada
Canadian Kennel Club, 2150 Bloor Street West, Toronto M6S 1M8, Ontario

Caribbean
The Caribbean Kennel Club, PO Box 737, Port of Spain, Trinidad

Chile
Kennel Club de Chile, Casilla 1704, Valparaiso

Colombia
Club Canino Colombiano, Calle 70, No 4-60, 3er Piso, Bogota, D.E. Colombia

Denmark
Dansk Kennelklub, Parkvej 1, Jersie Strand, 2680 Solrad Strand

East Africa
East Africa Kennel Club, PO Box 14223, St Andrews Church, Nyerere Road, Nairobi, Kenya

Finland
Suomen Kennelliitto-Finska Kennelklubben, Bulevardi 14A, Helsinki

France
Societe Centrale Canine, 215 Rue St Denis, 75083 Paris, Cedex 02

Germany
Verband für das Deutsche Hundewesen (VDH), Postfach 1390, 46 Dortmund

Guernsey
Guernsey Dog Club, Myrtle Grove, St Jacques, Guernsey, C.I.

Holland
Raad van Beheer op Kynologisch Gebied in Nederland, Emmalaan 16, Amsterdam, Z

Hong Kong
Hong Kong Kennel Club, 3rd Floor, 28B Stanley Street, Hong Kong

India
Kennel Club of India, 17 Mukathal St. Purasawaltam, Madras 600 007

Ireland
Irish Kennel Club, 23 Earlsfort Terrace, Dublin 2

Italy
Ente Nazionale Della Cinofilia Italiana, Viale Premuda, 21 Milan

Jamaica
The Jamaican Kennel Club, 8 Orchard Street, Kingston 5, Jamaica, W.1.

Jersey
Jersey Dog Club, Coburg House, Rue-es-Picots, Trinity, Jersey, C.I.

Malaysia
Malaysian Kennel Association, No. 8, Jalan Tun Mohd Faud Dua, Taman Tun Dr Ismail, Kuala Lumpur

Malta
Main Kennel Club, c/o Msida Youth Centre, 15 Rue d'Argens Str, Msida, Malta G.C.

Monaco
Societe Canine de Monaco, Palais des Congrès, Avenue d'Ostende, Monte Carlo

Nepal
Nepal Kennel Club, PO Box 653, Kathmandu, Nepal

New Zealand
New Zealand Kennel Club, Private Bag, Porirua, New Zealand

Norway
Norsk Kennelklub, Teglverksgt 8, Rodelokka, Postboks 6598, Oslo 5

Pakistan
The Kennel Club of Pakistan, 17a Khayaban-I-Iqbal, Shalimar7, Islamabad

Portugal
Cluba Portuguese de Canicultura, Praca D. Joao da Camara 4-3°, Lisbon 2

Scotland
The Scottish Kennel Club (the delegated Authority of the Kennel Club in Scotland) 6b Forres Street, Edinburgh, EH3 6BR

Singapore
The Singapore Kennel Club, 170 Upper Bukit Timah Rd., 12.02 Singapore 2158

South Africa
Kennel Union of Southern Africa, 6th Floor, Bree Castle, 68 Bree Street, Cape Town 8001, S. Africa, PO Box 11280, Vlaeberg 8018

Spain
Real Sociedad Central de Fomento de las Razas en Espana, Los Madrazo 20, Madrid 14

Sweden
Svenska Kennelklubben, Norrbyvagan 30, Box 11043, 161 11 Bromma

Switzerland
Schweizerische Kynologische Gesellschaft, Falkenplatz 11, 3012 Bern

United Kingdom
The Kennel Club, 1-4 Clarges Street, London W1Y 8AB

United States of America
American Kennel Club, 51 Madison Avenue, New York, NY 10010; The United Kennel Club Inc., 100 East Kilgore Road, Kalamazoo, MI 49001-5598

Uruguay
Kennel Club Uruguayo, Avda, Uruguay 864, Montevideo

Zambia
Kennel Association of Zambia, PO Box 30662, Lusaka

(Reproduced by kind permission of The Kennel Club)

USEFUL ADDRESSES

THE UNITED KINGDOM

The Agility Club
The Spinney, Aubrey Lane,
Redbourn, Hertfordshire AL3 7AN

Battersea Dogs Home
4 Battersea Park Road, Battersea,
London SW8 4AA

The Blue Cross
Animals Hospital, 1 High Street,
Victoria, London SW1V 1QQ

British Field Sports Society
59 Kennington Road,
London SE1 7PZ

**British Small Animals Veterinary
Association**
7 Mansfield Street, London W1M 0AT

British Veterinary Association
7 Mansfield Street, London W1M 0AT

Groomers Association
Uplands, 151 Pampisford Road,
South Croydon, Surrey CR2 6DE

**The Guide Dogs for the Blind
Association**
9-11 Park Street, Windsor,
Berkshire SL4 1JR

Hearing Dogs for the Deaf
105 Gower Street, London WC1

**The International Sheep Dog
Society**
64 St Loyes Street,
Bedford MK40 1EZ

**Joint Advisory Committee
on Pets in Society**
Walter House,
418-422 The Strand,
London WC2

**National Canine Defence
League**
1 Pratt Mews, London NW1 0AD

**National Dog Owners'
Association**
39-41 North Road, Islington,
London N7 9DP

**People's Dispensary for Sick
Animals**
PDSA House, South Street,
Dorking, Surrey

**Pet Food Manufacturers'
Association**
6 Catherine Street,
London WC2B 5JJ

Pet Industry Association
1 Lily Place, Saffron Hill,
London EC1

The Pet Trade Association Ltd.
151 Pampisford Road,
South Croydon, Surrey CR2 6DE

PRO Dogs
Rocky Bank, New Road, Ditton,
Maidstone, Kent ME20 6AD

**The Royal Society for the
Prevention of Cruelty to Animals**
RSPCA Headquarters,
Causeway, Horsham,
Sussex RH12 1HG

THE UNITED STATES

**American Animal Hospital
Association**
3612 East Jefferson, South Bend,
Indiana 46615

American Humane Association
(incorporating The Hearing Dog
Association)
5351 Roslyn, Denver,
Colorado 80201

**American Society for the
Prevention of Cruelty to Animals**
441 East 92nd Street,
New York,
New York 10028

**American Veterinary Medical
Association**
930 North Meacham Road,
Schaumburg, Illinois 60196

Animal Welfare Institute
PO Box 3650,
Washington D.C. 20007

The Fund for Animals
140 West 57th Street,
New York,
New York 10019

Guide Dogs for the Blind
PO Box 1200, San Rafael,
California 94902

**The Humane Society of the United
States**
2100 L Street, N.W.,
Washington D.C. 20037

**International Association of Pet
Cemeteries**
27 West 150 North Avenue,
West Chicago, Illinois 60185

Leader Dogs for the Blind
1039 South Rochester Road,
Rochester, Michigan 48063

National Dog Groomers Association
PO Box 101, Clark,
Pennsylvania 16113

The National Dog Registry
227 Stebbins Road, Carmel,
New York 1051

**Orthopaedic Foundation for
Animals**
817 Virginia Avenue, Columbia,
Missouri 65201

**Owner Handler Association of
America**
583 Knoll Court, Seaford,
New York 11783

Pet Food Institute
1101 Connecticut Avenue N.W.,
Washington D.C. 20036

Rare Breeds Association
31 Byram Bay Road, Hopatcong,
New Jersey 07843

The Seeing Eye Inc
100 East Kilgore Road, Kalamazoo,
Michigan 49001

Tatoo-A-Pet
1625 Emmons Avenue,
Brooklyn, New York 11235

RECOMMENDED READING

The Agility Dog by Peter Lewis, Canine Publications Ltd., Portsmouth, UK.

Best Foot Forward — The Complete Guide to Obedience Handling by Barbara Handler, Alpine Publications, Colorado, USA

The Complete Dog Book by The American Kennel Club, Howell Book House Inc., New York, USA

A Dog for the Kids by Mordecai Siegal, Little, Brown and Co., New York, USA

A Dog of Your Own by Joan Palmer, Salamander Books Ltd., UK

Dog Problems by Carol Lea Benjamin, Doubleday and Co. Inc., New York, USA

Dog Training for Kids by Carol Lea Benjamin, Howell Book House Inc., New York, USA

The Evans Guide for Counceling Dog Owners by Job Michael Evans, Howell Book House Inc., New York, USA

Happy Dog/Happy Owner by Mordecai Siegal, Howell Book House Inc., New York, USA

Homoeopathy for Pets by George MacLeod, The Homoeopathic Development Foundation Ltd., London, UK

Hunting the Clean Boot by Brian Lowe, Blandford Press Ltd., Poole, UK

New Knowledge of Dog Behaviour by Dr C. Pfaffenberger, Howell Book House Inc., New York, USA

Nosework for Dogs by John Cree, Pelham Books Ltd., London, UK

The Obedient Dog by John Holmes, Popular Dogs Publishing Co. Ltd., London, UK

Successful Dog Training by Margaret E. Pearsall, Howell Book House Inc., New York, USA

Training Dogs by Colonel Konrad Most, Popular Dogs Publishing Co. Ltd., London, UK

Training Pointers and Setters by J.B. Maurice, David and Charles (Publishers) Ltd., Newton Abbot, UK

Working Dogs by Joan Palmer, Patrick Stephens Ltd., Northampton, UK

Your Dog's Training by Charlie Wyant and Peter Lewis, Canine Publications Ltd., Portsmouth, UK

Your Family Pet by Maxwell Riddle, Doubleday and Co. Inc., New York, USA

Index

CREDITS

————— Artists —————
Alan Hollingbery and Clive Spong (Copyright of the artwork is the property of Salamander Books Ltd.)

————— Photographs —————
Special thanks go the Marc Henrie A.S.C.(London) who kindly supplied the majority of the photographs for this book. Many thanks also go to the following for their contributions:
John Daniels (Ardea London): 78(B), 158
Robert Estall: 12/13(T), 13(B)
J.P. Ferrero (Ardea London): 18/19(T), 182/3(T), 183(B)

Guide Dogs for the Blind Association: 18, 22/23
Roger Hyde: 164/5, 168, 169(T)
Dr Roger Mugford: 83(TL)
National Canine Defence League (Marc Henrie): 22(L), 80/81, 108/9
People's Dispensary for Sick Animals: 20
Rex Features Ltd: 79(B), 81(T) 158/9, 188, 189
Royal Society for the Prevention of Cruelty to Animals (Lee Tiller): 25(B)
D. et S. Simon (Ardea London): 20/21(T)
United States Air Force: 14(B)

The position of photographs on the page are indicated as follows:
B (bottom), T (top), L (left), R (right) etc.

————— Author's credits —————
The author would particularly like to thank Christian Gardiner, Alan Menzies and Elliot Wood for their invaluable assistance during the writing of this book.
 Thanks are also due to the following: Allbrooks Ltd., Barnsbury Pet Dog Training Club, Bobbie Edwards, Gwynne Hart & Associates

Ltd., Hearing Dogs for the Deaf, The Homoeopathic Development Foundation Ltd., The Imperial War Museum, The International Sheep Dog Society, The Kennel Club, The National Canine Defence League, The National Dog Owners' Association, Lesley Scott Ordish, Pedigree Petfoods Education Centre, The People's Dispensary for Sick Animals, Pro Dogs National Charity, The Society of Companion Animal Studies, Smith Kline Animal Health Ltd., and last, but by no means least, the designer, Roger Hyde, for his artistry, patience and unfailing good humour.